YESTERDAY'S SEASONS

YESTERDAY'S SEASONS

Memories of a Rural Medical Practice

by Gene Schulze, M.D.

HAWTHORN BOOKS, INC.
Publishers/New York
A Howard & Wyndham Company

The story on pages 28–36 originally appeared as "Conversation Piece Unspoken" in *Transatlantic Review,* number 10 (summer 1962), and is reprinted in this slightly re-edited version with the permission of *Transatlantic Review.*

YESTERDAY'S SEASONS

 All inquiries should be addressed to Hawthorn Books, Inc., 260 Madison Avenue, New York, New York 10016. This book was manufactured in the United States of America and published simultaneously in Canada by Prentice-Hall of Canada, Limited, 1870 Birchmount Road, Scarborough, Ontario.

Library of Congress Catalog Card Number: 78–53481

ISBN: 0–8015–0301–9

1 2 3 4 5 6 7 8 9 10

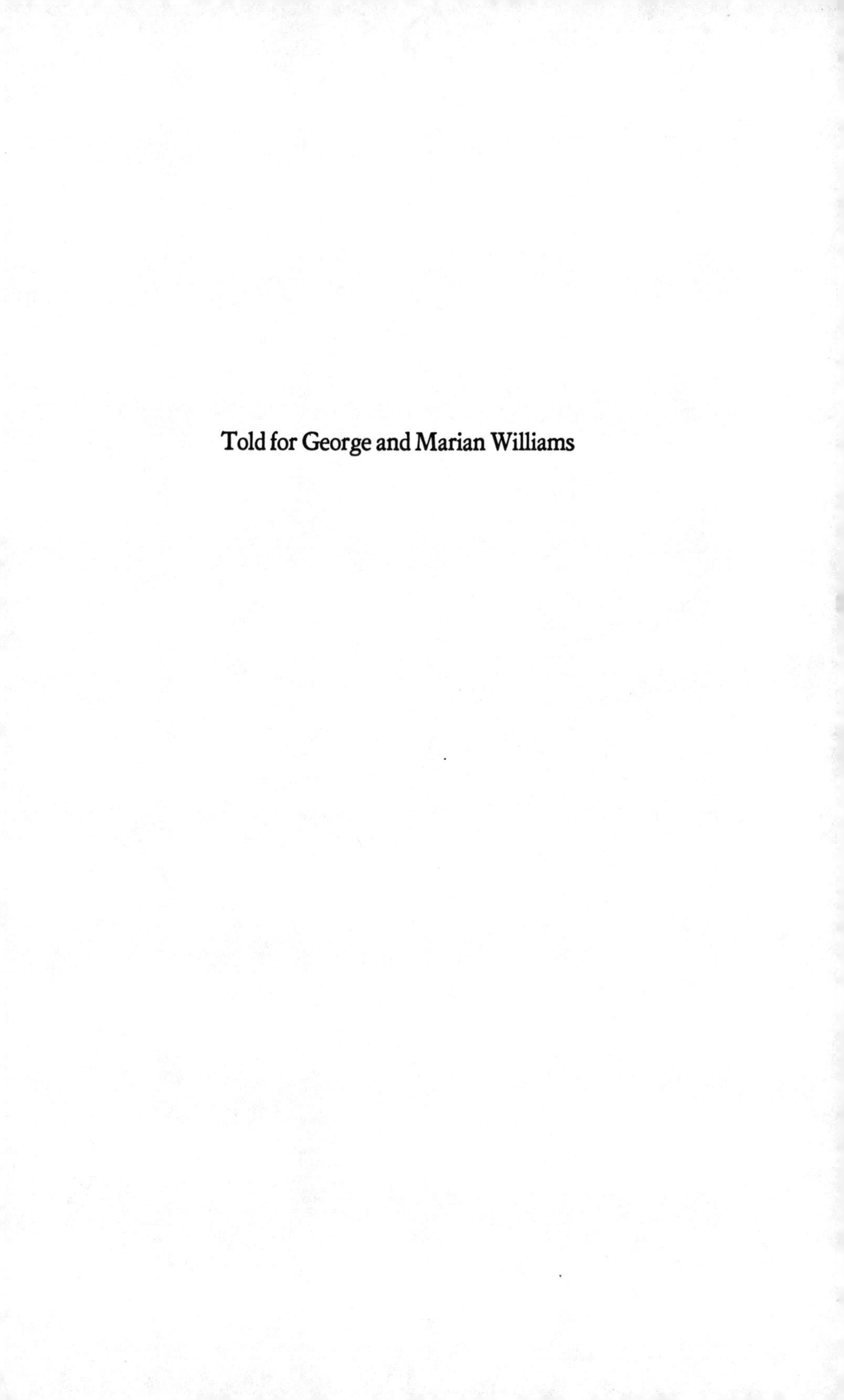

Told for George and Marian Williams

Contents

Every story told here is basically true. Names of persons and details of circumstances have been altered to protect reputations and privacies. Some persons depicted here have no counterpart—I have created them to animate a situation that, while based on one or more similar case histories, is in itself fictitious. So also, the town of Schulenburg, as depicted here, is not in all details the town that existed in fact more than three decades ago. But the truths of themselves, whether I understood or not, are in no way altered, only recorded. In that manner every person seen here is real to me. Each one of these persons and I exchanged moments, small pieces of our lives. We gave to each other. Whether well or badly or despite indifference, we gave to each other, and it made our lives.

These stories are parts of those lives, theirs and mine, experiences over a certain passage of time, but "time" not so much in the longitude of years as in the latitude of strengths or weaknesses in the moments and pieces of ourselves we exchanged.

A person dies completely only when pieces of the realities he lived are no longer remembered by anyone, are part of no one, are no longer being used. It is why I wrote this—so the realities of those portrayed here will continue a little longer, and also mine.

Although every story here is real, others were omitted—as anybody from around Schulenburg of the time can tell you.

Gene Schulze, M.D.

A Medical Bag with the Smell of New Leather

That first Sunday morning, early, the town seemed deserted—

In the small office I continued unpacking. James, the assistant pharmacist, stuck his head in from the drugstore, "A man called—second time." His dog, Nietzsche, wiggled through and came to me again, wagging and smiling; I patted and stroked his head. "Baby case. I told them you're not down yet. Guess they called the hotel."

"Who?" I asked.

"Name of Rhodes. Sweetly Rhodes. Timber people."

"Sweetly? A name like Sweetly?"

"Sweetly Rhodes," James shrugged.

I picked up my bag—new, never been used. The hospital where I'd interned gave one to each new doctor on leaving. The handle squeaked. "Hope I've put everything in—that I'll need. What's 'timber people'?"

"You going?"

"Sure. Why not?"

"Dr. Kotzebue never takes timber people."

"But he's old, isn't he?" It occurred to me now that I had never even thought of refusing to go to anyone. I had at some time, during school, thought of becoming a medical missionary. And still wanted to go work with Dr. Schweitzer someday, if I could ever afford it. "How do I get there?"

"Well, since you're going . . . Even if it should rain—and it might the way it looks—you can't get stuck. Nothing but blow sand and clay dust out there. But have to sure watch it out on the black land—get stuck easy right now. Deep."

Driving first through the black farmlands, open rolling prairie, one sees each hilltop house—its barns surrounded by a white speckling of chickens—with a straight line of green cedars planted always on the north side. You see neat kitchen gardens and a row of hazy pink where peach trees are beginning to bloom. The open pastures lie pale green with new grass, and trees glow light yellow-green even without sunlight splashing through them. Fences are straight and tight. Corner posts, large, always braced double.

And the plowed fields have long curving rows of tiny green dots—the first corn and cotton are coming up. "Groves Chill Tonic" is painted on one wall of a barn. I should be in church this morning. Everybody else is, I'm sure. I should be, too. Well, ox-in-the-ditch . . .

A black shiny cow stood near the tight wire fence chewing slowly. A calf with stilty legs and a swinging navel cord—must be less than a day old—looked at me with big eyes, its ears forward and its tail high, and tried to run—like "Mama! Mama! A monster coming! Run!"—and fell flat on its chin. The cow, her huge udder swaying, stepped over, nudged the calf, licked it.

Then, as if driving through an invisible wall, timber country. Sandy, dusty, almost chalky roads. Crowded bare trees thrusting gaunt crooked limbs into each other. Saggy two-wire fences. An exhaust plume of fine white cloud follows your car, lingering in the air long after you have passed. In this tight timber there is no wind. Cedar trees and evergreen brush along the roadside stand coated with the ghostly dust; you wish a good rain would come and wash them fresh so they could breathe clear again. And post oaks. Post oaks everywhere, thick, bare, their trunks straight but the crooked branches all twisted and snarled, gyrating in awkward directions. Like congenitally deformed arms ending in odd elbow-fingers.

Runty hogs on the road, with a bottom V-cut in each ear, nosed into the belly of a dead armadillo. Buzzards sat on the thin, crooked fenceposts, five in a row, then flew up, flapping wildly. The hogs retreated to the side and crinkled their bloody snouts up at me as if calling dirty names.

I drove fast. James had said they called twice.

The shanty leaned to the left. Two rooms. This would indeed be a mission of mercy—obviously no money would be involved here. I stepped out into the white cloud of dust, which now had caught up and, in its momentum, floated, passing ahead. Through this white haze I saw that a group of assorted twittering children and some curious chickens had met me. Now the group divided itself into halves, leaving a path for me.

I entered the shack, feeling the floor boards give, and also feeling under my shoes that the chickens were not always kept out of the house. In a sagging iron bed lay a big, strong woman with a big, strong belly. I hope this is not a multiple pregnancy. Her feet, dirty and coarse, on the filthy mattress . . .

In a rocking chair near the window sat a fat woman with dirty curly hair like an old wig that has been used to wax furniture. She chewed and rocked continuously, said nothing, and expertly spat brown juice out onto the dry, parched ground where it bounced and rolled into a ball of white dust. Sweat dripped irregularly from her face and also soaked into large dark areas under and around each armpit.

The children—with the chickens—had followed me right on into the house and stood around watching. All covered with layers of dirt or dust, clean only around their mouths as far as they could lick.

"Well, well, so you are the expectant mother."

She gave me a rather peculiar look. "I sho' ain't one 'm Catholic popes."

Suddenly she grabbed the iron frame of the bed above her head, clenched her teeth, and held her breath. I jerked around as the fat woman bellowed "Hallelujah! Go ye into all the world and preach the gospel." I couldn't see what possible relationship this could have to a full-term pregnancy. She rocked and spit as if she had done no more than her duty. Perhaps she's something like a cheering section.

I opened the case, which had my name in gold letters; it smelled of new leather. Inside lay the instruments, still virginally new, only the price tags removed. I carefully pulled on a pair of sterile rubber gloves, then looking at the children, said to the mother, "Have to examine you."

"Get at it," she replied.

To cover my embarrassment at doing a vaginal in front of such an interested audience, and still trying to manage my own Good Samaritan feelings of importance, I decided to keep the patient talking as much as possible. That would help allay any fears the poor woman might be having. And started with the old question, "What do you hope it will be—a boy or a girl?"

The mother again clenched her teeth and fists in pain. The fat woman screamed, "Hallelujah! He is risen!" That, I thought, might be appropriate for a new life about to begin. The mother released her hold on the iron bars and swore, "Hope it's a goddamn coyote and takes out for the canyon the minute it's born."

"Oh." I saw no further use for bedside manners and proceeded with the examination. Sitting on the foot end of the squeaky bed I reached in, amazed at how enormously she had been torn on previous deliveries, how loose.

"Anything in its way?" asked the mother from her disadvantageous point of view, being the only person or animal there who wasn't getting a look up into the pelvis.

"Not a thing." In fact, as wide open as this is, the child must be holding on to something in there to keep from falling out. Why, how does she keep the wind from blowing in; and how can her husband copulate with her anyway? It reminded me of an old joke I'd heard doctors tell, "He has to throw an ear of corn up in there, chase a hog after the corn, and then copulate with the hog." I summed it up for the patient in polite language: "You should be repaired."

She answered with a bellow, "Kids! Git outta here! Y'all shakin' the bed!" At which children and chickens—I wondered if they didn't think they were children too—scattered out of the door and window. But all heads immediately appeared at the window and around the sides of the door. A dirty-white chicken flew up into the window and settled itself between the children's heads looking in. The fat woman spat expertly over them and asked, "Doc, is it time to feather her?"

Feather her? What does she mean? I've never heard of such a thing. Since I had no idea what she was talking about, I answered in an authoritative, professional tone, "No. Not yet." She continued her rocking and chewing.

Feather her. I never heard of any such procedure in school. There isn't something I'm overlooking, is there? I asked the mother, "You haven't had any trouble with your previous deliveries, have you?" This one could ride out of there sidesaddle.

"Nope." She closed her eyes, pressed her lips together, and clawed the soiled quilt in her fists. I watched the abdomen contract into a hard mass. A tear squeezed from her closed eyelids.

"Hallelujah! He maketh me to lie down in green pastures."

The mother relaxed. "Nope. Last year this time we was still asettin' to the table finishin' supper. I stood up, yawned and stretched, thought I almost felt somethin' slip. Looked down, and there war Mitildy 'tween my feet."

"Well . . . I say."

"The year 'fore that I had one in the pot. War a right peculiar feelin'. Thought for a minute I war apassing gravel. Kid damn near drowned 'fore it come to me it be little Hedward and not no kidney gravel."

"Is it time to feather her now, doc?"

What the dickens could that "feathering" be? I used an almost haughty voice, "No. Not yet."

Got to figure out what that is. Let's sec—featherbed, perhaps—no. Feather her? . . . Hmm, I don't know what to do. Maybe I can say this case doesn't need feathering.

The patient fanned herself.

"It certainly is hot, for this time of year. Is it always so hot this early out here?" I almost added "in this timber."

No one answered. The fat woman spat out the window. "Hit's gonna come a good 'un."

"Baby?" I asked.

"Storm."

Maybe if I keep her distracted she'll forget about "feathering." "I certainly need a pan of boiled water—and soap."

She rocked on.

"To keep my gloves sterile—and instruments."

She spat.

"Could you please put some water on to boil?"

The rocking stopped. She turned to me, placed a small hand delicately near her fat throat like a duchess, and her look said, "Are you addressing me? Why, son, surely you jest."

"I'm sorry. But I'll need it—and for cleaning her and the baby later."

She spit.

The patient answered, "Tain't no wood chopped. 'E's off uptown someplace."

No sterile water? It never occurred to me I'd ever be doing a delivery without . . . Well, so much for Louis Pasteur and those fellows with their germs. I glanced at the floor, scattered with chicken droppings. Opening my bag again I took out an atomizer and sprayed the vulva and pubic hair.

"Ow! 'At's cold!" she scolded and clamped her knees together.

"Oh, I'm sorry. Should have warned you."

"Whatcha doin'? Baptizin' the baby afore it sticks its head out?"

"Oh no, not with Merthiolate—I mean, no, it's for sterility. To prevent puerperal fever—not get infected later. It's for . . . cleanliness." There, I had said the word. Didn't intend to embarrass them. My voice came almost apologetic, "It's only to keep out infection."

Still sitting at the foot of the bed, I reexamined her. Felt the cervix edge now thin and marginated around the head, fully dilated. Surely she would have the baby with the next pain or two, everything seems in order.

"Is it time to feather her?"

That again. Well, whatever it is, and if it should happen before the baby is born, it will have to be done now. "Yes," I stated seriously. "Now."

I watched the woman push herself up out of the chair, toddle to the bed, watched her pull a feather from the corner of the pillow (there were plenty others stuck on the floor). Then slowly she tickled it back and forth under the patient's nose.

"Ach—" she began. "Ach— ach—" and then it happened. Everything! "Ha-CHOO!" The baby shot out, hit me in the stomach—but not alone. With him came a copious splashing bowel movement, mixed with a gushing slap of amniotic fluid, that splattered over my good suit, face, and the wall behind me. At the same time a blinding slash of yellow light cut through the room! And a thunderous shock that seemed to bounce the house off the ground.

The thunder repeated itself again and again and again, and lightning cast streaks of yellows and blues and greens back and across the room. It rained hard. The kids came stomping inside and huddled at the door leading to the next room, a tarpaulin held over their heads.

The whole room glowed with a quivering fire. The mother's face took on a glaze of holy green; the greasy curls of the woman in the rocker wore a bright red halo that moved back and forth with the rocking. Blue flames radiated in all directions from the newborn child.

This is unreal! I won't believe it!

The chicken sitting in the window, with water running off its tail, wore a strange bright crown. The bedstead glowed purple. This is something supernatural. That holy glow—holy . . . holy . . . The second Christ? I delivered him?

I reached into my bag for the hemostats to clamp the cord and saw my fingers over the stainless steel instruments like a blue X ray of thin bones.

This can't be. It's unreal. Unnatural.

Under the blazing tarpaulin alternating purple-green-purple-green stood little "Saint" Edward, and little "Saint" Mitildy lay in the arms of an older Saint sister. They looked solemn and quiet and unbothered, just as saints are always pictured, even when being burned at the stake. The child lay screaming angrily, like if he could use words they would all be obscene.

Well, whatever all this is—no matter whether you are Jesus or what—I've got to tie your cord.

I picked up the husky baby and its blue cosmic aura. As I wiped him on the dirty quilt, he opened his eyes and glared at me as if he didn't like that.

Well, when the real One, the first One, became born, surely somebody assisted there too . . . And who really knows?

Actually, I had done nothing on this case. Tying the cord seemed like the only thing I came out here to do. I went through some routine gestures of making myself useful, such as spanking the baby, who didn't need it; gauzing mucous out of his lusty throat—I thought he tried to bite my finger. When I attempted to put the drops in his eyes, he fought me so, I'm not certain I got them in good enough.

I tied the cord carefully. I scrutinized the afterbirth to be sure it had all come out. I could remember our famous Doctor Cooke standing in the amphitheater: "Examine the placenta carefully. Make certain it is all there, none left adhered to the wall. It only takes a minute and may save the mother from a uterine infection or an epidermic cancer."

The fat woman watched me, spat out the window—a long blue spark which made an arc like a comet—leaned forward (her halo stayed right in place). "Whatcha doing? Telling its future?"

The chicken wearing the kilowatt crown hopped up on the bed and began pecking into the afterbirth.

"Any clothes for this baby?"

No one answered me.

She rocked, letting rain splatter on her from the window sill. Well, nothing else to do, there being no window to close. "Always rains when Salomie has a baby. Might' near every year."

"Do rains out here—in these parts—always begin with these . . . electrical fireworks?"

"Reckon they always has." (Months later I learned from James that meteorologists had long recognized the rather common occurrence in this part of the country of what is called Saint Elmo's fire.)

I could almost imagine the house floating along in the flood. Rain began dripping all over the mother, the bed, the baby. I picked up the big, naked child and stepped into the second room. All the children stood around a brand-new cook stove, which glowed purple with yellow trimmings, holding a torn tarpaulin over their heads.

"Here, let me have that," and I held it over myself and the baby, and as many of the smelly kids as could sit on the sagging bed in that room.

Suddenly the patient herself ran into the room, jolting the floor with each step. She snatched the tarpaulin off us and flung it over the stove, tucked the corners down and smoothed the sides in. Then, as if this behavior called for some note of explanation, she said over her shoulder as she stomped back, something about ". . . can always get more kids."

With the baby on my arm I huddled next to the stove, protected from the dripping water under part of the tarp. I felt something warm-wet on my arm dripping off my elbow and looked down at the baby's red strained face. It looked straight up at me and strained again.

The rocking and floor-squeaking from the other room continued steadily.

Gosh, kid, how big is your bladder? Well, I guess all Christs have to have their navels tied and have to urinate too.

Seeing the thick encrustations under my shoes, I tried to scrape them on the floor, without much success. Listen, kid, just a word of advice: when you begin to grow and crawl around here—oh, never mind. Well, maybe it's still better than being born in a barn. At least you're home, not traveling. And you own a sixth, seventh, eighth interest in a tarpaulin.

I sat there with the naked kid and his new-tied navel and listened to the rain, and the steady squeaking rocking coming from the other room.

※※※

Straining, I carried another crate of my books into the small office behind Hajovsky's Drug Store. I hooked the claw hammer under another nail and pulled. It screeched loose. Better save these good crates, store them out behind . . . just in case. The boards splintered and prized up, open, giving off the fresh odor of new lumber; I breathed it in deeply . . . and thought I heard somebody call my name.

I pushed open the screen door into the drugstore but saw no one—

only shelves and shelves of toilet articles and patent medicines. I asked where Black Draught, Groves Chill Tonic, and Carter's Little Liver Pills were kept—because there was a peephole somewhere there, no larger than a navel—"Did you call me, Papinku?"

"Yes," came muffled from behind rows of Lydia Pinkham's Compound, so I walked behind the counter and turned between the shelves. There sat cherubic druggist Hajovsky, surrounded by an odor of camphor, eating kolace from a neatly napkined plate that his wife had evidently left for him.

Since nothing more was said, I thought I had been invited to share in this delicacy of Bohemian cooking, when Papinku—his mouth too full to speak—pointed his fork at the waiting telephone receiver.

"Oh. Hello?" I kept my eyes on the kolace—only two left; maybe he'll save me one. "Yes."

Somebody came into the store; I stood a better chance now. I watched Papinku squint through the peephole and come around to the front. The lady wanted a package of Gillette razor blades.

"About how old is he?"

The old-fashioned bell of the cash register clanged so loud it surely could be heard in Hajek's Feed Store on one side and the post office on the other. The little cash drawer punched Papinku in the belly and nestled there while he scooped out nickels in change.

"That sounds very serious. And at his age."

The druggist returned to the kolace.

"I'd better come right away. What's the name?"

The second kolace was gone.

"Cernoch? Ivan Cernoch?" The druggist shook his head no and started on the last kolace.

"Where does he live?"

The druggist shook his head again, but it may have been in sadness, for now the last kolace disappeared. He touched his fat little mouth with the napkin, folded its corners together, and put the plate on the chest of thin, flat drawers marked "Thread," where he kept contraceptives for sale. The local priest frowned upon this, but perhaps since Papinku was a heavy and constant contributor to the church nothing was ever done about it. If the holy father knew anything about the bottom drawer where little blue pills were hidden ("almost guaranteed to make her come around regular again—five dollars"), he preferred to ignore it.

"Four blocks north of the high school, three houses alike, the middle house. Okay. I'll be right out." As I left the camphor odor, heading for the screen door to my waiting room, I nodded pleasantly to a lady coming into the store.

"Mr. Hajovsky, the window is closed at the post office and I understand you sell stamps." Judging from her good clothes and speech, she must be a townsperson.

Papinku began to rub his pink bald head—I learned he did this whenever he felt flustered. It always looked as if he were feeling for something, soft spots perhaps. "I do, Mrs. Galloway, to my regular customers. Why don't you go buy stamps where you buy your medicines?" She glared at him and stomped out.

Hardly the way to win friends and make customers, I thought as I dropped my bag behind the front seat.

And again I wondered: Would they accept me here, these Bohemians with their ways, and the Germans? They're still Europeans. The German part doesn't worry me—I can manage that, am used to it. But will I soon be crating those books and looking for some other place—the "doctor's office" behind some other drugstore in some other town?

Mr. Cernoch was sick, very sick. He sat propped up in bed, grunting for breath. A barefoot woman stood fanning him. His feet were swollen big, and droplets of serum oozed out of the thick legs, with flies sitting there licking at the juice. She waved the fan at them. His hands lay stiffly puffed.

"You obviously have been sick a long time, Mr. Cernoch. Why didn't you call a doctor before?"

No one answered.

"You should be in a hospital." I tapped out the size of the enormously enlarged heart. A hypertrophic sclerotic heart, the kind—when you recall a specimen mounted in its glass jar in Path Lab—that has many, many tiny scar tissues. Each scar takes away one or more of the tiny heart muscles, killing it off, turning it into scar, until finally there are not enough of the workers left to do the job well. And the weakened heart walls become slack and saggy and cannot pump the blood through the entire body. So the sluggish heart enlarges, "hypertrophies"—but it is a false growth, not a growth at all, more a collapse. Like a balloon filling with water bigger and bigger. The backlog of blood in the body stagnates and dams higher and higher, filling even up into the lungs, leaves the man gasping for air, literally swimming or drowning in his own blood.

This man is dying.

Wish I had a hospital here.

Will live only a few days more.

Unless I can actually reverse some of this . . . and at least delay his death. Maybe even for several years.

But he's going to die.

Even if I can delay it—and it's possible, quite possible—even so, this man, breathing and living now, is on the path to his death.

He'll die. Of this condition. Sooner or later, he will.

Suddenly it seemed another person had come into the room. An invisible one. Death, I suppose. Had suddenly appeared, just sitting there on the other side of the bed. Like a real person. Sitting, silent, as though waiting but also watching me.

That's how it felt. Exactly as if another person were joining us around this bed. Me; the barefoot woman, standing; the patient, propped up on pillows, laboring to breathe; and this other person, just sitting, looking on.

"I must tell you, Mr. Cernoch: You are very sick."

I glanced up to the woman, who stopped fanning to listen. "I think you'd best call the priest right away."

While the woman went into the next room and told somebody, I kept explaining, "I'm going to give you two injections, Mr. Cernoch. One is to make you pass off some of this water in your body, which is even up into your lungs—it makes that gurgling when you breathe. The heart is weak and cannot pump the blood fast enough, so the water—serum—of the blood has seeped out, leaked, and swollen your legs and abdomen, see? And you are like standing in water up to here, the lower lungs even. But the water is inside. The medicine in this injection drains this water off, through the kidneys. That alone will help the heart—it won't have to push against all that water. The other injection is for your heart itself, will make it stronger for now. You will feel stronger yourself." I spoke loudly, as to a deaf person, as if this would help the man understand English better.

The priest, Father Puziovsky, came almost immediately and began his ceremony. He lit two candles and put on a black robe—which smelled of being locked in a closed place too long—and a purple and gold ribbon around his neck and began saying something in Latin and touched the man's eyes and lips and hands.

I visualized the many small scars scattered through the heart muscle-walls. Was each created from a small infection? It is said that some of our emotions damage us as much as some of our infections. Did each severe disappointment that he had suffered cause a constriction and then scar? The pain and pay of it again and again and again? Was that the cause of the wearing-out of a tiny muscle, here, there?

I tiptoed into the next room where the old wife sat on a sagging bed looking down at the black beads in her hands, crying, and I whispered to the other woman, "Two prescriptions I shall leave at the drugstore; I will have the directions written in Bohemian so he can start on them right away. Each he must take before meals. Three times a day—whether he eats or not."

The priest droned " . . . in Your boundless mercy grant this man recovery from this illness, and if this is not possible in accordance with Your wisdom receive him, for he has . . ."

I whispered again, "I'll be back in the morning, but if during the night he seems worse in any way, please call me."

"Papinku? Are you here?" I called between the shelves. No answer. I glanced to the place where a key to the toilet is kept, but the key, wired to its short plank, hung there. "Papinku?"

"Here. In the back room."

He sat on a table with his bare feet in a chair, his round belly like that of a Buddha. The odor of camphor filled the room like incense. A man who calls himself Doctor David and travels through kneeled, trimming Papinku's toenails.

"Here are two prescriptions for Mr. Cernoch. The man is very sick. They will send for them."

He said nothing but rubbed his head.

"Got any knives or scissors you want sharpened, doc?" That from Doctor David.

"No, thanks."

"Sure fix'em up nice and sharp."

"No. I use those with the detachable—throwaway—blades."

First thing next morning a neighbor phoned through to Hajovsky's. "Mr. Cernoch is worse. They think dying."

He lay dead, mouth open. His wife had been taken to a friend's house. The barefoot woman still held the fan with a picture on one side of Hajek's Feed Store and on the other side of Jesus on the cross with purple clouds and yellow lightning. "He vas better, after you here, and all night. He passing so much vater and sleep in between. And his breathing so much better, he lay hisself more flat down."

"I don't understand why the medicine didn't keep him going—after a good start. How many doses of the digitalis did he take?"

"From vat?"

"The heart drops. Comes in a small green bottle."

"Oh such. No, they couldn't get those medicines. Mr. Hajovsky vouldn't let them have it only they pay kesh, and they don't have it."

"But he *had* to have it—digitalis. It's the *only* medicine which helps. For the heart."

"They ask it two times, once right avay after you, and once more later afternoon. He say no."

"But what I prescribed would only cost about two dollars. The digitalis only seventy-five cents."

She said nothing more and fanned the flies away from the dead man's mouth.

"The mattress? Ve should burn it?"

"No. It is not necessary. What he has—had—is not catching."

I drove back fast, stomped into the drugstore. I'm going to have a talk with that druggist. Just what does he think he is? Acting like God or something. "Where's Papinku?" I asked James, who sat reading a magazine.

"They're having their meeting." He indicated the back room without looking up.

"What meeting?"

"The annual meeting. It's the SJVKT."

"The what?"

"It's a benevolent Slavic order, like a lodge and insurance company together."

"And they meet here?"

"Sure. Then they don't have to rent a hall."

"When will they be through?"

"When they finish the meeting, they go to Mr. Hajovsky's house for dinner."

The door opened and they filed out. They had high stiff collars, untrimmed mustaches, dirty fingernails, and set their clean hats precisely straight upon their heads.

Papinku smiled big. One of the men patted him on the shoulder.

"I see their voting is finished."

"Voting?" I asked. James closed the magazine and slid it back into the stand.

"Oh yes. They always reelect Mr. Hajovsky president. Every year."

❋❋❋

I sat at my desk, idly thinking of how the land of all this area is so decisively sliced into two. There is the open, rolling black-land prairie where all the farms lie, and an almost sharp line marks where that ends and sand land begins, thickly covered and crowded with timber and brush—no farms.

I heard the side door open and thought, Good, I have a patient.

Victor Schlussmann, he said his name—tall, blond man—and we shook hands. He had tools hanging around his belt. Came to install the phone. We looked at each other, my thoughts saying, We look much alike—no, his shoulders are wide, his voice deeper. His hand felt rough. He walked about my desk and office with an easy certainty in his step, asked which side of the desk I wanted it on and would I be cranking it right-handed or left. "Nobody could tell us that about you, they thought right-handed." He finished quickly and left.

I sat at the desk. Looked at the telephone. It made me nervous.

Did I have any other choice but to come to a small Texas town, this one or any other? With medical-school debts and no money, I couldn't afford to start in a city and pay rent while waiting for a practice to build up. And buy office equipment and furniture. And I certainly couldn't buy a ready-made practice.

My roots were here in southern Texas. I came back from medical school with a diploma and dreams—of joining Schweitzer in Africa, at Lambarene, maybe building a jungle hospital of my own. Big dreams, but with nothing definite. An older brother, the oldest one, with a large practice well established, offered me a junior partnership in his office in San Angelo out in west Texas. But the arrangement he suggested made it clear that I would be "junior" forever, so I declined.

Rather be my own man somewhere else—anywhere else. So I leafed through medical journals week after week and read the ads and more ads, and began to doubt.

Then Mr. Hajovsky heard of me through an insurance salesman and asked me to come. He said the one doctor practicing here, a Dr. Kotzebue, seventy or over, had more than he could do. (I ought to go call on him.) Told me the doctor who had my—this—office before me had been an old man who died three years ago; that's why there's the cabinet and rickety examining table. (I'll give them a coat of white enamel.) The man was sickly for years before he died. His instruments rusted and corroded; I had to throw them away, have all new shiny ones. But he left a skull, a real human skull, which has a container, a can, sunk into the cranium. Now whatever do you use a skull for? To show the patient where sinuses are? Or nasal passages? Wouldn't it shock most people? And the can, for heaven's sake—was it for pencils, flowers, or cigars? Anybody who'd keep a thing like that around really was sick. It ought to be buried somewhere.

Holding it in one hand, way out, I pushed it up in the closet, high on the top shelf, far back, dark in a corner. And closed the door.

Dr. Kotzebue—Bohemian name. I have to go call on him; it's the polite thing to do; he'll appreciate that. My colleague. Maybe he'll want to say Welcome and give a few pointers about local traditions. Or tell a couple of amusing anecdotes about patient happenings. He's certainly the senior doctor, perhaps he'll be the kindly old uncle to me—glad to have a young man around to take some of the work load off. He might phone me later and say, "I'm taking the weekend off. Told my office and the telephone operator to refer all calls to you. Hope you planned to be around?" That would be nice, help me get started. And I can repay him someday—take good care of him when he's old and sick. Even take care of his office and insist all payments go directly to his office. It's been done between doctors. A few years from now people might be saying, "Those two, they were like father and son." Aw, I'm probably dreaming. But I must go see him. Might as well go now—haven't anything else to do. I'll stop by the lumberyard first for sandpaper and paintbrush.

His office is on Main Street, which parallels the railroad. Papinku's drugstore is on the perpendicular street, which crosses the tracks and goes on up the hill to the big Catholic church. I can't find a place to park right in front of his office—everything taken. My gosh, does he own *two* buildings? He's in one and his drugstore in the other—big buildings.

I entered the office and, my God, the waiting room alone was larger than my entire office space, and it sat full! They sat against the wall all around: women, men, old, young, children, babies. Like a bus station. Couldn't even find a place to sit. Seemed to me they were all Bohemian farmers. Would Dr. Kotzebue be Catholic? Most Bohemians are.

A middle-aged receptionist, nice looking, came and asked, "You wanted to see the doctor?" Nice perfume. Everyone in the room sat perfectly quiet, watching me.

"I'm the new doctor. I've just moved here, and I wanted to say hello."

"Oh yes, we've heard about you. That poor Mr. Cernoch. I'm sure you tried everything to save him." Must she speak so loud? Everybody looking, listening. "Wait here, the doctor's busy now, but I'll tell him. I'll have Raymond bring more chairs."

I stood waiting, everybody looking at me—like I might be some different species. They didn't come up and feel my suit or look in my ears or mouth, but I felt their eyes did. I nodded hello, but they only kept staring at me.

When Raymond came, I realized his was the only black face in the room. He looked so serious, sad. (Is he sick?) I took the chair from him and said, "Thank you, Raymond," and instantly his eyes opened big white and so did his smile.

I sat, waiting. Looked at my watch.

The receptionist kept busy, bookkeeping.

I lit a cigarette and saw no ashtray. I went to her desk, "May I have an ashtray?"

"The doctor doesn't like smoking." And she continued with her accounts.

So I went to the entrance doors and flipped a whole cigarette away. And came back to the chair and sat. And waited.

Is he deliberately keeping me waiting?

He could call me in to examine and review a patient *with* him. It would only be polite.

I had sat almost an hour before she took the next patient in and said to me—across the room, "The doctor said he will see you soon."

Surely everyone in this room knows by now that I have no patients waiting for me.

If I could only smoke.

At last: "The doctor will see you now, sir."

The man is certainly no seventy years old. Big fellow. Straight carriage. Expensive tailoring, beautiful cloth, but it did not altogether hide his large abdomen. Looked more like a nice mature fifty. He held out his left hand, almost pontifically, I thought; his right wore a pallbearer's white glove. "Oh," I pointed to the glove, "injured?" Some of the fingers were sewn closed, making it more like a single claw.

"X-ray burns." His voice, resonant with authority, seemed to vibrate through everything in the place, including me. "X-ray radiation. I've sacrificed my right hand to science."

Sacrificed to not taking the proper precautions, like wearing lead-lined gloves, but I didn't say it.

He looked at my hands. "So you've moved right in. I wish you had consulted me first. I would have told you: Another doctor here isn't needed. Won't make a living." His tone sounded like a judgment—sentencing: ". . . and hanged by the neck until. . . ."

"Sorry to hear that. I know I'm not . . . Catholic. You seem to be mighty busy." (I remember that old trick of examining patients so slowly that you keep the waiting room full. Then at five o'clock you see them all fast, one after the other.)

"Half of them don't pay."

His oversized long desk, like a closed casket, stood on carved claw feet—talons, each clutching a ball—stood in the same huge room with his X ray, a monstrous iron thing, black, with exposed wires overhead, and the tube nesting in a thick glass bowl above, almost like something sacred—maybe, to these people, like the eye of God, which can see through you. I had never seen one so old. "That's rare. Practically a museum piece," had already tumbled out of me before I knew it might sound derogatory.

"I was first to have an X ray. For my patients. But they don't appreciate one's efforts. You'll find out."

"Oh, a . . . [almost said "antique"] sterilizer—the old-fashioned kind where you step on a pedal and the lid opens like an alligator's mouth. This one so old its chrome was peeling. But—stupid thing to be doing—I had already tripped the pedal and the lid came up and I stood looking down in at a stack of bank notes. Notes or certificates or stocks, I had never seen such things before. "Oh. Sorry. I wanted to see if it still works." Clumsy me. "Sure sorry about the . . ."

"That druggist you're with—nobody likes him."

"Oh?"

"I could have warned you. And everybody remembers what happened there. They'll never forget it."

"Forget what? What happened?"

"About the boy. The tonsilectomy."

"What boy?"

"He didn't tell you? That'll be a blight on that place forever. The boy died without Last Sacraments. These people are devout Catholic. You're *not* Catholic, are you?"

"What boy?"

"He should have told you. He had a young doctor come in, about like you. How old are you? Twenty-two?"

"Twenty-four," I lied.

"Your record says twenty-two." I blushed red and forgot to ask, What record? "Got this young man to come here, only stayed a week. Did a tonsilectomy there in the office and the boy died. Right there where you are. Couldn't stop the hemorrhage. The family started screaming he killed the boy. They and their relatives—it was a mob. Someone ran over here and told me. I thought they might lynch him."

"Your influence calmed them?"

"I stayed completely out of it. Didn't want to get myself pushed around for trying to protect a wrong. He didn't tell you? Next morning that young man couldn't be found. Lit out during the night—packed and left. Everybody knows it happened right there where you are now. Didn't tell you?" As we neared the door of the next room, a nurse in fresh, stiff uniform stepped right in front of him and pushed the door open for us.

"Well . . . no. I didn't know." I glanced around. A black woman in white uniform leaned at a sink, washing test tubes and syringes and coffee cups. She did not look up as we passed. "The knob—handle—is missing from the cabinet." My voice seemed rattly. Such a stupid silly thing to say. Wish I'd said nothing.

"All the doorknobs are off. Haven't you noticed? I always have them removed. If I turn a handle, it breaks the skin open again." He held the white-gloved claw up. "The twist does it."

"You have so much space here. Nice."

"I have an entire clinic here, complete laboratory, X ray, treatment rooms, diathermy, everything. Too bad you lost a patient already. Like the other young doctor. That druggist you're with doesn't tell you everything, does he?"

I had no answer.

"I assume, then, he didn't tell you about the one before that—it might have scared you off if he had. That one went crazy—insane. Ran off, leaving a woman laboring in childbirth. She died and the child too. He's still locked up in the lunatic asylum—should be and always will be. And the last one, the old fellow coughing on his patients all the time—the few he still had, free ones—I think he had TB. People were afraid to go near him on the street. Who wants TB? Hajovsky kept trying to get rid of him. Everybody thinks that office of yours has TB germs in the walls everywhere. He didn't tell you *any*thing?"

I felt my face burning. My mouth flew open to speak, but at the same time the door opened without a knock and the receptionist stepped in. "Doctor, they called again. Her water broke. Strong pains."

Another nurse appeared—how many does he have?—wearing a white stand-up cap and a blue cape with red lining. She carried two bags.

"And by the way," he smiled at me, "what's your draft status? You're of military age."

"The local board in LaGrange already sent me a card—right after I registered. Deferred."

He didn't say good-by to me, nor glad-you-came. They started toward the back door, everyone opening doors for him. He did say something, either to the others or to me—I didn't catch it. Either he said to the others, "I don't think we'll be long," or maybe he said to me, "I don't think you'll be here long." And they left.

As I walked slowly into the drugstore, James, leaning on the counter reading a magazine, straightened up and kept looking at me as if waiting for me to say something.

"I've been over to Dr. what's-his-name . . ."

"Kotzebue."

". . . to say hello. That man *owns* this town, medically speaking."

"The town and all the countryside for twenty miles in every direction—and the bank."

"No wonder no young doctors came here: They figured they'd have no chance."

Back in my office I stared at the white walls and at the diplomas. I looked at the closet door and thought of the skull hidden up on the top shelf.

❋❋❋

While I still stared at the closed door, my new phone rang. "This is Mrs. Harmann, the operator. Mr. Freytag asked me to call you. They can't get Dr. Kotzebue—he's on a call. For you to come to the Jarosek farm right away. He and the sheriff are there already. Do you know where?"

"Why the sheriff?"

"First you pass the Catholic church and turn left. . . ." She gave directions clearly and I tried to remember them: turn left at the four corners, pass Pitman Cemetery, but it's only a small sign, watch for a big oak tree with a wire gap . . .

I drove through the beautiful land, over hills, down smooth valleys, across rumbly plank bridges flanked by tall, easy patterns of naked pecan trees. A swirl of birds turned in midair—if you could put them to music they would have made a symphony of pastoral harmony, swooping and turning again. As I drove the winding roads, over the rolling prairie hills, it was surprising how often I saw a church steeple. Always built on the highest place. Almost every one with a cross on the very top.

Farms everywhere, the buildings clustered on hilltops, sometimes with great live oak trees. Always white houses with black roofs, and red barns. Farmers in almost every field. This is planting time. Finishing spring plowing and starting the planting, following the curved contoured lines of fine furrows. Some ride behind their teams; others still have the old walking planters. In rare instances, there is a farmer on a red and yellow tractor, going fast, making so much noise the birds pecking in the fresh soil stay far behind and fly up again far ahead of his coming back.

But all of these plowings follow the contoured lines—curves, swirls, even circles around a low place: all parallel lines. They make each field look like giant fingerprints. On hill after hillside lay these great plowed fingerprints, as if some mighty being had laid his hands gently upon the land, leaving imprints of benediction.

And the directions came out right. I drove up to the house, the hackberry trees in front there all in a row, still naked bare, showing their green nests of mistletoe. A wall of thick green cedars sheltered the north side. Several cars were there already, and people standing around—must be having some kind of get-together.

Carrying my new black bag with its handle squeaking. "What is it?" I asked the nearest group. "Who's sick?" They pointed to the well. I had no idea what they meant, but thought I'd take a glance before going on into the house.

I leaned, looking down into the round, rocked well—at a man hanging there, his hands down at his sides and his shoes pointing down. New shoes, brand new. The body turned slowly, as if the rope were untwisting itself, and as he came around with his head back and to one side, the torn throat hung gaping open in a wide raw smile. An odor of blood and watery bowel movement. New shoes, shiny new. On the flat mirror waterfloor I saw a head that moved as I moved, with sky behind it, but something dribbled and dropped and the reflection wobbled.

I heard someone saying ". . . musta cut his throat before he jumped," and I remember thinking, nobody could cut their own throat that big. Hanging there, the weight of his body has pulled it wider apart. It smiled like a great mouth. "Brand-new shoes," I said, maybe aloud.

The body turned, and his face now came around with the eyes open, looking right up at me.

My God! What would make you do something like that to yourself?

I cannot remember what I did next—I did not vomit, nor lose sphincter control either. But the next thing I knew I came walking into the house—holding my bag against my chest, hugging it with both arms—toward a woman sitting on a bed.

More conscious now, I spoke to her as gently as I could. "Let me have your arm, please, I want to take your pressure first." It stood only slightly high for her apparent age. "I'd like to give you a small hypo. May I?"

By now I could dare think of the cut throat again—dare let it come back into me as I fixed the hypo, trembling. The long red mouth, the corners torn farther by the pulling weight, angled up, making this wide mouth into a broad red smile of raw-torn lips. Almost a laughing. I saw again the small clotted line of blood out of a corner of the real lips. And with the face looking up sideways, the blood had come up into the nostrils—but no farther—and in the turning they shone like two eyes there . . . of some monster that had come up into the body, claiming it, watching, looking at me. The big red gap laughing.

No, not the corpse, not him laughing, but something within him—maybe the same monstrous something that had conquered and possessed him and made him do it. Maybe that laughing. And slowly turning so it kept laughing all around, at everybody, all the world.

I saw again the clot of blood—or bowels—fall *splotsh* on the water. As if some deep and denied wish had at last lunged free. Or like some god laughing up from the bottom of the well.

Outside we heard a man's voice saying, "That water won't be fit to drink for weeks."

She fell to one side on the bed with an arm over the back of her head, sobbing into the mattress. No one could hear the muffled crying except me, and I doubt she ever felt the needle. Then I left.

❋❋❋

There's much advice around on what to do until the doctor comes. But what does the doctor do until the patients come?

The outside room is for patients to wait for the doctor. But first, the inside room is for the doctor to wait for the patients. So I stayed nights, after supper, just in case somebody should come, and I read—the thick heavy Gray's *Anatomy:* "To facilitate the anatomical relationships of anterior, posterior, medial and lateral, the cadaver is always described in the anatomical position, that is, lying on his back, facing the ceiling; the arms lie along the sides with the palms open and upward. . . ."

Or I'd go talk to James for a while—Papinku doesn't come back in the evenings.

I leaned against shelves of glass jars with gold-edged labels, saying again how the country so definitely divides into two, the prairie hills and the timber.

Shaggy Nietzsche, a white tip to his tail, lay on the floor, often looking up at us as if listening.

James picked up the thought. "Divides the kinds of people, too. Not the geography—the people make their choice. Prairie people are one kind: good people. German and Bohemian farmers, hard working, honest, peaceful, built the churches. All have credit if they'd ever use it, but they don't—buy only what they can pay for with cash. Except their land of course. Good people almost without exception."

A large man in farmer clothes, blue denim jumper—looked dirty—walked slowly by, stopped, looked at us through the window, went on.

"The timber: 'Sandies,' lazy, white trash, shiftless, always cutting and killing each other—man-wife, father-son, brothers—whereas the blacks and Mexicans, also always fighting, kill only their friends. Can't be trusted. When they come in the store, you have to let them know you're watching and stay beside them or they'll walk off with things—anything. They came first and made their choice; the Germans and Bohemians came later and chose the hard work—prairie."

He fanned a turkey-feather duster over shelves of bottles and the glass box over the scales. He stopped and looked toward the window. The same farmer had come walking by again, going the opposite way, paused, looking in at us, went on.

"Negroes have their own settlement, called Colony. They went way out there when they were freed from slavery and started it. Here on the edge of town, their place is called Happy Hollow. In their situation, I suspect their happiness is too often hollow."

I yawned. "Sure can notice it out on the farmland—the hard work. Everything taken care of so pretty, perfect; fences exact; fields all plowed; no weeds, even on the turn row. Like they had conquered nature and set it into boundaries and rules for themselves."

He had finished dusting and put the duster away. I got up to leave. He said a strange thing, "More like they conquered their own nature, fencing it into strict tight rules."

***

Hired a nurse. Don't know how, nor hardly why. Margaret. Hadn't even thought of hiring anyone. She came and applied entirely on her own, because I hadn't mentioned any such thing to anyone, not even to James. When she came I didn't know what to do. We talked a while, and I asked what salary she'd want, as I had never hired anyone before. She said forty dollars a month if it wasn't too much.

She was from an old German family in the town—old-maidish, neat, Catholic. Seemed industrious; seemed a good fifteen years older than myself (but I didn't ask her age). Had been a practical nurse for years—at one time or another nursed many around here in their homes. Stayed home and nursed her parents until each died, at eighty-two and eighty-eight. Only thing was she didn't speak Czech, and I didn't know much. And neither of us knew Spanish either. We both spoke German.

I said, "Excuse me a moment," went to James. And between the shelves told him in a low voice about her applying, and did he know her and would she be all right?

He answered "Sure" so fast I wondered if she might be his girl friend. But I knew he supports his mother and doesn't date girls. Goes to Miss Jessie's Chicken Ranch, near LaGrange, every Friday night with several other single men in town—they go together in one car. So I believed him.

I really didn't know what to do.

When I returned I asked her if we'd need a maid later, and she said she could always clean up before I came in the mornings. Margaret—in German it's Gretchen. I asked when she'd like to begin; she said as soon as she could go home and put her uniform on. I told her to come tomorrow, if that'd be all right with her.

I hoped we'd get a patient or two. It'd be so embarrassing to have a nurse and nothing to do.

I also hoped I'd have enough money by the end of the month to pay her.

❋❋❋

Mr. Theo Hajdik. Such a pleasant little old man—and didn't seem to be worried or even serious about his complaints. His attitude puzzled me. "Weakness and this big stomach—in here, a growth."

Margaret made a card for him, had brought her typewriter to the office and said she'd type out a card for everyone as they came. I wrote on this first one, "Pt unusually objective."

And what a growth! A spleen the size of a bucket. "How long have you noticed this?"

"Many years. Now so big I don't get my breath good—can't walk far." He smiled.

"Then—many years, hmm—you have had medical attention?"

"Yes. To Dr. Kotzebue."

"Oh? How did he diagnose this?"

"Enlarged liver. That's what it is. Enlarged like a growth." Smiling.

"It's the spleen. You can feel the typical shape of the spleen and its characteristic markings: the two notches. With the spleen involved—so enlarged!—we have to get a blood count and smear first."

"A blood test?"

"Yes, blood count—differential count."

Under the microscope, the large bluish cells with their characteristic "knotted-rope" type nuclei came easily into focus: myelocytes. And with their typical granules. And with the high white count. Myelogenous leukemia. "You have chronic myelogenous leukemia. That's a rare condition."

"How you say it?"

I repeated. "Why do you choose—why do you have—such an unusual—You are not a farmer, no, are you? What did you do?"

"Me? I taught school for many, many years. In the old days. We had little country schools, one room. All changed today, all different. They don't need me for years past. How you say it?"

"Chronic myelogenous leukemia. Now wait. I've heard of you. Aren't you the one wrote a book of poems? That intrigues me—that out here—"

"Only translations. Nothing more."

"Why, that's wonderful. James. It was James told me."

"No. Nobody was interested. It was for nothing."

"Oh . . . I'm sorry to hear that."

"Yes," he said sadly. It was the only expression of sincere emotion I had seen in the little man. "And I worked so many years on it. And taught so long, sometimes children from the first ones. All the years you work on something like that. You live with it so long it becomes part of you. It's difficult to swallow that nobody cares what you did. Like it won't go down, even after all these years." I thought he'd say "Every man has his dream," but he didn't.

I had to look in *Medicine* and *Current Therapy* for the treatment. Myelogenous leukemia is not an everyday disease. "You must take some drops—in milk. In water they would taste bitter—it says so here. If James doesn't have them, I'm sure he'll be glad to order. You'll have to take them over a long period of time."

The little fellow never asked if he would die from it, or is this kind of leukemia as bad as other kinds, or anything. Asked nothing. Seemed entirely unbothered, unconcerned. Smiled mostly. He left by the side door—which meant he wasn't going to have the prescription filled here.

Within an hour he came back. "Did you forget something?" Margaret asked.

"How does he say it? What I have? Would he write it on a paper?"

I did and he left again by the side door.

Almost half an hour later Margaret answered the phone, frowned, covered the black funnel mouthpiece, "For you—but it's Dr. Kotzebue!"

"... wanted to tell you of an interesting case I had today—a chronic myelogenous leukemia."

"That's odd."

"Made the diagnosis by a blood count—thought I'd tell you."

"Gosh. It couldn't possibly be that there would be two. Is it Theo Hajdik?"

"Yes, yes, that's the patient. Been my patient for years. It's an interesting case, and I thought I'd tell you."

As I hung up, Margaret still looked questions at me. I shook my head. "All I can say is danged if *I* know."

In the afternoon, Margaret had asked old Mr. Kalina if he had a bottle at home, to bring a morning urine specimen next time.

"Is going always to Dr. Kotzebue and all time get new medicines. Each time is changing it all new medicines. By the armsful I get it each time. I got it at home bottles like from a machina factory."

"If it had cough syrup or any kind of sugar, wash it out good."

After he left she opened a catalog—don't know where she got it from—to "Laboratory specimen jars, Wide opening, Graduated. With personalized caps."

"I wish you'd agree—I'm going to order three dozen of these."

"Okay. Okay."

"Shall it have Schulze Clinic or just your name on it?"

"I'd rather people's excretions wouldn't be labeled me."

"I'll make it 'Schulze Clinic, Schulenburg, Texas.' "

"Yes. Yes, I think I like that best. I'd rather be called a clinic—than an excretion."

She didn't seem to think it funny. Well . . .

❋❋❋

The grandmother rose and dropped several handfuls of corncobs and pieces of split live oak into the cookstove; the flames fluttered shadows across her face and lit up the dark room until she replaced the iron lid. She adjusted the handle of the damper and glanced toward the double bed at the far end of the big room, where Margaret, by the dim light of the lamp, busily arranged a patch quilt over the patient. "Yes," she spoke in Czech, "waiting on first baby to come makes the remembering to lookback."

"How many babies did you have, Maminko Konvitchka?"

"Ha. Not like peoples today: I had fourteen—only, two died."

"That's a fine record. How old were you when your first one came?"

"Fifteen I was in the summer, and the baby came at cotton-picking. I was all alone. My papa farmed for a German and he had a son. My work was to chase all the mules up from the pasture into the lot, and the German boy—nice blond fellow—would catch, holding them by the ear, and put the harness on, and bits and reins. So the boy and me we always meet at the barn by the mules, and so finally I begin growing me a little belly, and my mama she ask me about the boy and I say, 'Yes I think he nice fellow,' and she say nothing. Few months later, when my belly she is getting big like a cow udder, my papa asked me about the boy, and I say, 'Yes, I think he nice fellow,' and papa tell me to stay away from the mules. Next day the boy comes from the big barn to our little house and say he want to make marry by me and I say 'all right.'

"But next day boy's papa come and say wedding be by Lou-turn church, and my papa say No, he Kat-tow-lick in old country, and he come to work in new country to make it better life for his children and change from old church in new country is no good for children. Be wedding by Kat-tow-lick or no wedding.

"German farmer man say his people had much to carry in old country from Kat-tow-lick church and they go Lou-turn and they stay Lou-turn in new country."

I looked at Margaret and she answered, "Twelve minutes apart, lasting one minute—fairly strong."

"You didn't marry the boy then?"

"No. My papa move right away to another farm, and there I had the baby. I was alone in house and baking the kolace—Friday—for my mother, because everybody has to pick. I was afraid of not knowing, and ven the pains got the vorse I tried to leave the house and go to the field where my mama is. A Negro voman in a big straw hat is at the well in the yard pulling fresh vater for the jugs and she see me and she say, 'Child, you is in labor.' "

The old woman grinned, showing missing teeth but healthy gums. "I say always she was a black angel. She stay by me and help me, and ven my mama came from the field I was all in a clean bed and the baby vashed and wrapped and the kolace were done."

As if this reminded her of something, she went to a shelf where she turned back a white cloth to inspect three large pans of fully risen dough. As she began sliding the pans in the oven, I went to the other end of the room and pulled on a rubber glove to examine the patient.

"Only three fingers dilation," I said to Margaret.

"Where's Joe at this early hour?" I asked as I peeled the glove off. "Doesn't that big lug know you're having a baby, or couldn't he take it?" I teased—maybe it helps some—to relieve her anxiety.

"He's down at the pigpen helping his registered Hampshire sow have her pigs. He has to stay with her, or she'll eat some of them."

"Gosh. Wonder why they do that?"

"Some say nature makes the sow do it so she can nurse the right number."

Grandma Konvitchka had come to the sleeping end of the big room, but instead of asking about the patient, she took the lamp. The small, fine tremor of her old hands quivered the flame, and the glass chimney rattled. She held it low to peer into the oven, saying almost to herself, "These high-bred things, they are not natural at all. It must be difficult for them. They are not of the seasons." She lifted the round lid, stuck more wood into the fire, and sat hunchbacked in the dim yellow light looking down into her apron at her crude hands, as weathered as the oak trunks that sheltered the green-grown shingles of this cottage.

The pains came slowly. I sat on a bench, my elbows on the long, cleanly scrubbed table, looking up at a row of saints on cheap prints done in primitive colors: Red was barn red, blue was dark blue, and haloes were yellow gold. I recognized Jesus and Mary for sure, but the rest could have been almost any of the saints. But they seemed all to be in the same fix—each had his bared heart thrust through with swords and daggers, leaking large, simple drops of blood like a string of beads, and yellow and red flames radiated from each heart like a picture of the sun. Yet each saint seemed to look satisfied, almost happy, about the whole thing.

I walked over and sat in the warm corner by the old woman, where a cradle with its carvings worn smooth and its fresh covers waited by the oven.

"How many grandchildren do you have, Maminko?"

"Thirty-six." She pointed to the dark corner of the double bed. "Thirty-seven."

"Were all your other children born here?"

She nodded. "I see Konvitchka many times; once he buy a cow from papa. One day he ride up to the porch and say, 'I have paid it down on a farm and need a wife to help me work—a strong wife. Will you come?'

And I say 'Yes.' So he say, 'I will tell the priest today and we will go to church together the three Sundays as it is done.' I took from my mother's my yeast, and the next Monday morning we was married, and Tuesday morning I was baking bread. I work hard and many many times he whip me.''

''He did? What for?''

''I don't know.''

''What did you do about it.''

''I work harder,'' she laughed through her few teeth.

''Ven we were old we sit at the table vun day—he was smoking his old pipe vich gurgled its spit. On the table was some cooked cheese vich had not come out quite right for me. We were alone and I ask him, 'Old man, I have been your wife for fifty years. We are old now, we cannot work, and we may be only sands soon. I wish to ask you, have you loved me?'

''He gurgled his pipe and finally said, 'Vit you it was no love, but slowly vit the years—as slow as an acorn tree grows—it came and I love.' That's all he say, and we sit over there by the table vit the bowl of cooked cheese that didn't come out just right.''

I glanced over to that place. The satisfied saints were looking down. ''What did Mr. Konvitchka die of?''

''He slowly became white and the stone went out of his strength. His blood was thin and went to water.''

Pernicious anemia, maybe.

''Three minutes apart, doctor,'' Margaret called. ''Will you bring the lamp—it's the only one.''

I sat on the foot of the bed examining. The woman's bare knees angled into the air; the covers lay folded back on her chest. Just as I finished, footsteps on the porch shook the entire house. Margaret covered the patient, and the door sprang open with a cold thrust of air and there stood Joe—big, shoulders wide, red cheeks from the early morning, a small yellow flame in his squeaky lantern.

The old mother glanced at his muddy boots. ''Joe, you forgot to clean your feet.'' As he went slowly toward the bed without hearing her complaint, she smiled.

He looked down at his wife, said nothing, and licked his lips. ''Everything all right, doc?''

''Our patients are just fine, both, coming fine. How's yours doing?''

He grinned. ''Ten. I've got them in a separate pen.''

He looked at his wife again; she smiled back, but he said nothing to her nor did he go close. I saw Margaret watching them.

The old woman came to the bed and carried the lamp back to the oven to look at her bread. After she had clanged the iron door shut, the odor of fresh bread stayed. She began to make coffee in a big blue pot with sharp black spots where the porcelain had chipped off.

Joe stammered, "Well, guess I'll be getting back to her."

"Don't worry. Everything's fine. I'll call you when it's over."

Joe left quickly, his boots making only three big thumps on his way out. The old woman looked down at her ugly hands and smiled, "He knows he doesn't have to stay vit the sow now." I glanced at the saints as if trying to catch them at smiling. They weren't, but they seemed satisfied about it.

"Every three minutes, hard," said Margaret as she looked to the stove where the delicious odors came from and where the old mother moved in the yellow light.

"I'll simply have to be able to see," I whispered. "Go get the lamp."

Now I could make out the elliptical patch of the baby's head, glistening wet in the lamplight. "It's going to have black hair—like Joe's."

The mother smiled. "But it hurts so, doctor. Oh, now I'm getting another pain. Give me something. Oh, this one's bad."

"Take several deep breaths of this and hold the last breath in," Margaret instructed as she held the ether mask over Mrs. Joe's face. Now we couldn't smell the bread or the coffee.

"I'll have to do an episiotomy. Give her a lot with the next pain."

"Oh, it's beginning to hurt again— My water! I don't think I can hold it."

"Don't hold back. I just catheterized you. It's not urine, it's the baby. So push right down."

"Oh, it hurts." Her muffled sounds came through the mask and the drunken ether. "I'm floating. The bed's moving. Oh, oh, Joe! Joe . . ."

"Give her just a little more and I can cut."

But as I was ready, I saw the lamp rise and walk slowly past the saints to the oven. "Get that little flashlight out of my bag. It won't help much, but it's something. She's asleep now; let's put on low forceps. Get the lamp back as soon as you can."

In the half-dark I felt the forceps slip onto the sides of the baby's head and the handles lock together easily—it gave a good feeling. With this traction I lifted the baby's head up and out smoothly, now dropped the forceps as the baby's chin hung against the mother's rectum. As my fingers felt for the child's jaws and I pulled up to deliver one large shoulder, Margaret brought back the lamp and I saw a big baby slip out with a gush of amniotic fluid. It cried so lustily I know Joe heard it. While I tied the cord and wiped away the blood and mucous, I counted the fingers and toes—if you delivered a baby with an extra finger it would be embarrassing not to know it until the parents told you on the next visit.

"Put the baby in the crib. Keep the mother asleep while I sew up the episiotomy." I watched as Margaret, holding the baby in her arms, walked past the saints. They seemed to be watching her tuck the child in the cradle by the oven.

The grandmother followed Margaret back and took the lamp to her end of the room. She wants to get a good look at the new grandchild that I have delivered, I thought—her thirty-seventh—but she set the lamp on a shelf and with her knotted hands began to crack eggs on the stove and drop them hissing and spluttering into a heavy black skillet.

I tried to sew. The double bed swayed in the middle, making the place hard to get to. With only the small, weak flashlight, I could barely see. The mother's relaxed knees wouldn't stay up, kept slipping down. And she lay on a feather mattress, which bulged up right in the way. I hoped I wasn't sewing the sheet and protective coverings into her.

The grandmother came bringing the lamp toward this part of the room. Ah, she knows that now I need it. But she passed the bed; opened a door, letting in cold air; leaned into a pantry; and backed into the room holding a pan of milk in one hand, the lamp clasped trembly in the other. I sewed fast while there was a little light. She took the milk and the lamp toward the stove. The legs slipped down again and I pushed them back up.

"Can you make out with the flashlight?" Margaret's voice came from the head of the bed where she dripped ether on the mask.

"After she's awake, make her stand up."

"Stand up?"

"To see if the feather bed comes with her. I may have made them one, like a pair of Siamese twins." Margaret snorted like a person who has not laughed in a long time. The knee fell down again.

"Shall I call Joe to hold her leg up?"

"No. He wouldn't like this; let's not spoil it for him."

"I'll try to get the lamp again, but I don't think we'll be able to keep it long. The smell of that bacon and coffee gives me hunger pangs." When she brought the light I hurriedly checked my work.

"Probably the best one I ever did. Maybe I oughta always sew them in the dark. Let her wake up." I massaged her loose flat abdomen and pulled gently on the cord until the placenta slid out. The stink of afterbirth and blood mingled with the aromas of bread and frying eggs.

As Margaret finished cleaning her and turning her from one side to the other onto fresh sheets, the sleepy woman opened her eyes drunkenly and moaned, "Joe."

"Do you want Joe now?" Margaret asked. "I'll call him."

"No—no—don't bring him until it's all over."

"It is over. It's a boy."

"It is?" She seemed to awaken more. "Joe will be glad."

I laid the baby in an open diaper, tied two corners together—like the stork brings them—and hooked the hand scale in and held it up, reading the weight. (Margaret was the only person who knew I had set the small spring scale to read six ounces more than the actual weight, had practiced with it in the office using rocks from the graveled alley.)

And as if he knew just when to come in, we heard Joe's stomp on the porch and the shuffling sounds of wiping his boots on a gunny sack.

"You have a son, Joe," I announced as if I had had a great deal to do with its all happening. "Eight pounds seven ounces. Meat's worth eighty cents a pound; that makes him worth about six dollars ninety cents." I smiled—he knew that was more than doubling the price of meat.

Joe glanced at his wife, who lay quietly smiling, very sober now. He stooped to look at his small son, hefty shoulders bending protectively over the old family cradle. He looked back at his wife who watched him, smiling.

"Come on, doc, let's eat." Joe sat to the clean table, swinging a big leg over the bench.

He's a poor man, but he has the easy earth in his hands, the clean sky. He plants the yellow kernels of corn in the ground and the fuzzy capsules of cottonseed, to make them grow—creation, a work as fundamental and satisfying as planting his own seed in his wife's womb. He has everything. His life will walk smoothly calm as these gentle hills, for he depends on so little—and so much. He respects me for being a doctor and thinks me rich. Thinks I am important.

I saw the saints looking down on Joe as he mumbled and signed a cross on his forehead and chest.

I bowed my head over the empty plate.

The old woman had been muttering Bohemian consonants for sometime before I realized what she was saying. Seemed she was talking to herself. "His *krev* [blood] been so *slaba* [weak] for slow wasted months, but at last he get a congestion of the lungs, vere it gather. Ven he breathe there vas a gurgle like his old pipe."

Terminal pneumonia, I thought.

The picture of a man coughing into no relief and the lungs filling with pneumonia—strangling him, my mind translated—and I again saw old Mr. Cernoch gasping for air and saw the man hanging in the well. Maybe I knew a little better now what it is. Not the hanging nor that ghastly cut itself, more that other thing—that grinning, that laughing its superiority, its victory. It had been the first time I ever met him in the raw, so real. Warm. Pulsating, *red,* and hot as fevered breath.

Up to now I had always been protected from him somewhat—by the authority of teachers, my professors, by shields of only partial responsibility. Had seen so many of his specimens in the Pathology Lab in his unending forms—an esophagus in formaldehyde, sliced in two to show the knotty cancer; a stomach, now a bland gray, open and the crater ulcer looking harmless under clear alcohol; the black of a coal miner's lungs with a dissolving dark cloud like a formless ghost seeping out into the solution. All safely walled away from me in glass containers, on glass shelves, in the locked glass cabinets. Separate from me. Only colorless curiosities for teaching purposes—not live nor bleeding nor too close. But now I knew him, whatever he might be called. Laughing at my beardless new and ignorant nakedness. He had entered my life—alive.

Maybe he entered me, had suddenly been born into my brain through shattered doors splintered by shock—looking at me out of the man's nostrils. Now he stood here. He had walked right in with the memory of an old man's death.

So this would be it.

Joe here will not have to know any of it—fortunate man. Not even until it touches him. He will not have to know, never be forced to know.

But from now on, in varying degrees of severity and cleverness—so open and so secret—a presence had joined my life, would always be near. This my enemy, my only opponent. And yet my life—for all the rest of my life. He's here.

Always my enemy. Until finally . . . one day will come, like with Mr. Konvitchka, when even I will have to take that coldest hand . . . as if in friendship.

I refused to think about it further.

She was still talking, "After the priest put out the candles and leave, old Konvitchka called me. I question him and he say, 'Stay by me,' and I say, 'I have stay by you these years and I will stay by you.' He say, 'Sit by me, close by me.' He know it was near to the end. I sit beside the bed on this chair; the bed was over here. For a long time he was quiet and I sit and listen to his breathing and at last he say, 'It is good,' and he turn on his heart side and in a little vile he is gone."

The straight shaft of early morning sun illuminated the saints.

The old woman looked down, smiling at her ugly hands.

⁂

Even with the stethoscope in my ears listening to Miss Sophie's heart (through the layers of clothes—she shook her head No when I tried to unbutton, and then when Margaret stepped up Miss Sophie simply put her hands there, crossed, like some kind of saint), even with straining to hear her heart, I got sounds from all the commotion going on at the side door and the thump against the building—a car bumper? Margaret went. I kept trying to listen through the layers. But Margaret came right back, tapped my arm, "You'd better see about this. Looks terrible."

Four big farmers, like four Paul Bunyans—I think they are brothers—came carrying a door flat, like a stretcher, with Emil Trohajeck on it. Carrying it from a pickup truck toward the side door. His left leg stopped midway down, the bluish-white bones sticking out; the foot, in a big rough shoe, lay up against the knee.

"Is it off?" I asked, more out of shock than reason.

"Not yet off. Is only such stringy meat holding. You going cut him the leg off. You cut it off; ve hold him down. Is strong, by gory. You going saw him the bones off. Is vit grass and cow shits on."

"Tomorrow ve snitzel him out a vooden leg."

"You vant it—hey, Emil—you vant it from oak?"

"Too heavy for him, oak. Better is from cedar."

"No, pecan. You like it better pecan, no? Is plenty pecan trees."

My God, I had never seen anything like this. "How'd it happen?"

Standing out there in the alley, I kept trying to make out just what *is* left of the guy's leg.

"He try yump from the mule down. It throw him up over the brooder house down. Is in cow lot."

"He vork in Houston whole year already. Don't like it noise, but make it big money, Houston. Comes on wisits home. Mule is throwing him in cow lot down," they laughed loud.

There actually was new green grass and brown cow manure on the ends of the tibia and fibula. What can I do . . . ?

"You cut him off here outside, or ve should bring him inside?"

"Oh, this must be done in a hospital." I turned away. I despise the thought of amputation—any amputation.

"You hex-ray him? You got it hex-ray machina?"

The leg lay awkward, the big shoe with its thick sole toward the knee, like in some fantastic dance, some grotesque ballet. They all kept talking, laughing how funny he looked flying over the brooder house, kicking around in the air. I unlaced the dirty leather string, felt for a pulse high on the instep.

And found it.

"There's a chance!" I yelled them down. "A chance that it can stay on! The artery hasn't been torn!" I unlaced the shoe more and slipped it off the big, stinky bare foot with dirt between the toes. "But it's only a chance. I'll straighten this out a little—there, careful, easy now—so the blood can get through better." The toenails were a nice pink, and I squeezed one into white, testing. The pink came right back. "Good."

"Does he feel it? You feel it, Emil, ven doktor make pinchy?"

"Now I'll clean this up and give him a shot and we'll be on our way to the hospital. I'll have to put a metal plate and screws to hold the bones together."

A thought hit my head like a slap. Come to your senses, boy. All that dirt there? *In* the very bones? And you think that isn't going to be an infection? Ha! An osteomyelitis at best, septicemia at worst. You have no choice: amputate.

"Wish we had a hospital here." I turned to go into the office. Everybody in the waiting room is crowded at the door, and these four big guys must have thought they should follow me; they pushed the stretcher-door and couldn't go through. So they simply tilted it to one side and Emil slid right off.

I heard it and turned. "Oh my God no!" There's the leg and raw muscle on the gravel.

Margaret came with towels and I placed them under the leg and straightened the foot again and they kept saying: "Ve put him back and try again more slow. Emil, hold next time yourself more tight."

And everybody in the waiting room is telling them how, and I had to yell again: "Let him stay! Don't move him! The ambulance will come. I'll give him shots, right here. Put the door back on the pickup. Leave him lay."

It'll be infected. Blood poisoning. You'll have to amputate against the infection. Risk his life—maybe lose it. Why not be safe—amputate first?

At LaGrange Hospital we put him to sleep, cleaned the bone and the raw muscle with soap, ether, grain alcohol, tincture of iodine, then grain alcohol again. I asked the nurse, "Do you think it'll heal? Or be infected?" Nurses generally agree to any leading question such as this, are supportive. But she remained quiet.

We checked the tendons, used two metal braces with four screws each, simply set the thin fibula together (it doesn't carry any body weight), and salted it all down with sulfa crystals and started sulfathiozole orally as soon as he woke up enough and could retain. And double doses of tetanus—the lockjaw tetanus grows especially well in ground-under cattle manure.

Amazing. It all healed. Not a sign of infection. And in seven and a half weeks he came walking on it without crutches. His "uneventful recovery" (as it is named in surgery texts) did seem really remarkable.

"By gory, is somethink ven you can put a man his leg back."

"Thank you, Emil, but I didn't do the healing. *You* did. It's something, to be so strong and resilient as you are."

There was so much more I wanted to say to him, this bulk of naturalness. He seemed to radiate an entire wealth—warmth—of hunk strength, muscle, the odor of work sweat, of male energy. He walked easy in this glow and seemed to know nothing of it, nor that he was creating it. So natural, so easy with the earth.

It seemed so to me.

I knew I couldn't tell him this—wanted to, yes.

Seems there is so much people dare not say to each other. Wonder why not? But it stays the rule: No. Don't.

If we aren't allowed to say it, at least we can see it.

All I came up with was, "The mule—is it giving any more trouble?"

"No. Is fine mule. Good in single harness, good in double. No, is fine mule."

"Are you . . . going back to Houston?"

He hesitated, looking down at his leg, "Yes, Houston."

People, Carrying Their Symptoms Carefully

I don't know how it happened. The patient load gradually began and—almost like rain—rapidly became more and more. People came from Schulenburg, yes, but also from the dozens of small surrounding country communities I hadn't heard of.

Probably it spreads—like a contagion—by word of mouth: "I tell my cousin Yak-ob—lives by Ammonsville. They say they bring the girl Anna. Always she gets it the *ast*ma."

And even from other towns—Weimar, Flatonia, Shiner, where a small brewery makes "Shiner Special," Moulton, Waelder, Harwood. These are towns. Others are only small communities: High Hill, Migil's Gin, where the only thing left is some concrete foundations and huge rocks hardly higher than the weeds, Dubina, Moravia, Saint John's—all of them only a few houses, always a church, maybe an old country store left, and a few had a new smooth concrete slab for Saturday-night dancing next to the store and two outside toilets. Bunje's School, where there remained nothing at all, no buildings, no toilets, only weeds, but it is a corner—good for directions: "Turn left at Bunje's School."

They came from Praha, also only a few houses and a store, but there stood the largest, tallest, and oldest church of them all, built of stone. Inside, walls and ceiling were hand painted with vines climbing snake-like and barefoot saints and bulgy clouds and angels with yellow wings, all peeling off, like chickens in molting season. And every summer there was Feast Day on August fifteenth, with thousands of people from all over the state coming "home" to the mother church, Maticka Praha. Freyburg, a large German area "as big as New York City but not quite so built up, yet" (where Margaret and some relatives still own the family farm). Engle (means *angel* in German, but while the railroad was being built a mule-driver named Engle became caught under a wagon load of ties and was crushed, and they buried him on the spot—marked his grave with a sign, Engle) once had a post office, but now with more all-weather gravel roads, it's on a mail-carrier route out of Schulenburg. (It was James told me most of these histories, nights.) They came from these and many other small communities.

Armstrong Church, its white paint practically all gone, is an all-black area where timber country begins, far, far back in the woods past Cistern, Elm Grove, Black Jack (which is a type of tree), and Muldoon (named for Father Muldoon, *padre,* who later owned a league—four thousand acres—and gave a plot for the townsite. He came with the first settlers into this Tejas Territory—the Mexican government insisted the settlers be Catholic and own no slaves. Being the only priest, he refused to baptize or marry or bury unless they paid him twenty-five dollars. They say he seldom performed sober; had at least a dozen illegitimate children by young Mexican girls, some of whom had come to his church in their homemade white veils; fought "heroically" in the Texas Revolution, killing "more than his share"; owned slaves like many of the settlers; became excommunicated. To-day no one knows where he is buried.) Past Muldoon, Kovar, Rozansky—past all the white-people places—you come to Colony, started after slavery ended and planned to be a "new-life colony." It is still a far and isolated place where everybody is finally kin to everybody else. ("Bug? No, we ain't brothers. Guess he be my cousin. Guess he is.") Has a school, and a church where they are always inviting you to come out for Watch Night.

"What is it actually?" I asked little Auntie Callie, helping remove her jacket. She complains about her back and walks with a cane.

"Always the same. Christmas Eve. Every year. You come."

"What do you watch for?"

"Course we watch! Watch all night. For the Comin'."

"All night?"

"Till first light. Every year. Singin' and preachin' and testifyin', all night. Sisters and brothers comes from all over. Far's San Antone, Houston, Dallas."

"If it happened, would it be exactly at midnight?"

"Reckon so—hit could be. But could be anytime."

"What you do if . . . it actually happened—did come?" I teased. "Scare you?"

"But *you* come. Stay a while."

"Thank you, I shall try to, Auntie Callie."

"You come. I sure be proud."

They came. From these many places and others. Usually the illnesses or traumas they brought seemed selected from the more usual, the ordinary possibilities—infected throat; flu; ear; blood pressure; mumps; boy with broken arm at the wrist (ordinary Colles' fracture, easily reduced); measles (I always gave sulfathiozole, to prevent the complications of secondary infections); cuts from knife fights at Lupe's Lounge and Dance Hall (Mexican) or the Blue Flame Cafe (black), where in a fight one woman bit a flap out of another's ear, a half-circle notch edged with teeth marks (I cleaned it with straight iodine, gave her a tetanus shot *and* sulfa since the human bite is extremely infectious)—used a plastic-surgery stitching, and it healed nicely, hardly noticeable); many women with bladder and vaginal infections (always found it a delicate matter to tell them to wipe *backward,* never forward between the legs, because feces is almost a hundred percent germs and if smeared against pubic hair could enter the vagina and urethra). Mostly what they came with were these and other more or less ordinary conditions—"front-shelf" selections. But occasionally one brought something more unusual.

Finally the end of a long Saturday, already dark.

"How many did we see today, Gretchen?" I asked in German—she and I often spoke German when alone. "Fifty-five? Sixty?"

"All I know, it's a lot. Why is it people have to get sick? And fight! Hope they leave you alone, but it is Saturday night again. *Die Schwarze und Mexikanische.*

"Everything is ready if they do come," she switched to English, "plenty skin and catgut sutures, sterile needles. . . ." She kept talking as she went to the side door to latch it. She was forever latching and locking things. And saving empty boxes. But as she talked—" . . . skin clips, black silk and sterile pads . . ."—the door opened and she stood staring up at the biggest Negro man ever: His size took up the whole doorway, and wider and taller, too. ". . . bandage . . ." He stood before her holding his intestines in both hands.

". . . and tetanus," she said up to him.

"No, ma'am. I's Otis. Otis Moore. I's cut."

"Good God, man. I'll take you to the hospital. I can sew you up there."

"Ain't got no money. For no horspittal."

"It has to be done in a hospital."

"Ain't no money. They won't let you in, lessen you pays first." He kept standing outside, holding his intestines in both hands.

"Well—well, come in."

Margaret and I both turned around back into the office; she said, without looking behind, "Don't drop them—this floor is filthy."

After a large hypo of morphine and local injected along the cut-skin edges (a sharp clean slice, whoever did it)—the only anesthesia—"You'll feel some of this as I handle the intestines, but I do have to check every inch to see if there is a cut *anywhere.* If I should forget and pull too hard, you tell me."

Now starting at one end—at the appendix (normal: small, skinny, dangling). I knew my location there and came on up the small intestine backward, searching both sides, dipping my brown-gloved fingers in a bowl of alcohol, with Margaret showering the tiny crystals of sterile sulfathiozole on after I had slid it through my fingers. And putting it back into the abdomen. And never letting go, so as not to lose my place—what if I miss even one minute, small stab?

And again came that thought or voice or odor or rumble growling from a deeper bowel than my own—or is it one's own very voice of fear? *Even if you sew up every nick perfectly, or if there is no cut at all, he'll still get peritonitis. Worse than from a ruptured pus-appendix because this leaks, seeps silent, until too late. And then, of course you know, he* dies!

Margaret wiped the sweat off my face and sprinkled sulfa. "Makes it look like salted-down sausage," she whispered in German.

I searched inch by inch along his intestines' both sides—dare not miss even a pinhole prick—and sweated. This should be done in a hospital, under a proper anesthetic and under proper lights.

I tried to talk cheerfully, hoped my voice wouldn't quaver. "Otis, we're supposed to have about thirty-five feet of small intestines. I do believe, you must have a hundred yards." And looked along, and Margret sprinkled and wiped my face . . .

As you know, doctor, there is no cure for peritonitis.

"I always thought the intestines were one long, loose tube," Margaret said in English, "like a garden hose."

"No, it's like a border on the bottom end of an apron, the omentum. If I'd pull hard on *that,* Otis wouldn't like it."

"It's like a hem."

"Don't worry, Otis. I'll keep my eye on her so she won't be making a skirt out of it."

Your silly talk may disguise your fears from him, but you know.

"Where do you live?"

"Live?"

Nice sounding words, aren't they?

"What's your address?"

"My what?"

". . . where you stay at?"

"Oh, sure. Out a ways, close to Colony, other side Armstrong Church. Know where it's at?"

"Yes, yes, the doctor knows. He's been out that way lots. Made calls to many. Do you know Henry Neville? Makes tombstones."

Good God!

"Sho'. Not far atall. My mother and me, we bought from Henry when our father—my daddy—passed. Sho' made him a nice one. They was friends for years—long time."

We talked; neither Margaret nor I asked about the fight; nor did he say.

And I looked and looked and hoped Margaret wouldn't run out of "salt." There it is, the end, the pylorus, the stomach; no cuts, everything intact. So far. Now if he doesn't get peritonitis, everything will be fine. I sewed the thin peritoneum closed first, then the thick fascia, with both continuous and interrupted sutures—so he'll be sure not to have it all rupture out on him later under strain: He does heavy work I'm sure.

If he recovers.

If he recovers. And the skin. Each layer of closure had also been washed good with alcohol and sprinkled with sulfa. Now the big white dressing. "So there. You did fine, Otis. Your gut may get tight with gas tomorrow—from all that handling. It'll go."

You hope.

"Now let's take you home to bed for a few days. No solid foods, only liquids—soups, milk, juices—until you can pass gas. You will be sore, probably for three days. So take these for relief. Before mealtimes—remember, no solids. Three times a day."

He got up, buttoned his shirt, turned backward to Margaret while he stuffed it down into his pants, and buttoned and buckled up. "Sho' thank you—and you, lady. I knowed y'all was ready to go on home. I'll find me a way. Thank you the same."

"Now. One thing, please, Otis—I don't know what you're thinking. You've had a big dose of morphine and that makes a person feel good—for a while. Feel like you could whip the world, but it isn't true. It's false. It even slows you down. So if you're thinking of going after anybody tonight, don't. Some other time—if you must. After all, you have had major surgery. Don't try tonight."

"Ain't studyin' nothin' like that."

"I'll come see you tomorrow—every day, for three days."

To check his temperature. And when it starts straight up? With chills?

"Hates to trouble you. Can walk it. I always walks it when my pickup quits."

"Let's get in the car."

"Hates to trouble you to carry me back."

"Know this night for the victory it is, Otis. You won."

"Suh?"

"You won. The other person thinks he won; he'll be so surprised to see you well and going about with nothing wrong. It's your victory. He thinks he killed you, that you'll die of this—let him believe it, if he wants. He'll be so surprised. Remember that. *You* won."

I saw that he listened, even through the morphine.

Fine pep talk. But will it do?

(Also it's pure selfish on my part: I simply don't want him coming back tonight with my nice stitching all cut open—or sending somebody else who needs sewing up.)

While we stood waiting, Margaret kept washing one more thing and putting it in its place.

In leaving, he and I waited with the drugstore screen open for Margaret to come first, but she went tippy-toe back to latch the side door as if sneaking up on it, saying in German, "Now try it once more."

❋❋❋

In each ear she wore a small tuft of cotton. Mrs. Schneider came, I saw, well protected against the spring air. The small dark glasses made her hollow white-powdered face more skull shaped than usual. But no one, no one at all, still wore an overcoat on this unusually warm morning. Even Papinku stood in the drugstore in a white short-sleeved shirt.

She hadn't worn glasses on previous visits, so is this merely an affectation or is it actually needed—photophobia? "Are your eyes troubling you?"

She opened her coat and tried to drape the stiff cloth over the chair arm. I waited.

She talked first about the last time she had come and how she still had not gained any weight, although she had followed my instructions "completely." Said the last time she weighed, she'd even lost two pounds. She spoke longingly, affectionately, about the two pounds—you would have thought they were twins. I listened patiently—I hoped it looked patiently—as she talked on and at the same time folded and unfolded a handkerchief in its creased squares and occasionally touched the glasses near her temple daintily.

Nervous as before. She will talk all day, and there are some waiting. "Yes, but what about your eyes."

"I'm coming to that." And continued folding the handkerchief. Again how "terribly much" weight she had lost and long explanations of just how she had prepared her food, and at what time she had gone to bed two nights back and how she had awakened the following morning, yesterday, with her "eyes stuck closed—pasted shut." Her lipsticked mouth illustrated the point to a degree.

At last she raised the dark glasses. What a shock! Large pus pockets. Not only one like a sty, but pimply ripe rows marched along each lid edge—all four lids. And the conjunctival covering of each eyeball glared lacy with tiny red tongues licking toward the center coloring. There is nothing neurotically "imagined" about this!

"I know it makes me look terrible," she stated looking at me, showing me her inflamed eyes.

"This is serious. Most serious." I did not tell her it is possible to lose both eyes from this if it spreads into the eyeball itself, into a panophthalmitis. Her nervous system is too shaky as it is to give her a scare about going blind.

"My sister and my son, Arnold, said it might be important. They made me come."

"Made you come?"

"Yes, I thought it would go away." She smiled, revealing a missing tooth; as I looked at the empty space she quickly closed her lips tight, like gluing them back together. This is puzzling. Because a few weeks ago she came every day trying to gain weight. No other complaint. Came much too often, even pestering me and Margaret to let her be weighed and to reexamine her diet chart. Yet with an eye infection, enormous, a dozen small abscesses along each eye, she comes reluctantly.

"Eyes are too precious. You must stay in the hospital—"

"What?"

"You'll have to stay in the hospital a few days."

"Oh I couldn't. I haven't got the . . . the time."

"There are two beds empty in the county room—I learned about it—so don't worry about money. It won't cost anything, and then you'll get well in—"

"If I had a husband, I could afford to go to the hospital like people should. He ruined my health."

"It won't cost you anything. I checked recently. They keep two—"

"He ruined my health, and when I couldn't have more than the one baby he left me. That must have been the reason. But I'm not old, you understand."

"Of course not. But you must go to the hospital."

"I couldn't. People would hear about it. Then it would be hard—harder for me when I went home. Maybe just a little salve to apply? . . ."

"Salve won't be enough for this, this is serious. Can't you go to the hospital? It isn't too far, not for this. We need one here—a hospital."

"No."

"Are you trying to defend—keep—this disease? It may be the difference between—"

"I can't go." She turned the handkerchief into a cylinder and fitted it on a finger. "Just give me something to put on it."

I sighed. "I'm going to give you an injection now—Vitamin B-12. Doesn't cure anything, but should help your resistance fight this. Go home and stay in bed with boric acid as a wet compress over each eye—hot. Take these tablets"—I wrote the prescription. "Rather large tablet—take two before each meal. It's a big dose. Sulfathiozole. Before meals, three times a day. Drink a large glass of water with each dose. And this eye salve. I'll come by your house this evening to check and give you another shot."

As I came up the front steps of the small white house, a stiff-starched curtain moved and sounds came muffled of quick scurrying about inside, and a commanding female voice. A tall, pale boy—probably the son, Arnold—unlocked and opened the door. Does he always look like that, or is he afraid? His features, although similar to hers, somehow made him handsome.

Mrs. Schneider lay—more like enthroned—in bed with the wet towels across her eyes and forehead like a slipped crown. A large woman—looked strong; must be the sister—nodded to me as she dipped other towels into a steaming basin—how can she hold them with her bare hands?—and laid them slowly on Mrs. Schneider's forehead.

"Hurry! Somebody get him a chair!" The words snapped sharply. Both the sister and Arnold rushed out in opposite directions, and each returned immediately carrying a straight wood chair. "Watch the fire in the stove—this last pan is only warm." Her words cracked like whips, and the sister and son bumped together in the kitchen door.

I looked around the room—habit, I guess—for something to comment on favorably. But the room sat gaunt, practically empty. Smelled of homemade soap. Everything clean, the grain of the wood floor splintery from frequent lye scrubbings. "This house is spotless. What excellent housekeepers you ladies are." An oval picture with convex glass of a young woman in bridal veil—maybe it's a deceased parent. "Is that a picture of your mother?"

"No," she answered in a nice voice without seeing, "my wedding picture."

I made no comment about an equal-sized oval area of fresh-looking, nonfaded wallpaper directly beside, like a missing twin. "This infection—has anybody else had it? Anybody you were in contact with? In a grocery store? At the post office?"

"No, doctor. Nobody. Only me." She sighed.

I peeled the towels off—the infection looked no worse—and layered the cloths back on. "I'll give you a shot now. Pull your sleeve up, please." I turned to reach into my bag.

"Come here!" she screamed out to no one in particular, but both Arnold and the sister came running to the bed, crowding together. "Roll up my sleeve."

I jerked the needle from her bony arm, "I still don't understand how you could get such a severe infection in both eyes at once."

"Get him something to wash his hands in! Do I have to tell you everything?"

"Thanks, but that's not necessary."

They brought a basin of steaming water, a fresh towel, and a new bar of soap still in its fragrant wrapper. "Thank you very much," I waved it away. "I take it you're Mrs. Schneider's sister?"

She smiled broadly, nodded, but said nothing.

"You're taking excellent care of her. You should have been a nurse."

She laughed giggly, said nothing.

"My being sick hurts her work. The washings she does for people is all we have to live on since Arnold's father . . ." The part of her face not covered by towels showed no emotion.

"Keep up the good job you're doing," I nodded to the sister. "Continue the compresses during the night, and I'll be by in the morning. Hope you can get some rest in between."

Both the sister and the son moved draggy and looked at me with reddish thick eyes. Had they been up all night?

The inflammation had definitely improved; many of the pusheads had already ruptured and spent themselves. "Your sister will be well soon," I said to the shy one, trying to give her credit. "She'll get along fine now; so you get some sleep today—"

Mrs. Schneider interrupted: What could she eat, she asked, how should each item be prepared, and what should she take for elimination in case she needed it. And could she sit up with the towels on her eyes, should her back be rubbed, with what, should they keep the room dark, and would the wet towels wrinkle the skin about the face, and? . . .

The eyes and eyelids cleared, healed. Thank heaven! The thought of a person going blind by a bacterial destruction of the inner eye, turning the wondrous miracle of eye into white blanks, like dead fish eyes. Or like two opaque pearls, regardless of price worthless and blank as eyes.

And how could she ever adjust to blindness, with her unstable demanding condition?

And what would that have done to the others?

Is the illness a way of saying something?

Why have such an illness, why choose? . . . Is she saying she wants to be "blind," unmindful to something? To what? To herself?

Anyway, it's healed now, the whole thing over with. At the very last visit of all, the sister, showing me to the door, said, "We thank you, doctor—"

"I didn't do the healing, she did."

"We can't pay you anything—"

"You already have. A blind person? No."

"I'll be glad to do your laundry."

"Thanks so much, but the hotel takes care of it."

"Yes, Mrs. Zapalac washes for them," and she put her fingers to her cheek as if she shouldn't have said that.

I called back into the hard empty house, "Thank you, Mrs. Schneider." It echoed back, "—eider." "Goodby now." "—eye now."

Less than a week later she came again with exactly the same thing.

"This is incredible! Both your eyes at once. So suddenly. And so bad. I can hardly believe it.

"Well, we had luck last time. Let's do the same precicely and hope it goes well again. I'll be by tonight on my way home."

As I came into the dimly lit house, which smelled of freshly ironed clothes and of kerosene lamp, Arnold, closing the door, said, "Mama's got that eye trouble again."

What an imbecilic thing. They seem like a nest full of blind mice, hiding in this empty house, ruled by this hostile woman. Trying to peep out at the rest of the world. They have their eyes, their sight. They should *use* it—see their situation and do something about it. That boy should get out of here and get a job. I'm sure they're scared of her. I don't blame Schneider for leaving—probably couldn't stand it; probably the only sane one in the bunch. Except the shy sister, she's trapped here. And this anemic boy . . . The pathosis living in this house is certainly more than that eye infection. And the truth is, I don't know how to fight it—I'm only dealing with one of its symptoms. "Yes, Arnold, that's so. And I sure wish I could figure out what's causing it. Where does she get—"

"Bring him in!" As if she meant a bundle of laundry. And there she lay—in state, the blinding crown again over her eyes. A chair placed exactly beside the bed, for me. A bouquet of yellow daffodils stood on the crowded bedside table with the pan for washing my hands.

"Lovely flowers you have, Mrs. Schneider."

"Yes, I had to make them put the bulbs in. Now I always have to be after the others to take care of them, or else they would only let them dry up and die."

"Did you pick these yourself today?"

"With these towels on my face? No, Arnold did, and I wish he hadn't. They're nicest in the yard, where neighbors and everybody can see them. Shouldn't be cut."

The boy grinned at the floor, but quickly turned his head and wiped his eyes.

"He ought to know I can't see them, and they give such a musty odor to the room. It almost chokes me." She coughed.

Arnold, grinning at me, blinking his tears, hurriedly carried the flowers out.

"Pull up your sleeve!" I commanded, almost angrily.

Immediately I knew I had committed a sin—fractured, fissured something against her. And against myself. Not the rudeness by itself, but deeper—I was standing in judgment of her.

How easily and instantly, when one does not wish to see a thing, does one hide it, pulling across the curtain of judging. What snaky, slimy crawlings must be eating silently inside us, excused under the clean skirt of judgment.

I must not be blind—to her loneliness.

Thank you, Mrs. Schneider, for teaching me a little more . . . of myself. My voice came gentle. "This will be only one small stick—just a little pinch."

⁂

As I drove up—thank heavens!—I could see the lights still on in the drugstore and the light outside over the door. Good, James will give me some Pantopon *if* they have it. If not, I'll have to drive all the way to one of the hospitals—either to LaGrange or Hallettsville. A few bugs circled the light and I stepped over those on the sidewalk. He did not look up from his book until I closed the door. Nietzsche lay stretched out on the floor, only swished his tail.

Too much is happening. It's always that way now—can't get finished. This evening it's several more, all contrary to themselves. Anton Kopecky, husky, broad, farmer, middle-aged, looks strong as the old rock house (which his father built), shaking in the chill spasms of passing kidney stones. And I couldn't relieve him because he's highly allergic to morphine—I had nothing else.

In driving to his house and leaving—both—you pass the red-brick and tin-roofed ruin of Kopecky Gin, which Anton himself built—just before the cotton crash and farmers planted less cotton and more and more of their fields went to grain. Lost everything, had everything mortgaged, and would have lost the very family farm (from his father) too and have no place to go, but he took bankruptcy. (The law allows a man to keep a homestead of two hundred fifty acres and a team of mules.) But bankruptcy here is a curse forever, can never be erased. Suicide is more acceptable to the community. He's had to live with it ever since, daily seeing the neighbors who brought their savings to the investment. Even from his bed he has to see the high, hulking ruin.

He clutches the sheets, his face sweating and burning red in pain. The brass bed trembles, the hanging fringe edge of counterpane shivering—and he's allergic to morphine! I've got to get some Pantopon from somewhere.

And the Kobza twins, girls, we delivered yesterday are not doing as well as . . . Their fingers and toes and ears are bluish, also lips and tongue tips. And I don't know why. Their lungs are clear, there is no patent (congenital) heart valve (from the foramen ovale not closing at birth), their heart sounds are perfectly normal. Why are their extremities bluish? It's circulation—vascular—but what? And why? The young parents are plainly nervous, afraid about it; they've only been married six months and now twins . . .

And Anita Zurek—Mrs. Johan Zurek—is cramping and bleeding. A threatened miscarriage—at six months! With such a "green" unripe cervix, a large six-months miscarriage could mean one hellacious rip-tear and hemorrhage!

As I closed the door, James said without looking up, "Of all the animal species on earth, man's only enemy is himself—which is the most deadly. Having none—and it is probably the first law of nature that each must have his enemy—he assumes the job himself. He destroys himself. He must. It is the law. As if in the beginning the law was there. And he must obey. Must destroy. Himself." He stood, removed his glasses, polished them with the backside of his necktie. "Does he sound logical?"

I thumbed my mustache, wanted to say, "Philosophizing about the animal species of this earth is not what I had in mind just now. Anton Kopecky, for some reason, needs more than the usual substance to relieve his pain—is allergic to the ordinary morphine. His blood rejects it. Why a strong man about fifty-five should 'need'—should grow extra 'stones' low in his back and into his groin? . . . And also I do not know why twins born yesterday are hanging around the door half-deciding at the threshold whether they're going to come on into this life here and try it or not, and I don't even know their excuse—the diagnosis. And if I can stop Anita Zurek from miscarrying and maybe dying of a hemorrhage . . . and she refuses to go to a hospital . . . and Anton Kopecky may go into shock and actually die from sheer sharp pain."

"Pantopon," I said. "I must get it. Do we have it?"

"Thirds?"

"Yes!"

"Want six or twelve? More?"

"Thank heavens! Twelve." I stepped over Nietzsche. "Then I'll have some ready for the future." I scribbled my signature across the bottom of a blank prescription pad—James would fill it out later. In the morning Papinku would leaf through, counting who got what during the night, and sometimes he changed James's charges, adding fifty cents or a dollar.

James finished counting, said, "You need a hospital here."

I started to tell him, absolutely—that'd be the greatest thing on this earth—to start a hospital. Yes. And yes, I want it. But there isn't time to talk.

Clenching fist-tight the small glass tube, its straight row of tiny tablets all in a stacked column . . . This strange small chemical which stops pain, relieves—like morphine—but does not cure the cause. Does not cure anything—only masks it blind, says "It is no longer here." But it is still here, waiting . . . to be solved. What strange little tablets, tiny white wafers of a strangely holy communion—but giving an unholy mask that makes a lie seem true. And so terribly believable.

I closed the door and stepped wide across the fat wobbly June bugs on the sidewalk.

***

He came around often, sort of adopted me right from the start. Asked for jobs. A handsome young Mexican, always very serious. His full name Peter Immaculate Conception Estrada.

Whenever Pete was out of work, he'd come ask me for a job. Actually I had none. But I'd let him wash my car, although I liked doing that myself, with a hose, behind the hotel Sunday afternoons. Also I didn't like to have him do it because I'm sure it wasn't the kind of work he wanted. But he'd never say so. He had to use buckets and wash it in the alley by my office, and if I had to go on a call quick I used it half-finished and came back from the dirt-dusty roads and he'd have to start over. But he'd never complain.

I asked patients if they knew of work needed—everyone who had had him agreed he was a good worker and fast—and we'd get him on to where somebody was rebuilding a barn or repairing a line of fence. (Mostly people had their own relatives to come help—who helped them back—and didn't hire "outside.") When it came into chopping time, everybody had to be in their own fields—the whole family—so those needing an extra hand hired Pete. And he always did a good job for them. I felt it my obligation each time to try to find work for him—simply because he asked me, I guess.

He always called me "Mr. Shoes—Dr. Shoes." "Dr. Shoes, can I have a dollar? Pay you Sabbaday."

There was absolutely nothing immaculate about Pete—that I could see. Except that irritating, almost childlike, sincerity—always completely sincere. Otherwise, nothing. I treated his gonorrhea, and his blood came back from the lab positive four-plus. Syphilis. "Mr. Shoes—Dr. Shoes, I think maybe I catch me the drip again." So often that I wondered if these were new infections or periodic flare-ups of a chronic case. I told him the only reason he didn't have yaws or granuloma inguinale was simply because there's none in the county. (He didn't smile—never smiled.)

When I hadn't seen Pete for a while and Adelita, his wife—she always looked angry; seems it's simply her features—would bring in a child, or several, sick again, I'd ask, "How's Pete?"

"And *I* should know? He's gone again."

"Working somewhere? Houston?"

"Huh! Comes home with no money. Maybe he comes back in a week, two weeks. Who knows?"

Adelita—Indian-looking woman—came with their four children, very beautiful children. They seemed to have much more than the ordinary number of diarrhea attacks, of sore throats, ear infections, colds, upper-respiratory infections, and flu—usually all at the same time, sometimes in succession, one at a time. All of which made me wonder if this was a vague language in which, unable to focus in on the real thing, they tried to speak with tight chests, the mental confusion of high fevers, inability to breathe right, choking—tried to cough out their trouble, their hurt; to vomit it, cry it out, say it in the pain of throat and ear infections, eliminate it in diarrhea. Whether these organicities were only the surface symptoms of a permeating overall sickness of the home, whether they got these illnesses for a reason, I'll never know, of course. But I did have these thoughts from somewhere. When Pete or Adelita brought one of the children—they never came together with the children—all I could treat was these organic results anyway. We always had a lot of drug samples on hand for practically everything and saved them for these children. Papinku would never have given Pete credit.

On Saturdays—even if he worked all week—Pete would come by, sit and wait his turn so drunk he'd keep going to sleep on somebody's shoulder, who'd move over and he'd wake up. His alcohol breath stank. But the waiting room often smelled like garlic anyway (eating garlic buttons straight is a Bohemian home remedy for high blood pressure). So now, garlic and alcohol. Come his turn, Margaret'd wake him, he'd come in, look perfectly sober like he always does, borrow a dollar—completely ignoring the fact that he was supposed to pay *me* a dollar this Saturday—and leave. Every time he left the office, Margaret'd pull up her sleeves and scrub her hands.

And just about the time that all this would begin to be a nuisance, he'd disappear and be gone for weeks or a month. Then he'd be back. Once I said, "This time I hope you didn't catch leprosy—you seem to get everything else. Did you?"

He answered seriously—he was always like that—"No, Mr. Shoes—Dr. Shoes."

And here they'd come again! Saturday night. Everyone bloody. God!

It's the only bad part about knowing Pete—all his relatives and the tradition of theirs: the feud with the Salases. No one could tell you exactly why or when it began. I asked Pete—he shrugged and said, "Always." I asked James. Some said two generations back (that would be in Pete's grandfather's time), an Estrada killed a Salas. Or the other way around? In the next generation (Pete's father's) the payback was one Estrada (Salas?) shot, which should have closed the books—even. But no, another Estrada received a cut in that fight and he bled, so the payback again must be a Salas (or is it Estrada?) should bleed. Must bleed. Well, both sides have now been doing a lot of that, on Saturday nights—and a good deal of it in my office, where I have to sew them up. There have been so many of these Saturday-night cuttings that both sides, surely everybody, have lost count completely as to who made whom bleed and how much, and the whole thing has turned into an almost regular exercise.

And although everyone in town deplored this feuding—they said so—I noticed, each time, you heard much talk and discussion concerning it. People asked me on the street, "Is it true, Julio got his jugular neck cut Saturday?" And "Was it? John almost bled to death this time?" Their talk always exaggerated it. Their questions rushed at you always with excitement and expectation in the tone. I'd reply "Only a few skin cuts," and you could see the enthusiasm sink away in a letdown—I don't know why I always made it less than it really was. But everyone swore it was such a "terrible" thing, those "Mexicans always fighting."

While they sit in the waiting room, they say hardly a word, any of them. Maybe that's best. Both sides sit there, in various degrees of disrepair, while I tend the worst cases first. I look them over, say, "Hay-sus, come in first." They have always accepted my referee decision where to begin. But that's another thing I dread because: (1) half-drunk they might not know how injured they really are; (2) their rules seem to forbid a lot of unnecessary talk, so they don't say they are hurt here or there or anywhere; and (3) sitting there across from each other is the very last place one is going to admit he's badly cut. Suppose one of them received a deep stab into a kidney, or spleen, or liver—is sitting there looking like "Who? Me? Don't be silly, I come only because my cousin is here"—and is quietly bleeding internally. And when I say "Come in" he'd be sitting there dead. So in my refereeing I have to keep this in mind, and anything that looks suspicious I take first. Each side chooses to act as if the other is not there.

It appears as if the seamy scars they inflict are like curses, derogatory graph messages written on each other, written in another language easily read by everyone. On Pete I always used a subcutaneous stitch, so there'd be as little scar left as possible, sometimes none. But he never said anything about it one way or another.

John, one of Pete's older brothers—Pete is the youngest—an extraordinarily handsome man, went for throats, produced cuts on throats, necks, ears, cheeks. But another brother, Slim, tall, who always looked half asleep—looked like an Indian, a sleepwalking Indian—seldom had any cuts and then only small ones; maybe he had some special defensive footwork. John, unbelievably handsome—everybody said "That's the real mean one"—often sat in jail, would beat his wife to the point of "attempted murder." And they'd go back together and it would happen all over again. And every one of them—Salases, too—each wore either a silver or gold chain with a crucifix or religious medallion on his chest. Sometimes it had blood on it.

It's aggravating to think about Pete. And yet, such simplicity makes him endearing somehow. But here he is: capable, sensitive, reliable, thorough—and not *doing* it. What's holding him back?

And if symptoms are supposed to say something, do say something—more than merely "I have some gonococcal germs"—what does it say? That I can't use my flesh for love? There's something wrong with my ability to love my wife? Or I'm afraid to love: it shows weakness? Or something wrong with my manliness?

I must admit: usually I do think of him as a boy.

And this cutting business. Does it say "See what a big brave man I am? See how manly I fight and suffer wounds?"

I told James one night, "They're children. But I'm afraid they'll kill each other yet."

As I sewed—Salas or Estrada, made no difference—I'd keep looking. Where do they hide their knives? You never saw a knife. But you knew they were there, always there, and ready. Where are their knives? You never saw one.

Always had that apprehension. Suppose, in all these alcoholic cloud fumes and smell of blood, this whole thing would burst wide open and they'd start it all off again right here?

. . . with me in the middle.

I sewed.

❊❊❊

There have been lots of rains. The talk in the waiting room says crops should be good. "But now it comes too much," they complain. Roads, they say, are bad; it's too wet to keep the weeds down; no place to hang wash; water is seeping out of the sides of hills making temporary running springs. "We can't get out no more; he keeps now the car on the hill and we walk barefoot home."

And they phoned to come to Leroy Strassman's.

It had begun with a severe headache, they said, his wife and mother and aunt telling it for him. Began in the cow lot while he kneeled on the wet ground milking. He thought he might have a fever and opened his jacket even though it was damp-cold. On the way to the house he vomited, but didn't know he was going to, so sudden. His mother and his aunt had said it wasn't much milk tonight, what it ought to be from two freshened cows, and he could not remember if he had milked the second cow or only turned the calf in. That's what frightened them all—that he couldn't remember about the second cow. Made them know this is something more than just the flu, and they rang and rang—"always three long and one short"—and finally got through to Elray Ehlers—he has a Schulenburg phone—and he called me. It was already after dark.

Leroy lay in a fresh bed, all clean sheets, fresh-smelling pajamas, hair combed damp. A pan of clear water stood on a table with towel and new bar of soap. The children were told to go stay in the kitchen; his wife stood by the head of the bed. A pretty woman, young, maybe a little too pretty. We spoke German.

During the examination, when I told him to put his chin on his chest, he couldn't. "It hurts."

"Wo? Wohin?"

"In the neck and up in the head. And down the back."

I tried to act like this wasn't so important.

Reflexes were exaggerated, jerked far too big. I did them again to make certain, maybe hoping it wasn't so.

To examine into his eyes I needed only to blow out the lamp to have the room dark. Retinas normal, but his other symptoms obviously show intracranial pressure.

With him positioned on a side, head pulled down, knees pulled up, and me kneeling on the floor to get to his naked spine, and with her holding the lamp near, I did a spinal tap. Had no way to measure the pressure, but it did seem to dribble faster than it should. Holding the test tube up by the kerosene lamp, I could see the fluid murky—it should be perfectly clear. This man is much sicker than he knows.

No, they couldn't recall anyone having a similar illness; they had been noplace—"He doesn't like to go, hardly anywhere"—except to church last Sunday. The children are too young to go to school, so they are home all day. No idea where he got it from.

Leroy being the only man in the house, I had no choice but to discuss his case plainly, openly, directly to him and the others—but I made it sound as mild as possible. I said, "This simply is spinal meningitis." I did not say, a very dangerous disease condition from which you might not recover. "You have the whole set of symptoms complete, including the small red spots on the abdomen," which he hadn't noticed but are described in every textbook. "You should be taken to a hospital. We need a hospital here."

"No!" his wife gasped. "Please leave him here. We want him home."

Quickly I went into details about "sterilization of everything he touches" and "isolation" and what his medicines would be and how often—everything. (I wanted to light a cigarette, but I feared they'd notice my hands shaking.) His dishes must be scalded as soon as they come into the kitchen; the children must be kept out—also the mother and aunt. And again, it would be best if he'd go to a hospital. But they said they wanted to keep him at home. And lastly, I explained that I would phone for the serum tonight—it should be on the train and here by noon—that we had to give it every day for three days.

Oh yes, and to keep the room dark for sunlight—if there'll be any. Can make his eyes hurt and headache worse. And that she should sleep in the room, on a separate bed, if he wants something—and easier to watch him.

"What should he eat?"

We went into all that too, in detail.

And finally: If the sickness should make him vomit any of the medicine, wait a while and give a new full dose, even if you're not sure it all came up. If he should have a convulsion, do not be afraid—it will pass. Only have a spoon ready, wrapped in cloth, and quickly thrust it between the teeth so he doesn't bite his tongue (I didn't say "off"). I will come tomorrow with or without the serum—I must see him. They must start the medication tonight. How can they send for it?

She said she'd walk over to their nearest neighbor, Dennis Hagens, and ask him to go.

Again I said, "It would be best to be in a hospital."

And she said, with him nodding agreement, "We'd rather have him home, and the undertaker probably can't get that big ambulance through the mud anyway."

We had talked about this disease almost as if it had become another person and was coming to live here. Like getting the guest bed set up in this room and ordering special foods for this visitor—strange. And when would he leave? And how? Defeated? Or as an invisible "honorary" leading the pallbearers and the coffin?

"Doctor, have you ever attended a spinal meningitis before—on your own?"

No, of course not!

Have you ever seen one—before now?

But I have read about it in textbooks! I answered my ghostly inquisitor and snapped my bag closed tight.

While driving up that sloppy, slick hill, it began raining again, thumping on the car roof. Sitting on my bed at the hotel still with my hat on, I phoned the prescriptions to James at his home and told him the neighbor, Hagens, would pick it up later tonight. Finally got hold of a detail man at his home in San Antonio who said, "We have an emergency call-service and the serum will be mailed, in dry ice, tonight."

I had told James to call me back from the drugstore—I couldn't find my key—so I could get in my office to examine the spinal fluid and mail the rest of it to the lab in Houston. Margaret always locks the side door and somehow I always misplace the key. I'll have to do something about that—put it on my car-keys ring.

Under the microscope, there lay the many small cells. Like so many zeroes. James came in to wait, and I showed him the small cells in the scope, telling him, "It might just be too bad for Leroy Strassman." Nietzsche looked serious and stopped wagging his tail. "And if he . . . dies, who's going to support all the rest of those people? The wife, the kids, the mother, the aunt?"

Second visit: fever higher. One hundred three and two tenths. Give more aspirin and more fluids. He took the shot in his buttocks without a flinch. Maybe he didn't know too well what was happening—today he couldn't remember when he got sick. Mental confusion. Is he getting worse?

"But he sleeps so much. It is good . . . is it good?"

I hope the "sleep" is not periods of semicoma. Were they? Beginnings? Am I losing him?

It's as if I were asking that other person sitting there, unseen, silent . . .

And as if the silence is his answer.

No one else had become sick. All the children were okay—not even a sore throat.

"I'll be back tomorrow. Remember: absolutely no visitors."

I did make it up the slippery hill.

Third visit: two days of medication. No better. Fever didn't go over a hundred two and four tenths, but held it down better by using more aspirin. Chest is still clear—means the sulfa is keeping out secondary pneumonia. Or his resistance is doing it. The second dose of serum, in the other buttock. "You must get some sleep, Mrs. Strassman, or you'll be sick next."

Each day the older women in the kitchen with the two children—now there is a bed in there—had the coffee ready, and after seeing Leroy we had a cup. They have a set of old-fashioned china with a part of the Lord's Prayer in German in the bottom of each cup: *Vater Unser der Du bist im Himmel*—and on in the next cup, *Geheiligt werde Dein Name.* It was supposed to be a set of twelve. I got a different line every day, but not in proper sequence. They talked, saying Leroy had got sick—that the whole thing—is because he won't listen, and I should tell him it is because he didn't dress warm enough for outside; that they are always after him, but he just won't hear; and they tell him over and over he should wear two pairs of socks, double, to keep . . . Also, he didn't always eat everything on his plate, and they've told him food is . . . And sometimes he stayed up too late, reading at the kitchen table, and that isn't good for a person's eyes and takes more kerosene . . .

If I would imagine this disease condition in a human form and had imagined him sitting in the large chair, watching, he might have said, "In telling her to rest and in examining the children's throats each day, are you saying you're afraid of losing *more* than one?"

And I would have answered, "Who invited *you* in here? And why?"

But he would only have answered with a silent grin, like a skull.

Meninges are the covering of the precious spinal cord tissue and brain tissue: spongy interlacing, filled with fluid, a supportive cushion surrounding this rarest and most highly specialized of all the body tissues. It's protected first by an encasement armor of bone—the skull and backbone—then by a tough fibrous sheath like an envelope or sleeve, then suspended in fluid (against shock, jolt), supported there by the scaffoldinglike meninges. Brain and spinal cord—the most protected, treasured tissue of the body. As if nature said, "*This* is the very essence of this creature." (And even today, it is the least understood tissue. As if man's brain balks at disclosing itself to man. As if its secrets, too precious, too dangerous, must also be guarded.) Saying, "*This* is the zero center of man."

This rare, finely tuned tissue does not regrow itself in healing, as do other body tissues. Any damage to it, by trauma, infection, or result of these—scar—is permanent. All the other tissues, except one other, the highly specialized heart muscle, regrow.

This is his very being.

meninx (pl. *meninges*) *-itis*, "infection of—." Meningitis!

I do hope everyone in that house is praying for him.

My ruts up the hill now were little streams of running water. I spun and spun and with the door open pushed with my left boot and made it up the hill onto the solid gravel road that is an all-weather milk-and-mail route. It rained on me most all the way in.

Fourth visit. Late afternoon—what will I find there this trip? More rain this morning; still drizzling. Downhill is okay but more like a slide. Dreary day.

As I pulled off my boots in the kitchen—with the old lady saying each time I should keep them on (I'm sure she makes Leroy take his off)—even here, from their quick step or sudden eye smiles or busy attitude or the children playing more freely or something, I knew Leroy was improving. Knew it before I saw him.

And he was. Fever ninety-nine and six tenths with no aspirin. No more headache, felt weak, didn't have to take any more codeine, ate well, mind clear, insisted on shaving himself, bowels moved, wanted to get up—"my neighbor is doing all my work for me; I can't lay here."

"You'd do the same for him."

Today I drank several cups of coffee. The women said maybe it was too weak for me because you could almost "*Vater unser*" through it and they laughed. They always made it weak on purpose. "Leroy, he always drinks too much coffee," they whispered, and no matter how often they told him, he drank too much. So he doesn't know it, they make it not so strong—I should tell him he shouldn't drink it so much.

And today I said something that I had wanted to get off my mind—and said it loud for Leroy to hear plain in the next room. "Maybe when you're down sick it's nice to have so many women to wait on you but, oh my! How is it to be well and try to please all of them!"

And not a one laughed. When I said it they hushed still and it was completely quiet from Leroy's room too. Well, I had to say it. Maybe it's only a foolish idea, but I felt anyone who—unawares—elects to risk spinal meningitis could be saying something vital, like "I don't have the backbone (stamina) to cope with my situation, can't stand up to it."

Maybe they thought it rude of me.

"Hell!" I said it aloud. In blue socks I stomped back into his darkened room, with the flame of the lamp standing so flat, yellow, and still. "I must say this, Leroy, either for you or maybe for me: We mustn't live too much alone. When we're much alone—and feel alone—it turns us too much in. In on ourselves. I believe other people give us our lives. It may not always be good; may even be bad. But still, our life is given to us by *other* people. It's the only place we can get it. We don't *live* without other people.

"Since it is our—*the* most precious treasure, we must always be aware. Sometimes we must guard, must protect . . .

"I don't know why I had to say this, but I did."

I pulled on my boots and shook hands at the door and all three said good-by quietly and I called out, "So long, Leroy," and he answered big and loud, "So long!"—which is not a German expression.

That muddy hill was really a mess now. My ruts from these days were nothing but straight downhill rivulets and I buzzed and buzzed up slowly and pushed with my boot and slid in and out of the slick, watery ruts, and all at once the car slid sideways and the back wheels sank deep in the ditch. I buzzed and buzzed and mud flew up behind, but the whole thing was mired down hopelessly. I kept trying and buzzing and it was nothing. When I stopped, whiffs of smoke came from under the fenders, smelling of burning rubber, and steam exhaled up from under the hood. Now what?

In exactly the same moment of helplessness, there to my left coming across the pasture out of the foggy dusk is Herman Umlang with planks on his shoulder. And at the same time on my right, coming down the hazy hill, Dennis Hagens, a shovel on his right shoulder and an armful of tow sacks. And up the road right before me on a big red tractor with yellow wheels, clean as brand new, one of the Roy Bucek boys—the youngest, I believe—sitting high on that big machine. This boy, backing it down the narrow lane. Got off, clattered a chain to something in front, and drove uphill pulling my little car along as if it weighed nothing. That small boy did it, with that machine. On the gravel road he got off, unhitched the chain, drove off and never said a word to me at all. I kept calling out the window thanking and trying to hand him a dollar bill and he never looked nor answered.

Lots of rain. In the waiting room they said "... puts the season in the ground good."

❋❋❋

"Gretchen, I don't want to sound critical, but they don't like to be called Bohemians. They want to be called Czechs. So let's don't use the word *Bohemian* anymore. And never say *dumb Bohunks*."

"I never have."

"I know. Nor *Polaks*—absolutely never. Only *Czechs*."

"Why do they want *Czechs?*"

"Guess it's a better, higher grade of Bohemian."

"I have to remember. And we must always say *colored*."

"*Negro* sounds too close to *nigger*."

"Yes. Or blacks."

"Blacks? Call them blacks? To their face? They may not like that." (I did not foresee the trend of a quarter century later.)

"But in German we have always called them *die Schwarzen*."

"Maybe so, but for now we'd best call them colored—it's what they call themselves. And we're not to say *Mexicans*."

"Not *Mexicans* either?" She leaned back from the typewriter. "Well then, what are they?"

"Mexican-Americans. Spanish."

"They've never been to Spain. Why *Mexican-American*?"

"Guess so it's plain you don't mean *wetback.* Or call them *Spanish-speaking*."

"They don't speak Spanish. They talk Tex-Mex—it's not real Spanish."

"I know. But we don't speak perfect German grammar either."

"What should I be careful about . . . that I don't call us Germans?"

"*Krauts.* Don't call us Krauts. Nor Klabberheads. We don't like that."

"Of course not! We're German."

"There you are: German—that's the cream of the Krauts. Just like *Czechs*."

But after a moment she stopped typing again and said, in German, "I wish also not to criticize."

"Yes?"

"It is being said you gave Anita Zurek something. So she should lose the baby—make a miscarriage."

"That's absurd. Just the opposite. I did everything—"

"I know. But it is being said."

"That's absurd. How could it be?"

"Dr. Kotzebue started it. I'm sure."

"Oh. Oh yes, I see. But surely the woman, Mrs. Zurek, knows better."

"No, she's saying it, too."

"Good Lord!"

"They believe what he tells them."

"But she knows better."

"People believe what they want to believe."

"Even when it's . . . ridiculous?"

"Certainly."

"I wonder now—wonder if that's why she started in the first place."

"What?"

"Like if she wanted to, to begin with. No wonder nothing stopped it. Hmm. You say she believes I . . . made her to miscarry?"

"She's saying it."

"Is she saying she wanted to miscarry?"

"Oh no. She's saying you caused it."

"I see."

⁂

Margaret unfolded a thin newspaper, the Schulenburg *Stayer*, open big and laid it out before me. "Today's Thursday. I'm keeping score."

"Score?"

She pointed to a heading "Card of Thanks."

I read aloud:

> Wx wish to xxprxss our hxartfxlt thanks for thx many acts of kindnxss xxtxndxd us at thx loss of our dxar mothxr and grandmothxr, Mrs. Alois Mikulxncak.
>
> Spxcial thanks to Dr. R. B. Kotzxbux and assisting doctors and thx kind nursxs at Rxngxr Hospital.

"What's all this *x* business?"

"Don't pay any attention to it. That's Gus. He ran out of *e*'s years ago, but had plenty *x*'s. He's too *schlop* to do anything about it."

> Wx also thank Rxv. Fxlix Bxaxda for consolation and tributxs at thx funxral; to all who attxnxd thx funxral sxrvicxs, sxnt floral tributxs, and sympathy cards, to thosx who brought food to thx family dinnxr, and anyonx who hxlpxd in any way, wx also wish to thank thx Brosch Funxral homx and thx pallbxarxrs for thxir kind sxrvicxs.
>
> May God blxss xach and xvxryonx of you is our wish.
>
> —Hxr childrxn, Mrs. Rud. Vavrusa, Mrs. Gladys Bludau, Alois Kilulxncak.

"Do they always—when somebody dies—put it in the paper? Like this?"

"Sure. The family does. Read this one here."

> Card of Thanks.
>
> Our hxartfxlt thanks to Dr. R. B. Kotzxbux and nursing staff of thx LaGrangx Hospital for thx xxcxllxnt carx givxn our bxlovxd mothxr, Mrs. Cxcxlia Koncaba, whilx shx was a patixnt thxrx.

"He doesn't always get the paper out on time, Thursdays. And sometimes the Christmas ads are still in on Washington's Birthday.

Schloppie. He inherited the paper, of course. Half of it, beat his sister out of her half. His papa sent him to college—everything—but he came back here to work under his daddy on this dinky paper. And then beat his sister out of hers yet. Everybody knows it. *Schlop.*"

Wx xspxcially wish to thank Monsignor Rudy Martisak, Rxv. Pxtru, Rxv. Psxncik, for thxir prayxrs, bringing Holy Communion, also administxring last sacramxnts and last ritxs.

"What's all this got to do with us? What do you mean *score?*

Thanks to thx Brosch Funxral Homx for thxir kind sxrvices, also thx pallbxarxrs and altar boys. Wx gratxfully xxprxss our thanks to thx many rxlativxs and frixnds for thx food, Mass offxrings, floral offxrings and all who callxd to pay thxir last rxspxcts.

—Childrxn and grandchildrxn of Mrs. Cxcxlia Koncaba.

"What do you mean? Score?"

"He lost two more. Two for Dr. Kotzebue, none for you."

"That's absurd."

"You're winning."

"I'm not so sure."

"Certainly you are."

"I hope so," I mused, drumming my fingers, "but—I wasn't thinking about him."

A later Thursday. Margaret opens the paper wide. "Two for him, none for you. Two cards of thanks. And under Births, it's two for you and one for him."

"Aw, that's— Mexicans and blacks aren't put in the paper either way—neither born nor dead-thank-you."

"He doesn't take them."

"I know. So this silly scoring isn't fair either. And besides, it's not the real score."

"In any case, who's next?"

Margaret belongs to something—Altar Society, I think she said—at the church, and asks people for flowers. She had asked me if it's all right; she keeps them in buckets in the little toilet. "Do me a favor," I said to her. "Of the flowers you bring and people bring in here every

Friday-Saturday for church, do me the favor please: Never bring oleanders. Pink oleanders."

"What's wrong with oleanders? Allergy or something? Why not pink?"

"Unh no—well, in a way, yes. Just don't do it, please."

She looked at me strangely. But—for once—said nothing.

A Thursday afternoon. Margaret had picked up the Schulenburg *Stayer*—I saw her reading it between patients and while I examined. She didn't say a word. Now she folded the paper back into its creases and dropped it on my desk, saying she was going back to the post office again—"The rest of the mail ought to be up by now."

Soon as she was gone I opened the paper and looked down each column. "Card of Thanks." One for Kotzebue, none for me. Under "Births" were two for him and two for me.

I folded the paper and laid it back exactly as she had left it.

⁂

As she talked, chubby Babicko Fajkus unknotted her shatek at the chin and slipped it off her head. She sat on the examining table (it wobbled), letting her easy bigness sag as it pleased. "I'm talling! Visiting by me is the flu last veek; but I didn't take me down in the bed and I couldn't come. It rained. And rained. Like a cow making her vater on the rocks—such splatter; I couldn't come from such slotchy roads. And I am veak, like fuzz on baby chick, so veak. Everything aches me all over, and my knees is shaking. They not knowing to stand or sit down. Is the flu. And in my head it turns around and around and pushes me on the brains.

"So I take from them pills, twinklelizers, like you give me for rest?—those vich tastes like fefferment?—and I sleep. Oh, how I sleep. You could throw me from the bed down and I vouldn't know it. I sleep.

"I know I have it the fever last veek, but now it all gone. Only in my head is turning."

And ate garlic buttons—needn't ask. "Did you, by any chance, lose a pound or two with this? Or did your appetite stay good?"

"Appetite? I eat everything. I eat till I scare myself. Poppy seed don't hurt, do it? I make poppy-seed kolace. I vish I bring you jar from my zauerkraut—sour, sour. I bring you next time pickles—oh, sour; it is making you close the eyes.

"Appetite? Everything is growing. My begonias, my camellias, everything grows by me. I put something in, it grows. All grows by me." She patted her abdomen.

Pulling the stethoscope out of my ears, "Sorry, Babicko Fajkus. It is your blood pressure again. Today it is two hundred thirty over a hundred."

"Vell, it is the spring and everything is coming up. My flowers, my veeds, my tomato plants is up . . . vit the blood bressure is, too."

On her next visit: "Did you take them? Regular? Three times a day?"

"Oh sure. With the clock I am vaiting. Like you said it. Today is better, no turning in the head. I could bend me down and put shoes on myself."

"With all that stomach?"

"Is empty stomik, doktor. Maybe I put me too many odder things in, but is empty stomik: Is no more babies. Old man is too veak and by me is old, too. Don't catch no more babies. Is empty basket." She slid her hand over the large abdomen as if she were smoothing her skirt. "Is spring but is no more spring."

She folded and unfolded the shatek in her lap. I waited. "I know vat is, vat it makes me sick," she spoke without looking at me. "And is no medicine." She folded and smoothed it across her knee. "Is everyveres spring—peach trees is so pretty pink, plum trees vite like dumplings and vit bees, and smells it so nize, and little green leafs on trees. All around me is spring. But by me is no more spring." She folded the shatek.

❋❋❋

As I came out of the Schneider house—eyes again—John Smaistrla stood with a hoe between the rows of small blue cabbages, "Good morning, John. *Dobre Rano*."

He came up between the rows to the fence, "I see you going last night to Schneider again. Is bad?"

"Oh, things are improving. Again."

"Is Mrs. Schneider, no? Is always vit the eyes."

"Why yes."

"I know it long time. I know is coming. Always sick. From Lent I thought me so and I tall it to her she is losing veight."

"You? Told her that?"

"I see her go by to store every day. Make such little steps. So ve talk sometime. She don't look me healthy. Like she don't eat. Is bad ven no eating. Cattles has to eat gut to be gut stock—is same thing vit peoples, same like cattles, no? Eat gut and shit gut, yes?" I noticed that his eyes were not inflamed.

"You certainly keep your place looking nice," I indicated the freshly hoed garden, the neat white house, the picket fence.

"And the odder vun? The sister? How is she?"

"Oh, she's—"

"Fine strong vomans. Vorks hard and hangs op gut vite vash—and so much. Gut strong womans—no?"

"Yes—yes. She's working day and night—takes care of her sister's eyes, too. And her work."

"Gut. Strong."

By the end of the week, the infection disappeared completely from Mrs. Schneider's eyes.

Was it only two weeks later? Mrs. Schneider—back with the same thing.

"I don't understand! Do you have any idea where you are getting this infection? Nobody could get such a severe eye infection overnight. And if this keeps up, one of these days it'll get inside the eyes and you're blind—Forever." Gosh. Shouldn't have blurted all that at her. Only shows I'm scared.

She touched her bobbed hair delicately and did not answer.

"We'll use the same treatment as before. It may be late before I can come by."

When I knocked, knowing what's inside, it became almost as if something else would be opening the door, smiling, saying, "Welcome to my little house." Saying sarcastically, "Come in, come in."

As I heard footsteps coming—Arnold's—I took several deep breaths before going in.

❋❋❋

"*path(o)-*. Word element, *disease, morbid condition.*

"*pathologic*. Pertaining to or caused by disease.

"*pathology*. The scientific study of alterations produced by disease."

I need a word. Some kind of word to describe it—this force, this unseen will, this power within (yet far out of reach and control). A word to describe—a word deeper than *pathosis.* Maybe it's the parent of pathosis.

People come wearing their symptoms (1) on the surface and tell of them freely—the fever, cough, rash, malaise—yes. Almost all visible. Surface. "Symptoms" is the first layer.

But hidden underneath from themselves in a deeper stratum, is (2) the cause of the symptoms, the *pathosis.* The symptoms are, of course, clues as to where and what the pathosis is. They are as puppets on a stage worked by strings, or as hounds on long leashes held in the hand of pathosis. And the pathosis could be a bacterial infection, an allergy, a tumor (fibroid, cyst, aneurism, or cancer), a fracture, a malfunction of an organ (as with diabetes, or anemia—blood is an organ—or thyroid, or liver). And it is not always visible. As if sinking deeper down into the hidden unknown, it is not often seen.

"Symptoms" has many languages of its own. For example, a certain kind of wheezing cough is characteristic of allergy. While a coarser, croupy cough with bloody phlegm is almost the clear voice of lobar pneumonia. It's somewhat as if "Symptoms" is an actor on stage speaking his lines, but directed by a second person in the pit, Pathosis, whom the audience seldom hears or sees.

Between pathosis and the symptoms are many stopgap way stations, resistance poles against the pathosis—to protect the person. These include all kinds of mechanisms: a vast standing army of white blood cells to combat infectious invasions, enzymes to digest intruding foreign bodies, signal systems of pain, and the anesthesia of the shock mechanism which temporarily "shelves" the injury. And many others. However, when pathosis is strong enough, it overrides all safety fences and levies and expresses its victory in a stage flooded full of its symptoms.

But (3), what *causes* the pathosis? Who hires this director? Where's he from? I need a word. Who has him come and select a "suitable" pathosis? Why should one person come with a mild kidney infection and another with a leukemia? Who selects which? Why should some tumors of the breast be benign cysts and others malignant? Everything has a cause: So what causes the pathosis?

I need a word. There is (a) the subconscious mind, which stands like a lock system in a canal, allowing some thoughts of perceptions through, screening others, sending the rejects off into dreams or unlabeled deposit boxes like unmarked graves. And (b) the unconscious mind of anesthesia and deep natural sleep and severe shock, but which still retains a *consciousness.* The mind has many layers. And (d) down to the decerebrate mind of deep coma and down to brain stem, where there is no mind at all past the frog's level—a blind frog at that—where there is nothing but instinct. The mind has many layers, like a sheer cliffside that shows its structure of rock layers, laid down or eroded from many rains—prehistoric, antedeluvian rains.

So, as with the man in the well, what tidal wave force overrode the stop stations, flooded the locks, commanded forth that he murder himself? So who, or what, commands pathosis, "Be a fibroma." Or "Be a virus." "A suicide." "A murderer." "Be a sickle-cell anemia." "Be a dislocated intervertebral disc."

Or does everything just happen?

I want a word.

For I have felt him—that presence—now, too close and too often.

Him in the third stratum (or lower yet?). Totally invisible, neither macroscopically nor microscopically nor chemically plumbed. An invisible presence, a consciousness, a will, with its own might.

A word.

I'm looking in Stedmann's *Medical Dictionary:*

"*path*(o)-. Word element, *disease, morbid condition.*

"*pathologic*. Pertaining to or caused by disease.

"*pathology*. The scientific study of alterations produced by disease.

"*pathonomy*. Science of the laws of disease.

"*pathophoresis*. The transmission of disease.

"*pathosis*. A diseased condition.

"*-pathy*. Word element, *disease, morbid condition*."

No word that says it.

But the two word elements lie there as if waiting. If I join them, patho- and -pathy, forming *pathopathy* . . .

Maybe it is a word. Maybe I have found it.

And maybe its meaning, its definition, is waiting.

❋❋❋

I hurried through the drugstore. "Right cool this morning again."

James didn't look up from his book; nodded his balding head twice.

Nietzsche, without raising his head either, swept the floor with his bushy tail twice—swish-swish, hel-lo. (If Nietzsche is with him, it means Papinku is not coming today. Probably off with his state senator friend again.)

The waiting room is jammed, people standing everywhere, no more chairs. "Morning everybody." While Margaret got the first one ready on the examining table, I thumbed through the stack on my desk, pitched the samples into a box to be sorted later, threw the rest of the whole pile—all advertisements—into the waste basket and was ready.

At times the crowded rush feels almost like a river of frothing rapids. I don't like it. There is no time to know the people, only their symptoms. And that's only skimming along the surface. The whole thing becomes more like bottles on an automatic capping machine—no chance to learn them as a part of you, nor why they became ill. No chance to learn them, either as an extension of yourself or an involution, neither bulge nor bladder, but only as two parallel lines passing each other in opposite directions. I don't like it. You get nothing but symptoms. But you still try to inhale some of the essence of each, almost snatching at it as they go quickly past. If some of the people can possibly be seen in the office without having to use the examining room, Margaret alternates them, helps things go faster.

Case of bleeding piles, big as fists. "Is vorse from shopping."

"Worse? . . . From?"

"Bleeding ven I go out. Yes, from shopping corn the veeds out. Shop cotton."

Chronic bronchitis in old man Kalisek. (Examined him in the office.)

The open-leg ulcers of old Maminko Vanicek. (In the examining room.)

Six-month-old baby in (office) for a smallpox vaccination. "There. But don't buy any of those clear shields to put over it. They're made from horses' hooves, and some people got tetanus—lockjaw—from them."

Clarabell Green, a black woman, forty-five but looks sixty, in for a dressing. I did a hysterectomy on her at LaGrange hospital for fibroids. Big ones, like three fists. Blacks are a more "fibrogenic" race, have more fibroid tumors than whites, develop keloids in old scars (overgrowth of the scar tissue). I remember she had said, "When it first come on me, thought I might be pregnant. It stopped my periods, and I could feel it somethin' growin'. Thought I might be pregnant. My man sho' woulda been proud. When it come on me—when I first noticed it war on me. I hates to turn loose' it. You say hit gotta come out?''

Cataracts in an old man who said in Czech, ''Is Holy Spirit telling old man, 'You see it already enough ugly things in this vorld.' '' Will refer him to an eye specialist in Houston.

Child, seven years old, bed-wetting. Examination normal. ''Don't blame her, don't criticize. It's a nervous condition. She's trying to say something by it.'' The mother doesn't understand. ''Okay, then give her this; she will be all right.'' Elixir phenobarbital, mild dose.

The phone rings constantly. Why did they ever have to invent the thing?

Hearty farmer, thirty-eight, John somebody—they call it Yon or Yohon—had pushed back the bulky feather mattress this morning, got up and reached for his overalls. He stooped to put his shoe on and then ''got it like a pitchfork in the back,'' so painful that he could not straighten up. They brought him in, leading him bent over almost on all fours. ''Is walking like a mule. Is backbone knuckles? Snap from the joints out?'' It's a typical lumbago, which is an infection settled along the muscle sheath. Extremely painful on movement, but not a serious condition—hardly more than a cold. I gave him a hypo and in about ten minutes, reddish in the face and constantly rubbing his nose, he straightened up, walked about, began telling how he would plant two hundred acres more of cotton and he would build a new barn for ''peks'' and get himself registered Durocs. Maybe this year he would make himself ten thousand dollars—or more.

His friends in big shoes and loose overalls looked at me and one got behind a chair. ''It is only the medicine—it is a dope.'' I explained. ''He is like drunk. Let him talk. Now he has no pain. In four or five hours the pain will return—and his senses, too.''

I scribbled the prescriptions. ''Give him these tablets—two before each meal, three times a day. It is sulfathiozole and it will kill out the infections—in three days. And this one is for pain only. Use a heat pad of some kind. Heat pad? Well, use a brick—from on the stove? Wrap it first in old newspaper, then in a towel.''

Next patient.

Margaret explained, ''I got her in as soon as I could.'' Girl with measles. She's probably given them to everybody in the waiting room who isn't immune. In two weeks, we might have an epidemic.

Ruby Dallas, unusually dark for a black woman—they live in Happy Hollow between the city dump and the Blue Flame Cafe and have walked all the way in—bunched her five stairstep children in. "It's Roland," she pointed. "He the one got it worstest—just examine on him. He scratchin' most alla time."

"Do the others have it, too?" I studied the scratch marks at the wrists, between the fingers . . .

"Not so much as he do. Mostly at night—scratches in his sleep. Just examine on him and tell me and I'll give it to the others, too."

"Do they all sleep in the same bed?"

"Oh, yes sir."

"Then they have all got it. It is scabies. This will be a salve. Smear it on all of them for three days, then boil the sheets. Smear each child from the neck down—it never gets on the face—every night for three nights. On all. Then bathe them all good and *boil* all their clothes and sheets. Else it will come back." In case she might be embarrassed, I added, "They may have got it at school and brought it home. Remember, *boil*."

"How much that medicine gonna cost?"

I stepped to the screen door, peeking into the drugstore; James still there alone. "Oh not so much," I said loudly. "A precipitated-sulfur ointment isn't expensive. Enough for five—no, seven—a dollar or so."

James nodded—without looking.

"What I gonna owe you?"

"Fifty cents."

"Apiece?"

"No. In all."

Next case of tonsilitis—bright red throat and clean white spots. No danger of getting the diagnosis mixed with diphtheria, which is a shaggy dirty-white.

With the door closed, Margaret says, "That cleared a bunch out. At least they can all sit down now." We're also grateful for a pause—have to wait while old Mr. Kalinec (low backache, possible bladder or prostate) passes a urine, and he's in there trying, slow to start. Margaret left the water running—perhaps it helps.

"That Mrs. Greely," she sighs, dropping into a chair, "I can't stand the woman. I have to put up with her in our card club—says you're the only white doctor who takes blacks. She calls you a nigger doctor."

"Fine. Any day Mrs. Greely says something good about me, I'll know I'm doing something wrong."

"You still have to go to both hospitals, too. Why don't you start a hospital?"

"God! That would be the greatest. A hospital! A dream. In fact, the greatest thing a man could do. And also save me all that driving. But no . . . That's one helluva big order. Not for me."

"If you set yourself to it."

"No thanks. I don't have the—"

"The town could have had a hospital a few years ago—it got the underpass under the railroad. WPA would have built it. So, instead, they dug out under the rail—"

"You mean they did want? . . . PWA? Public Works? . . ."

"The government wanted to build a hospital here, and all they asked was the city to give the land and for all the doctors to sign they would use it. That's all. And the old doctor—the one who had this office and died?—he signed right away, but Dr. Kotzebue wouldn't."

"No. How could he possibly refuse? Everything that it would have meant for the town."

"Some said it's because he can't do surgery."

"Yes—that hand."

"That's not it." She can sound so sarcastic at times. "He never did do surgery, even before he lost the first finger. He refused. Everybody said it was because he didn't want new doctors coming in who'd show him up. So the town didn't get the hospital. Instead, we got that . . . hole in the ground."

"What a pity. And I suppose the people have forgiven him. They're very good people. And I'm sure they have."

"Whether yes or no, we did not get the hospital."

Mr. Kalinec came out of the toilet with the empty specimen jar. "I can't go. Tomorrow I bring it you some."

The waiting room stood full again. Almost nobody looks at magazines—they visit. They meet uncles and cousins on their papa's side and neighbors "from vere ve used to live" and their sister-in-law's aunts. "Sunday before Mass ve had two-tents but Friday we had inch and four-tents." "Oh, you say it. Friday ve had only seven-eights and Sunday all day nudding. But by us yesterday nize clouds." "How is Zelma's boy—the one vat is going to marry vit your cousin Gledysko?" "Oh, so you heard it already, no? We got to help by baking—ve on bride's side; Gladys is Joe's cousin." "By you corn comes up good? Good stand corn? By us such rain, vashes us the seeds out. Papa gotta replant low in fields, maybe ten acres." "You saved from last year plenty seed corn? For replanting, too?"

Child who had passed a long white worm (nematodes). They brought it along wrapped in a white cloth. Probably has pinworms too. Piperazine syrup—teaspoonful every morning for seven days; skip a week; repeat.

Vaclav Herzik in the waiting room held a clean cloth over his eye.

"I open the door to feed the cows and, by gory, right avay hits me something and it hurt like hell. My vife she don't see nudding. She make me flaster from cornmeal, but it don't help nudding, so I tell her 'Get me clean pants. I go doktor.' Maybe a little piece"—he looked around the crowded room with his one eye—"little piece cowshit, but I had it poppy seed drying on tin roof." They nodded for poppy seed. "Poppy seed—yes." With the door open I'm hearing all this.

"But you're hurting," Margaret insisted, although he protested he wasn't next.

"Yes. Vaclav, yes," they urged. "Go, go in; you emmajancy. Go."

He and Margaret came in, Vaclav holding his eye closed with the cloth. "Me. This time I emmajancy."

"Emma who?"

"So she take me first."

"Emergency," Margaret translated.

"Something is me in eye. Maybe cowshit in eye."

"Really?" I laughed. "Vasicku, whatever were you doing on your back under a cow? Sit there."

"No. It flies me in eye when I open door. Barn door. Maybe is poppy seed."

"No, Margaret, the light has to come from the side. To see a foreign body in an eye, light must come across, obliquely." I moved the stand. "If it shines straight in, you can't see it."

Vaclav returned to the waiting room showing the tiny black speck on the white cloth. Margaret came rushing past where I washed my hands, "So many standing. I'm running out of clean towels. I washed some last night but they were still too damp this morning. I ought to keep folding chairs here, like we do in church, for those times when it gets so— Oh, doctor, don't spit in the lavatory."

No? Huh, dear girl, when you're not here, on Sundays, I even urinate in it.

A black man wished ''to see the doctor alone.'' Margaret stepped out. ''I have a small growth—down there.''

''Where exactly?''

''Guess about ten inches back from the head.''

''What? . . . I don't know where that is on you, but on most men that'd be hemorrhoids. Let's see.'' And it was almost as he said. It was a small papilloma, easily cauterized.

Old man who said loudly he had become ''deef.'' Margaret held the bowl while I washed out his ears with a bulb syringe—huge wax blob out of each ear. ''Vot makes it vax?'' Still spoke loud.

''Nature. Nature puts wax in our ears to keep bugs out, so bugs don't crawl in.''

''What makes it bugs crawling in ears?''

''Looking for a place to lay eggs. Or to hibernate—sleep for the winter.''

''Ha?''

''A place to sleep during winter.''

''Is bad, bugs sleeping in ears. If snoring, make it noise inside head like new tractor.''

For the little man's sake, I tried to laugh. My eyes met Margaret's and I'm sure they said, suffering saints, how much longer? But I asked her, ''Many more?''

''Full.''

***

Clarice did not look at me as she mumbled through thick lips, ''I comin' cause I want y'all to hep me . . . if you will.'' She looked at the floor, showing the many short pigtails which needed to be recombed.

''I'll do what I can. How are you sick?''

''Oh I ain't sick. It ain't nothin' like that.'' She scratched her fuzzy scalp. As she scratched again on the other side, I thought of head lice. Or nervousness.

''How do you want help then?''

''It's my daughter.''

''She's sick?''

''Oh no, sir. She ain't sick.''

''Then what? Is she here?''

"Oh no. She be in San-tone."

"San Antonio? How old is she?"

"She three year. Be four in August."

"And she's not sick."

"Oh no, sir."

"What's this all about, Clarice? I haven't got time to beat around the bush. What's the matter? I'll do what I can, but you seem too bashful to tell me. Now speak up."

"Yes, sir. No, sir, I ain't zackly bashful, I guess—I jes' don't know how to splain it all."

"Well— Try to tell me what's on your mind—maybe there is something I can do. Do you need a health card?"

"No sir. It's nothin' like that either."

I'll wait, give her time. So I waited. And waited. She scratched her head. "Now look here, Clarice, damn it! I haven't got all day!" Her eyes widened, she seemed to back down, shrink into the large chair. "Well, it's just that there are a lot of people waiting. Please try to tell me what it is you want."

"I don't know—I mean—yes, sir. It's . . . I don't . . . Maybe this here letter'll tell you." I took the dirty ragged thing, hoping there's nothing crawling on it. The worn edges looked like it had been carried in a sweaty hand and felt of, in a pocket, for days. But the inside pages were perfectly clean and neat and written in an easy hand.

". . . and when we go for a drive she rolls the windows up and down by herself. . . ." I rearranged the pages: "Dearest Clarissa, we received your letter and of course we can understand how you feel. But I would like to tell you of the things she has here. This morning she went to the clothes closet and looked over her little dresses and selected a blue and white one with ruffled pinafore. Then she got into the bathtub and adjusted the hot and cold water herself, but of course I always watch her since I am with her every minute of the day and night."

"You stay below the Methodist Church, don't you—close by Sewella Jackson?"

"Yes, sir," she said to her lap. I've seen it, like others there, a small shanty sitting high on leaning blocks—you can see straight through under it. And no electric wires nor water pipes going into it at all. "This child the woman is writing about is yours?"

"Oh yes, sir. She mine. I birthed her."

"Are these people relatives of yours?"

She became completely obsessed in examining her dirty fingernails. "No sir," she said to them.

I read: "She turns on the radio and selects her own station. When she wakes up from her nap she has milk and cookies or fresh orange juice and when we go for a drive she rolls . . ."

"How does it happen that they have your child?"

For a moment she carefully studied the nails, as if she had found something wrong with one of them. "I lent her out," she murmured.

"I see. And now you want her back?"

She made a fist and put it against her lips as if she were going to blow into it. "Yes, sir."

"How many children do you have at home?"

"Six," she said into the fist, never looking at me.

"Are you married now?"

She looked down into her lap and said, "No, sir."

"How do you support these children?"

"I wash. But now they got thet new rulin' and the welfare is gonna hep."

"Yes, it's Aid to Dependent Children. It'll pay about twelve dollars a month for each child until they are fourteen."

"Yes, sir. That's what the welfare lady told me, too."

"Now I see. And you want to draw welfare for this child, too, but she's not here. So you want her back."

It wasn't exactly a sigh, more a short smothered sound. "Yes, sir."

". . . she is learning to pick up her own toys. She prefers the stuffed animals which I bought at Joske's. On Sunday she attends Nursery Sunday School. She is never out of my sight. Won't you. . . ." I folded it shut.

"This is your child and you have the legal right to have her brought back to you."

She scratched behind her ear.

"Do you? Want her brought back here?"

She studied her fingernails; the thick lips mumbled, "Guess so."

"Guess? Clarice, if you have six of them at home already!" My voice came harsh—she's taking up so much time! Surely she saw all them waiting, and we're hurrying all we can! Her head went down and in the same arc forward words flung together with one great sob: "I know it be best for her."

She was quiet, leaning forward on her hands, tears coming from between her fingers and running down her arms.

And everything was quiet. The rush was gone, the telephone didn't ring, Margaret didn't come in, no sounds from the waiting room—the whole world lay quiet, drained away, and left nothing in the universe but silence, circling around this hollow dead center . . .

"I'm sorry. I've done it again." I waited. It may have been a long time or a short one, I don't know. I stuffed my handkerchief into her hand. When she stopped crying, I said, "I'll tell you what. It's so busy this morning. Could you leave this letter with me for a day or two? And I'll think about it and write to them. Is their address plain enough on the envelope? Will that be all right? As a first step?"

At the door she paused, stood, like there was still something she wanted to tell me. Her finger began to draw a line along the door frame and her eyes studied it, lips together, like pouting—

"It's all right, Clarice. I understand. It's all all right. Let me write first. I think it's going to be okay."

As I left through the drugstore, James, by way of "Good night," said, "Heavy day."

"Yes, and I don't like that. Too fast, too jumbled. I don't get to know the people. Well . . . it's difficult to explain, but I don't get to *see* them, really."

He stood looking at me like expecting me to say more. "Aw," I said. "Good night."

That night I was back in the office a while to type a few late insurance claims and I came to the worn envelope. I turned a letterhead into the typewriter—

". . . and if a regular monthly gift of about fifteen or twenty dollars to assist with the others . . . would help for her to bear this, also occasional snapshots." I typed fast. ". . . if you have not already done so, please see that she receives the usual vaccinations, especially diphtheria. And remember about avoiding crowds during the polio season."

I finished, put on my hat, and at the same instant as I snapped the light off the phone rang.

"You should come to Ignac Faltisek. You knowing Ignac? Is by him baby coming."

"Where? How do I get there?"

"Is by Breslau. You coming now? I tell him you coming." And the voice gave me directions.

⁂

No moon. I am driving like crazy and I'm asking Margaret, "Where in God's name is this Breslau anyway?"

"Far out towards Sweet Home. That's a bad sign."

"What's bad about it? Other than it's so far?"

"That's it. They're much closer to other doctors. It might mean those doctors wouldn't go to them."

"Oh, that can't be."

"You let everybody talk you into anything. Go anywhere. Take care of everybody. I'll bet this is another no-pay."

"The real bad thing is they said she's bleeding. Could be a placenta previa, or partial one. Or varicocele. Or a torn cervix. Man, I hope we're not going to have a dead mother after all."

She says nothing.

We looked for the mailbox: Ignac Faltisek. The gate stood propped open.

The room was bare, floorboards scrubbed splintery and almost white. By the lamplight—Margaret now keeps two flashlights and extra batteries in the OB bag—looking for the baby clothes and clean rags to go under the mother, Margaret came back saying, "Doctor, you must see this cute sight. In that room." Five children—sleeping in one bed, sleeping crosswise. But as I turned around, the flashlight found another bed. And full, too.

"How many?" I asked the father.

"Eleven."

"Man! This will be her twelfth. A dozen."

When he was out of the room, and with her back to the patient, Margaret mumbled in German close to me, "They are really like spoons—too thin. Spoons in an empty bowl. They aren't getting enough to eat."

"I can't worry about that now; her heart is leaking. A loud, gusty leak, each beat. Mitral. I've got to tell him—I'll get him off in the kitchen. Have the glucose ready for IV, and adrenalin and a syringe handy if we need it. Wish we had oxygen. I don't know how this is going to come out."

I doubted he was really understanding me. "I have to tell you, your wife's heart— Not so good. Bad. If it becomes a long, hard delivery, the heart may get too weak, not hold out. Also she is losing blood with each pain so far—this is from big veins there, from having so many children."

"Should I send kits for priest?"

"I don't want to be an alarmist— So far the heart is not failing. But if it begins to come down, yes. I'll watch it close. Is it far? To the priest?"

"Only is mile."

"Do the children drive?"

"Drive car?"

"Yes."

"No. Walks."

"Well, we'll wait a few pains first, okay?"

"We Catholic."

"Yes, I know! Eleven—twelve kids."

With each pain the blood gushed out of her. I must do something. I tried packing around the cervix, making like a doughnut, using the thickest gauze. In a hospital and with lights I could have found the ruptured veins and tied them off. The packing helped some but not much. "Give her one more ampule of Vitamin K—might help yet." I kept listening to her heart, which ran slightly faster. But so far the blood pressure stayed.

"Only good thing that's happening is the cervix is dilating fine—the pains are really doing some good. If it—baby—comes along pretty quick now, we'll scrape through yet. She's going to be weak . . . from loss of all this—"

But then it began to happen.

The pains continued, strong; the loss of blood, too much; and the head just stayed there. No progress. No further dilation. "With this many kids, why doesn't it come on out? Down? It's a good position. What's the heart rate now?"

"Average eighty-eight between pains. A hundred during."

"It's gradually getting faster. Weaker. The pressure is only a little lower, but that is on the way—lower. Gosh. To lose a mother." And I looked toward the bedroom where we had seen the beds. "Eleven."

Margaret asked quietly in German, "Are you going to send for the priest?"

"That would be the safest. Okay." I told the husband and went into the bedroom. A tall, blond, skinny boy left out into the night.

And the useless pains came regular. Margaret scooped huge clots of congealed blood into the slop jar and the husband took it out, brought the jar back clean, and I wondered what he did with the blood.

The priest, a very old man, and the boy came in. The priest asked nothing, said nothing. Set up his candles—his hands shook badly (Parkinson's disease?); Margaret lit the candles for him. He hung the ribbons over his neck and began intoning out of a small book—don't see how he could read anything in it. And more of the skinny kids, some in nightgowns, some in clothes, stood in the door.

The pains continued. Also the blood. The odor of blood and candles and kerosene lamp . . .

Then the priest finished. He fumbled and folded everything away and shook hands with the husband and with me (I could feel the tremor) and with Margaret (I thought she was going to curtsy) and left.

The skinny kids stayed in the door. Their long nightgowns swayed. They looked like elongated anemic angels, all blond.

Good God . . . maybe twelve . . . and without a mother.

And I wouldn't blame her—for checking out of all this. Dying by "natural causes" is such an acceptable exit.

I tried pressure with my fingers, kept pushing a new packing against the cervix veins during pains. Lady, please don't check out, please don't go. Blood smeared up to my elbow and inside the rubber glove. I muttered in German, "This is worse than at hog-butchering time. Never saw so much blood. Go ahead now, give her an ampule of Pit. Have to risk it. Can't let this bleeding go on all night." Lady, maybe you want to, but please don't die, not yet—the kids are too small. You can't leave eleven, please don't . . .

The first three pains were no different than before. No further dilation. And more blood. And then it went.

With the next one, the cervix began to flatten and slide back, stretching open. The vertex of the baby's head—the pointed back end—came wedging in. The bleeding stopped to almost nothing.

Or is it now bleeding inside—into the uterus? It shouldn't be.

And three good pains later, here it came, the head bulging down and on the next pain the baby came sliding out, shiny bloody wet, and cried before I could hold the slick fellow up and wipe his throat. And the uterus contracted hard with no more bleeding. And we tied the cord and cleaned her, and Margaret—who always stuffs more and more into the OB bag—now put two Kotex on her. And the bed all cleaned. And the kids still looking, but whenever the baby cried again the smaller ones hugged onto the others.

In leaving I told the father:

"In a hospital we could watch that the bleeding does not start again. So here—these little white tables? Ergot. Be sure the children don't get hold of them—poison if they eat them all at once like candy. Give your wife one tablet three times a day. Before meals. It is for three days. It is so she won't bleed, hemorrhage. She can die from such hemorrhage, especially with her heart.

"Now the next thing is:

"No more pregnancies. You should get yourself cut to make sure it doesn't happen. You can't tell the difference. If you'll come in, I'll do it.

"Or:

"In six weeks, I want to check her and the baby both. Come in. At that time I'll fit her with a diaphragm. And show her how to use it.

"And last:

"Margaret has already got all the information for the birth certificate." (She does that beforehand, between pains.) "All we need is a name. Send or phone that in as soon as you know. Or take it to the courthouse yourself.

"Oh yes: no working the fields. That heart must rest and recover. No chopping cotton or corn. She must stay in the house.

"And:

"No—more—pregnancies! None. Good night." We waved to the kids and left.

Driving home it began daybreak. I said, "She couldn't possibly *want* more children."

Margaret answered, "The priest—whatever his name was—won't let them."

"Won't let what."

"Them have a diaphragm."

"I sure hope they never call us again. That ran too close. She's going to die in a hemorrhage. And such a heart murmur . . ."

We stopped at Frank's Place for coffee and breakfast. They're on the highway and stay open all night.

And Rosine, as she brought the cups, asked, "What was it this time?"

"A boy."

"Whose was it?"

"A family way out near Sweet Home. At Breslau."

"That far?"

❊❊❊

You listen to symptoms. And listen. And finally you begin to hear something. The causes?

There are often cases of back sprain or strain. Women as frequently as men. Muscular Mrs. Slovanek, who smelled like Vick's Vap-O-Rub, tried to show me. "I got ketch all time here in back." She tried to reach high on her own back, but her stout arms couldn't make it. She spun me around and ran a strong thumb into my shoulder. "There. Right *there*."

"You can stop now. That's enough, Mrs. Slovanek. Ouch. I know what you mean. When did it happen?"

"Almost two veeks. I smear me first hog lard. And then liniments, from Vatkins man. He telling me Vatkins liniments good—same like Vatkins Corn Remover. But by me is staying. Then by drugstore I buy me such kind flaster. It makes by me nudding—ketch don't go avay. So I come see you. Is here in back. *There*."

"Ow! That's enough. What work were you doing when this came on?"

"Vat vork? Alvays vorking. All time."

"Is it work you like? Enjoy?"

"I should like it? Vork? You choking? I *got* to vork. How you not going vork—four kits, old mans, house, garden, vashing, shickens, milking, vood shopping and carry up steps in, vashing, ironing, baking. I should vot, you say? It comes *there*, in the—"

"Ow! That's enough now, please."

Am I sometimes hearing an underlying theme of "turned inward"? An undertow of something internalized, sucked in on itself? I try to think back.

"Come in, Mr. Woytek." Margaret handed me his card. Only twenty-nine?

"Hello, Mr. Woytek. Did you hurt your leg? It's not often one sees a young man on crutches. An accident?" He came slowly, his wife following.

"His knees. Art-tritis," she said over his shoulder. "It's what Dr. Kotzebue always say. Ve heard it you did Yacob Stryrenka good vit his."

"How long have you had it? Recent?"

"On crutches now I been for three years, valking vit sticks."

"Before already you vas, it vas coming on him. One year before," the wife said.

"For three years vit these sticks I been going. These *berla*."

"Longer you vas already. And can't vork."

Am I getting it again? A feeling? That theme of turning inward. He hasn't said anything to make me think it, has he? Is it from his attitude? The way he hangs his head? Something about his hands—the way he holds onto the crutches when he's not standing?

"My vife has to do it everything. Drive tractor too—I can't get from it up and down."

I believe he's chosen to turn it in. On himself. Sounds so, to me. But what is he saying? The symptoms talk—they tell. Should tell. But what?

If one could only read it.

The knees themselves did not seem to be too involved—not swollen or red, no obvious fluid buildup. The causative pathosis, primary infection, must be elsewhere. He's too young and not fat enough to suspect a gallbladder infection. "Appetite okay?"

"He eats good. Not like ven he used to vork. He likes everything I fix."

Or digestive tract? "What color are your bowel movements?"

"I never looked at his—"

"I'm asking him."

"Color? Natural color, I guess. Like alvays."

"Brown? Black? Light—cream color? It's important."

"Brown."

Normal. Gonorrheal arthritis attacks only one joint at a time; he complains equally of both. Besides, these people don't get gonorrhea. I haven't treated a single case yet among the Bohemians and Germans.

These are, equally, weight-bearing joints. Infection . . . from bladder? Prostate? "How often, through the night, must you pass your water?"

"I keep him such kind fruit jar by the bed. Always wake me. Oh, many times."

That's a point to check further. "Does anything else bother you? Pains, aches somewhere else? Toothache?"

"No . . ."

"No, he never say something is hurting—only knees."

"When is it worse? What time of day."

"When is first getting up. In the morning first he can't get from the bed down."

"After you move around? Gets some better?" That fits with an infection. From somewhere.

"Yes, then he can put himself the pants on and take the *berla* by himself and come in kitchen. But not going by the steps down and outside yet."

"Do you—" I glanced at the card—"Frank, do you think it eases up the more you move around?" That would also indicate infection. But still doesn't point to why.

"Yes, he goes better by night-milking time—he comes down to the barn. But vit the hands he can do nossing, has to hold by the *berla*."

"Do *you*, Frank, feel it that way?"

"Yes he does."

"Oh sure, yust like she say."

"And no other place hurts you? Not headaches, not teeth, not stomach?" (Didn't realize I keep asking nothing but leading questions.)

"No."

"But on your back. You do sometime say it. In you back, yes. I rub it him vit Vatkins the liniment. Is good?"

"Where in your back?"

"Show it— Turn yourself so; I show him."

"Let him show me. Nothing wrong with his arms, is there?" (That part came out sarcastic. I should have cut my throat. Judging this poor country woman!)

He scratched his thumb across an area, more over the kidneys.

I began the examination. On a strong twenty-nine-year-old farmer with big shoulders, there isn't much to find wrong. But the infection had to be coming from somewhere, not primarily in the knee joints. His tonsils looked okay; so did his teeth and gums. No tenderness over the gall bladder. Even his prostate wasn't enlarged or tender—was firm as it should be.

"Let's also get a drop of blood—only a little stick now." I sucked the thin column of blood up into the red and the white pipettes. "Frank, at this time, all I can tell you is the knees can be cured *after* we find where it's coming from. This, in the knees, is secondary. Come back tomorrow or the day after. Bring a urine specimen. We'll know, too, what the blood says."

"No medicine?" his wife asked.

"No medicine?" he asked.

"Not yet. Later. After we know what we're treating. This is not the real bad arthritis. This one can be treated. Maybe cured."

Margaret handed him one of her new urine bottles. She had written his name and tomorrow's date on the cap. "First in the morning, Mr. Woytek. First when you get up."

"No medicine today?" the wife asked again. "Ve go so much to doktor and always pay and pay and nothing help and no vork and ve owe money for tractor and for Yersey cows. If Frank can't finish plowing and planting we have no crop." She looked near crying. "Maybe ve lose it yet the tractor, and he can't vork, and all time pay doktor. And medicine. And no medicine? Now? How he should vork vit no medicine?"

"Look, he hasn't been working. Let me first find out where his trouble really is. Sometimes the sickness is sneaky—he hides. And we have to find him first. If I can."

They left slowly, looked back at me several times. With the door open I heard them in the drugstore talking with Papinku, her voice saying, "He give no medicine, the doktor."

"I'm not going to fool them with red or blue or green aspirin," I told Margaret. "Who's next?"

As she went to the door she said nothing, but her attitude exuded the expression "It wouldn't have hurt any."

Mrs. Kobza—one of the many families of Kobza—ready, about to sneeze, and trying to tell me about her "undarable day fever" and about the sneezing. And "always in sprig dime" and of ordering two "filters," which she was to keep stuck up in her nostrils—filters, like two small milk strainers.

"It's like you're crying. Your symptoms: running nose, dripping eyes. Do you have something you wish to cry about? A worry?"

Now she did it—sneezed. Sneezed them right out at me. They stuck to my chest, one on each side, like nipples. She didn't even apologize while I was trying to get the gooey things off of me. "Uf my teef come yump out—don't fit so tight . . ." She was getting ready for the next sneeze. *Here it comes . . .*

Auntie Callie set her walking stick against the wall, then looked at the new white table with its stirrups and attached light and swing-arm tray. "Sho' feel skaryfied from such a thing. Do I hafta climb up there?"

"It's only one step—let me hold you. There. See? It's easy."

"Skaryfied from all these things lookin' at me.

"It's this here kneebone joint. Swole up on me. I wrapped it up tight. Used a little turpentine—just a few drops and stirred it good in some lard I had there. Hep it some, but not enough."

"Did you fall? Or walk a far ways?"

"I does it all myself—hafta. I carry water. I'm alone out there. Nine chillun, but they all grown and gone."

"But you didn't fall."

"No. Not as I recollect. Don't know what I done to it to make it do me like that. Seems if I ain't got one thing, it's another. Seems like a person make theirself have somethin' ailin' alla time. Now it's in this here kneebone."

The last thing, as she was leaving: "Sho' countin' you come out on Watch Night—be with us. Want you to promise you'll try to come. I know you busy and all such, but you try."

"I solemnly promise."

"To try to come. That you *try* to come. Dass all anybody can do."

"To try to come. You know I want to and that I'll almost surely be there."

"Hope so. Be together. Watch Night."

After everyone got cleared out—already dark—and with Margaret gone, I did the counts and differential on Frank Woytek's blood. There is a higher number of polys than normal, but that doesn't say anything definite, and the RBC and WBC are within high-normal range. Hmm, so that's no real help. Wonder where the infection *is* coming from?

❋❋❋

"Good morning. Good morning."

While I'm in the waiting room shaking hands all around, one of the new faces I'm looking down into is black, with lots of rouge—far too much—across the wrinkled cheeks and a hairdo that stood frizzled way too high. A filmsy, thin dress that started too far down, and a fur coat lumped beside her, all of which said she didn't come here straightaway from choir practice. She wore a heavy brooch, which pulled the dress down farther—the big blue stone was cracked and a part chipped out. Her sister—she introduced herself with "I'm her sister," the tone of which, in a way, struck me as saying, "She needs someone to come with her to see after her"—was dressed neat-plain, with a white scarf around her neck tucked evenly into a straight, gray coat, no fur.

The one with too much paint said, smiling up, "All I want is for you to take some of these bullets out of me." And I thought, that's all I need on a crammed morning like this—a real ripe customer; and I answered as smoothly as if I didn't think she was plum looney, "Certainly. Be happy to. Did this happen recently?" And the sister spoke in, "No sir, two-three months ago. She was in the hospital in LaGrange first."

Oh. So maybe she isn't entirely crazy, or maybe they told the sister they didn't find anything, that the bullets were imaginary, and she'd have to take her elsewhere—maybe to the state hospital. Well, it's days like this that will wear me out. But I said nicely, "See you soon as I can," and I went back and told Margaret that we had another "one of those" out front.

And she said, "Such a day it will be: her and that Mrs. Greely, too, even if she is in our Bridge Club. It is enough you should keep some *schnapps* back here for times like this"—which is strange indeed coming from Margaret, because she doesn't drink, not even beer. Oh well, bring the first one in.

And—when we finally got to her—sure enough she wasn't insane. She did have bullets in her. Birdshot. You could feel them under her skin, pebbly.

"But it's these here in my right tittie that's bother me *so* much—"

The sister spoke in between, "Shh, don't talk like that to the doctor—say *breast*."

The patient said, "Aw, he know what a tittie is."

"Come, let's go to the X-ray room for the fluoroscope." (When we are alone, Margaret and I call it our "new Hex-ray machina.") Because I couldn't feel any in her right breast where she said they were bothering her the most. With the room entirely dark and her standing behind the fluoroscope screen—my Lord! You never saw so many sharp clear dots. Hundreds. Like some odd unknown iron measles.

"Shot," she said in the green darkness. "All in this arm and up both legs and into my pussy it—"

"Shhh, don't talk like that in front of the doctor."

"Aw, I reckon he know what a pussy is—"

"Shhh!"

"How did you get shot? I mean—never saw so many."

"I was shot twice. Blam and I fell down, and blam again."

"How? How come? Who?"

"My son shot me."

My foot jerked up off the button, maybe by reflex, and the room blinked off, totally dark. "Your *son*?"

"Sho' was him. My own son. He shot me," she said in the dark.

I stepped again and the skeleton and hard dots shining in the green glow of the screen were back. "Why?"

"Oh, he were drunk. Drinkin' did it. And it were about money. Got it in his head and the drinkin' did it."

"Can't understand that."

"It were the drinkin'."

I said, "There's only a few—a few birdshot in your breast. Stand more sideways. Yes, only two, three in all. Not many."

"Yeah? But 'at's the ones bother me the most. Can you take 'em out?"

"Your son? Where is he now? Might he start drink—"

"He's in the pen. They put him there. He gonna be alongst there pretty good while yet. It were the drinkin' done it."

"Want me to take those out? The breast? These in the arm—this big bunch—I could get more at one time."

"No, they's ain't worry to me. Just get these. Sho' worrysome. Is it festered? Do the X ray tell if it festered?"

"Why did he shoot you? I can't understand."

I saw the skeleton hand come up to the breast. Its movement was strange—is it a pulling movement? "Mus' be festered. Sho' hurts."

"Can't tell this way, but don't think they are. Why did he shoot—?"

"It were about money. He claim it his, 'cause he brought 'em there, but it were mine. They paid *me*. But it was the drink got in him and made him do it. Thass all." The bones of the arm and chest and hands, speckled black, glowed and moved in the dark. Macabre.

"This is sure a lot of shot."

"Oh, 'course it is. Sho'. Shot me twicet. Woulda been lots more hadn't been for that heavy coat and the weeds. I fell down in the weeds. First one was all this arm and it tore the sleeve plum off that coat and I fell down in the weeds. And musta been curled up over this arm—that why the next shot is all up my legs and into—"

"Shhh!"

"That's why. Hope you can get these ones outa my tittie. Hurts—"

"Shhh!"

"Certainly. We'll do anything we can." And we did. Took them out. In the examining room, under the big light, a little local, and with a little cutting. And out peeled the shiny beads, perfectly round, one after another.

"Now looka dar."

"Ummm, see that."

"Look like new."

"Will you looka that."

"Ummmhuh."

"I don't see how so few bothered you so much, when all these others—so many . . . Don't you want me to get some of them out of your arm, too?"

"No, they ain't no worry. Was these 'uns festered up?"

"No, no, just like the others. It'll be all right." I put on a small bandage. "But I'd like to ask you something. One thing, if you don't mind: How do you feel toward your son now? I can't understand . . ."

"Oh, he what he is. He be there a long whilst yet."

But the sister, standing behind, nodded—kept nodding, big. "I know what you mean, doctor, you right. You sho' right. It's like amongst cattle—you know how they do. You been amongst cattle?" She kept nodding. "The cow still 'low for the calf." She kept nodding and looking at the back of her sister's head. "Still 'lowin'. Callin'."

"I think it feel a little better already. That you got these outta my tittie." She dressed, pulling things over her shoulders, with no sign of embarrassment.

As Margaret opened the door for the next one, I saw Pete. "Is it Saturday? Already?" Pete, squeezed in between several on the sofa, leaned against them, snoring drunk and drooling and still holding a white-star blossom—the wild onion flower. It was about to slip from his fingers.

You can tell right off if he's been working all week: He'll be drunk. If he's sober, it makes you worry a little: Has his family been fed?

But he asks for a dollar either way.

"Why does he always do that?" Margaret spoke German and closed the door. When it's about anything confidential, she automatically switches into German. Between us. I do that too. "Drunk Mexican." In German it sounds worse.

"He wants something. From me."

"A dollar? Even when he makes good all week?"

"No. The dollar must represent something else."

"*Aber* it adds up. Never pays you back."

"Does it symbolize? . . . Something he wants from me? Approval maybe? They get rejected so. Always looked down on."

"He won't pay you back. And someday he's going to get himself killed; then you can't collect anything. *Schrecklich.* Always fighting themselves."

"Yes, it seems to me some people push *out*. Spew their symptoms—their hostility—out. Fight. Murder, too. Others seem to turn it inward somehow. Get sick. Kill inward. Seems to me like each person follows, chooses, either one or the other pattern. Have you noticed any such . . . anything like that?"

"Huh. In-out, up-down, he's *in here* too much. You can't trust them."

"I wonder . . . how much asking there really is, behind hate."

She started to open the door, turned back. "*Schloppie* things. I say, asking to get killed."

"Here," I gave her a dollar. "Next time you're out there, just slip it to him. So he won't have to wait so long."

And there came the worst case of athlete's foot ever: blebs, water blisters big as dimes—even on the instep and ankles! Both feet. And between all the toes everything is totally raw.

"Use this salve three times a day. Wear only white socks. Bathe the feet once a day with this blue germicidal soap—keeps out secondary infections. By the third day the healing will begin. I understand why you couldn't walk."

Margaret came back, handed me a dollar bill.

"Somebody paid?"

"Pete. Wouldn't take it. Said he wanted to see you."

"Maybe it's his gonorrhea again."

She began rolling up her sleeves. "I asked if he was sick; he said no, wants to see you. Frank Woytek's urine is ready under the microscope. Sugar and albumin, negative."

I looked—there it all lay, solid pus. Like a scene from a saucer factory. The hundreds of small circles touching and overlapping. "That's fine, Gretchen. He's had this a long time. It's in the urinary tract, could even be kidney-pelvis involved. And it's the poison makes the weight-bearing joints hurt. Good. We'll start him on sulfa today. That'll clear this out. Then if it comes back—"

"They're probably out of money by now," she interrupted. "Been going for three or four years. Ready?"

She opened the door. "Come in, Mr. Woytek. You're next."

I explained about the kidney infection, and the poison settling in joints. Had them look through the microscope. "See all the little round dots? That's pus cells—shouldn't be any at all." I explained also that I still didn't know why he had the infection, but that these tablets would clear it out. "Now if it comes back then we have to take X rays to see—"

"He had it hex rays. Both knees. By Dr. Kotzebue."

"No, I mean X-ray the kidneys. Called *pyelogram*. To see if there's stones there or constrictions or kinks—any obstruction." (But there is no X ray that can show why he chose the kidneys.)

"He got it rocks? In kidneys?"

"I don't know yet."

She looked at the prescription.

"That's the medicine. Take it regularly. Let me know in five days. Bring another urine at that time. Drink lots of water."

She held up the single prescription by a corner. "Is medicine for kidneys?"

"Yes. Two tablets four times a day. Before meals and at bedtime."

"Is for kidneys only?"

"Yes."

"What should he take for the knees?"

When it came Pete's turn, all he wanted was to borrow a dollar. "Pay you next Sabbaday."

"Sure. Something else, too, Pete?"

"No."

"Nothing else? You don't need . . . medicine?"

"No."

"You want to sit awhile? Cigarette?"

He stood, smoking. I handed him the dollar.

"I think I go, Mr. Shoes. Dr. Shoes."

"Take one three times a day, before meals. Do this regular. Don't miss. And don't be worried if for the first two days you notice no change. Because on the third day and after that, you should find that the soreness leaves. Usually not until the third day."

I hear myself saying that to people very often.

As we left the office Margaret latched the side door, as she always does. "Did you know? Today old Mr. Holubec—after you injected his knee again—forgot his crutches. Forgot them. Sat here and talked and talked and got up and left. Had to come back for them. Didn't you hear everybody laughing? That's what it was."

We laughed about it again together, and then took our leave of each other.

I hopped into my car for another trip—a house call—to the Schneiders. (The house calls that are not emergencies—the ones that can wait—are made after work.) When I'd arrived I sat down on the straight-backed chair that had been placed beside the bed, opened my bag, and to relieve the heavy silence winked at Arnold and started teasing the sister. "I saw a great admirer of yours. Sometime back."

"Admirer? Me?"

"Yes. John Smaistrla—next door."

A wet towel slapped the naked floor. "So! That's it! That's why you don't hold the clothes pins in your mouth anymore. Now I see!"

"Sister."

"While I'm laying here sick—maybe losing my eyes—you goggle yours at the neighbors. You could stay and help me get well."

"Sister. I have hardly been out of the house since—"

"Have you no shame!"

"Mrs. Schneider, wait. Please. Did I—?"

"I know now! Behind my back! And me laying here, suffering! While you—!"

"No, Mrs. Schneider. Wait! Have I said something? . . . But is there anything wrong with that?"

For an instant the red eyes with their pimply edges glowed at me ready to explode. Then suddenly they calmed. "No. There is nothing wrong with him. After all, he *is* a widower."

I gave the injection, examined the eyes, tried to sound encouraging, said goodnight, and tried to leave. The sister accompanied me to the door, as if to let me out, but followed onto the porch and closed the door. "Doctor, I wanted to tell you we had an aunt who lost her mind during the change. Could it—"

We both heard it—a floorboard creaked behind the door.

"I must go," she said and entered the house quickly.

⁂

Over the phone—the line buzzes and I can't hear even though I know they're yelling loud—they say old Mr. Stryrenka has been shot, come quick. I can't imagine a Czech or German farmer being careless with guns.

Must be in the foot. It would be either a .22 rifle wound or a shotgun. Maybe he was chasing crows off the young corn.

So I'm driving fast over the country roads through the Freyburg area. The corn is waist high, a dark, hearty green, growing—shouldn't be a problem with crows now anymore. A cloud of birds, thousands, arise from a pasture. A dark cloud of them—are they cowbirds? They look more black. In the air the cloud changes direction—all of them, at the same instant—and flashes the clear sky through, as if for an instant they are invisible. Then they become the dark cloud again, flying away; flashing clear, dark again, a breathless moment of motion.

The ground is all cultivated, showing its black-black richness. Wild flowers are scattered along the roadside, mostly pink-red paintbrush, but lots of white dots, too, which will be the wild Dewberry. All the trees are green except the pecan and the mesquite, which is putting out its yellow buds only now. (They hold back until last—often until after Easter—after dangers of a quick last freeze are past.) And the curving rows of tiny cotton plants—two tiny flat leaves each, on a stem, like "Hel-lo" freshly popped up out of the soil.

Winding road, small pastures, fields. Wild plum thickets make clouds of white blossoms along the fence lines, mingling carelessly with the steel thorns of the straight-taut barbed wire. Down hills and rumble over the wood culverts. To my left in a pasture, not far from the fence, stands an old iron bed—the black burned skeleton of an old iron bed and its curly springs—with wild thistles growing up through and blooming blue on long stems, nodding. And a beginning of pink near the houses—rows of pink blossoms along the bare branches.

It's a far way out here, to Stryrenka's; I haven't even come to Freyburg Hall yet, nor the church there.

This rolling black land is checkered by small farms, each tended like a garden. The farmers walk the hills slowly, behind their team and planter. These are the Germans and Bohemians—I read the names along the mailboxes: Schumann, Meyer, Hobizal, Umlang, Ahrens, Jochen, Baumbach, Roitsch, Bohot, Dieringer . . . These are the "prairie people."

It tells you a lot about them right there—when someone says "prairie people." It means their house is in perfect shape, painted; the roof doesn't leak; usually there's a picket fence along the front of the house and it is *white,* with not a picket missing. The barn will be large, always painted red, and stocked high with summer hay and corn tops. The house is always white with a black roof and some flowers along the front—or between the house and the garden. It means the owner has water piped into the house and also out into the garden, chicken yard and cow pen—his wife and children do not have to *schlepp-schlepp* every day with the water buckets. And always the straight line of cedars, always on the north side.

Everything is paid for, except maybe the land. The farmer owes on that but is always right on time with payments—always comes a few days ahead. His implements are clean, oiled, sometimes painted yellow or red, and brought under roof. His wife has a good garden growing early (with rows and rows of lavender-blooming poppies if the family is Bohemian) and still has many shelves of jars of this and that left from last year's canning, and hangs the clothes on a good, strong clothesline that no prairie winds will ever push down. And she has chickens—chickens and garden are part of "woman's work." And her children are clean and well behaved, never too forward yet intelligent in school. And there's no use driving up to a house on Sunday morning to ask directions, because the windmill is cut off, and the dogs will come bounding out barking with nobody to call them back—everybody is in church.

There are hogs in the pen, a calf in the cow lot means a freshened cow with plenty of milk, butter, clabber, and homemade cheese. Wood is stacked ready beside the black wash kettle built into brick, and there is an aluminum-painted butane tank for heating, but still a flue on the roof, too, because there is no heat more satisfying than a wood stove—one that draws properly. A well-fed team of horses or mules grazes in the pasture among a few chunky beef cattle and one or more milk cows. Diversity is the security of the farm: some of everything—hogs, chickens, beef, milk, fruit, vegetables, corn to use, cotton to sell. Then no year can be wasted, no year can be a total loss.

How far is it to Stryrenka's?

You often see the entire family in the field: the man sitting on the cultivator, watching down between his knees and working the pedal guides with his feet, watching as the small green plants pass beneath him, maneuvering the sweep blades. Each horse wears a wire muzzle.

The farmer's wife, often pregnant big, with close bonnet and long sleeves, which are sometimes made of old black stockings and pinned at the shoulder. She stands with a hoe or walks the rows chopping here and there an occasional weed or start of grass that has escaped the first chopping.

And often here are young children, half as tall as their hoe handles, along with her.

And the birds that follow them.

Prairie people.

There are still some of the old walking cultivators. On these the man walks with the reins in a loop across his back. He walks long broad steps, straddling, looking down always.

When you honk and wave, those with hoes run and wave, but those on the cultivators or walking do not look up. Or they stop the team first. Only here and there you see a farmer on one of those yellow and red machines with big black tires. He is always a young man. But if you honk, he can't hear you, and the birds stay far away from him.

I haven't missed Stryrenka's, have I?

Sometimes instead of prairie people they are called "black landers." Or the "four-wire people," because of their fences—always a good tight four wires. Never three. That's not enough to discourage a determined cow. And five is unnecessary, wasteful. And six is absolutely a squanderer show-off and never ever used by prairie people. But a rich Houstonian might put up six—doesn't know better, and with him it's a deduction. He is not a farmer, he's a money man.

Prairie pastures are never overstocked so that grass would become grazed too short, and the cattle are never skinny, hungry-looking. That would be the ultimate crime against all that is natural and right.

A pond lies smooth, surrounded by the lanky patterns of tall willows. Three ducks keep bobbing down, turning their tail ends up, showing white. The car noise makes them swim along, cutting wedge-shaped designs on the water, and then they run on the surface and fly up, swerving off. Next to the road, I look down on a thistle plant patterned like a giant snowflake with an ivory blossom center. A black butterfly with gold tracings spreads its wings flat and raises them like some ceremony to the sun, raising them together like hands touching in prayer. Beyond the flower lie white bones of a cow or horse, scattered, disjointed, with the red Indian paintbrushes blooming among them.

As I come up over a hill near Herman Ohnheiser's farm, I see before me here and there white hilltop patches of the blooming wild onions that pop up after a good rain. They grow only on the hilltops. The flower is a small white star on a stem. Three white petals, wide, pointed. And when I come over the next hill the scene in the morning sun becomes a sheer joy. Solid white hilltops. Millions of the little white stars one against the other, poking and nudging like naughty children.

My, you're beautiful, I say to my right.

Like new snow, to my left.

They wiggle, nodding. They sway and twist like twittering. Wild onions. Called *Schlatten* in German. They make it feel like driving through a cloud. There is an old Lutheran church, Schlattenberg Church, standing alone weather worn and empty, with tall green blinds that have been folded closed for years and are pocked with birds' nests. The rows of old hackberry trees with dead limbs are where people used to tie their buggies and wagons in the shade. And the entire hilltop is covered with white. With tiny, three-pointed stars.

After a rain they make these hilltops clean with pure white. But only on the hills. They grow only on the washed-off poorer land. They live only on the weakened sandstone soil, keep it from washing and wearing away. They serve it—save it.

You are so beautiful.

No one likes us.

Oh that can't be true. There is such an element of purity in you.

No one eats us. Not cattle or hogs. People dig us up and try to throw us away. They say we are not productive, nothing eats us. They say we are worthless.

You are stars, trillions, as in the galaxies. You are like some gift from the saints. Always lovely. Thank you for being. Come again.

We will come again. After every spring rain. We have always come.

There's Freyburg Hall at last. It's a community affair for dances, meetings, feasts, and can be rented for family reunions. It used to be a lodge and Mutual Insurance. The church comes next. On the hill. There. Now only down to the bridge, a small bridge with two boys in faded blue overalls fishing with cane poles. Second gate, left. There. Why, it's propped open. That means something serious. Hope it wasn't shotgun—it could mean amputating part of his foot. Open gate like that means they sent a member of the family—probably one of the children—to open it and to chase the cows out of the small pasture in front of the house into another or into the lot.

Hope he's not bleeding much.

As I drive up under the naked hackberry trees, a barefoot woman runs out of the house letting the screen door slam, flapping her apron, waving her arms and pointing. "Down in the field—he's in the field. Follow the fence. Go along the fence—you'll see."

That's odd. Why haven't they moved him to the house? Never heard of this. I drive along in the pasture beside a field of corn—nice corn, dark green, almost knee-high. Over there several cars are bunched beside the fence.

I climb through the wire, and under a large tree where the corn won't grow, a group stands around looking down. They have brought a mattress and put him on it. One shoe is off, but nothing is bloody. Only a dirty foot, no sock, with a long green corn leaf tied around the big toe. On his forehead a small dirty spot—a tiny hole. The .22 rifle lies under the tree.

One of the men is a deputy sheriff from LaGrange, and there is another man with him. "He's still breathing, doc. We couldn't call the coroner."

And the old man's son—broad, barefoot—who keeps saying without anyone asking him—saying over and over, his eyes looking blank—"Ve hear nodding and come to bring him vater, and he is sitting by tree and gun vere is now and one shoe off and with toe he pull trigger by corn leaf. Vy he do it? Ve bring him fresh vater, and he is sitting by tree and ve don't know it nodding that he shoot himself in head. Vy? He don't tell us nodding like this. Ve shopping cotton odder side corn. Is too hot for old mans sitting—is not in vind—so he say he going in shade under tree, and my vife and me ve bringing him fresh vater and ve don't hear nodding—no shot. Sitting by tree, ve don't know . . ."

The blood pressure does not register at all. The heart weak, faint to hear, fast and irregular. The hole so tiny. And the burn only a smudge on the forehead, like when they come from church on Ash Wednesday. "Go call the coroner," I said. "By the time he gets here . . ."

We stand around and look down, and the son keeps saying it. "Vy? Vy he do this?" And when the priest comes we hold the wires apart, but he gets hooked anyway. He lights the candles and sets them down in the earth and puts the ribbon around his neck and intones, and we stand bareheaded, and the son drops his broad knees into the loose black dirt and folds his hands and his eyes still look blank.

If the pathopathy could have become visualized, I think he would have been sitting against the tree smiling up at me, saying, *This one for me. But cheer up—you might save the next one. Would we care to keep score?*

Behind us the field of young corn waves its long green leaves.

***

One Sunday morning I'm running through the drugstore into my office, James is dusting, the church bells of the big Catholic church on the hill are clanging. "Beautiful sounds aren't they, James? Deep sounds."

"The church bells? Kotzebue donated them. Very expensive."

I stopped. "Wish I didn't know. Now they won't sound nearly so beautiful. Was it purely for business reasons that he donated them?"

The feather duster—turkey feathers—stopped. "Maybe." He continued with the duster. "Maybe not."

Sunday afternoon. They come all dressed up: coats, ties, dark suits, dresses, hats. Smell of moth balls, shoe polish, and garlic.

I wrote prescriptions for Frank Pechacek—wanted to increase his aminophylline and to add elixir phenobarbital. (Nothing seems to really help his high blood pressure. In the textbooks this kind is called "essential hypertension." Wonder how they got the word *essential*?) But now it is noon and the drugstore is still closed, and they are waiting. Some come after early Mass and others hope to be examined quickly so they can get to late Mass.

But now it is noon—afternoon in fact. So I am phoning James at home.

"Number plee-yuz."

"Six-two, please, Mrs. Harmann."

"Doctor, are you calling James?"

"Yes."

"He always bathes his dog on Sunday afternoon, now that it's warm enough; I don't think he can hear the phone. If you wait a second I'll look out the window." She was back in a moment. "He's still in the garage, stooping over the tub. Can you call back later? Fifteen minutes?"

"How do you know all these things about people?"

"You'd be surprised."

"I'll be careful."

She laughed. "Number plee-yuz."

Later in the same afternoon, a call to come to Frank Kubena. "The vife is sick for ten day already"—fever, coughing.

As I thumped out the dull area in her chest, entire lower-left lobe—the skin felt hot under my hand and her cheeks had the "red apple flush" described in textbooks as often seen with lobar pneumonia—they brought several bottles of medicines and boxes of tablets and explained that Dr. Kotzebue had been giving her these for it.

"Then why did you call me?"

"Because he don't come back for four day—his mother is sick. She old vomans, nearly ninety year, and he gone. Alvays stay with the mother ven she is sick. He say he getting her to one hundred yet. Ve vaitink, every day. And my vife too bad sick—she cough it now up vit blood. Call you."

It was not only lobar, it was a solid one. "I have to tell you, she is seriously ill." I wrote a prescription for sulfapyridine (it concentrates in the lungs just as sulfasuxidine concentrates in the intestines). "You must give these tablets very regularly, every six hours. Wake her up to take them. And we have to also get this high fever down. This one is for fever, only." (It is nothing but powdered aspirin in a red elixir so anybody can swallow it, even children, and it works beautifully; James knows to add "Shake Well" because it settles out.) "It will control the fever right well, but this pneumonia! She's had this too long.

"You keep record now every day how much the fever is—write it down. On the third day the fever should really come down. Should. But with so much in there! I'll come tomorrow, but anytime you think she's worse, call me. And if she gets worse, call the priest too."

On the first day there came no change, neither better nor worse. I tried to talk them into taking her on to the hospital, but Mr. Kubena refused. "People vat is going horspittle is die there."

"That's not true, Mr. Kubena! More get well—many more—than die."

"Is only vat you sayink. In horspittle—die."

I tried more but got nowhere in attempting to convince him. Finally gave up.

At the end of the second day, I felt maybe she might be some better, because her temperature stayed a degree less all day, she coughed less and no more fresh red blood in it. And she took more soup and juices. But the whole lobe still echoed back the thump of solid tissue, and no breath sounds came through.

On the third day, before I could get there, he came in to pay the bill (which meant I was discharged). He had nothing but smiles.

"Why?" I asked.

"She doink much better and eatink somethink vat is real food. And Dr. Kotzebue come and put her back on her old medicines. She much better already and beginink happy."

"Now look, Mr. Kubena, your wife is not well yet. It's those little tablets—the white tablets? Two, four times a day? Every six hours? Wake her if you have to?—it's those. They are what's helped this. They and her change of attitude. Sulfapyridine. Keep on with them; tell her they will cure her. This isn't finished. The disease—the pathosis—isn't conquered yet." And the pathopathy hasn't even been sighted. "We've won a battle, not the war. Before meals and at bedtime. Keep taking them only three more days. Tell her. Please. Then she will be well."

He kept smiling all the while.

"Ha, no. Is no more. Oh vife: She saying nize thinks from you, vant you should come some more. But Dr. Kotzebue always my doktor many years. He don't like it your medicines from Hajovsky. Say, 'Throw it by the door out, out in yard.' Say, 'It is poison. Out. Don't let the chickens eat. Dig it in the field down.' Ha. How much is it?"

"Why chance it? Mr. Kubena, you know she was getting well on those tablets. Papinku would sell you more, enough for three days only. Please. She had it bad—very bad case of it. Mr. Kubena, she was on her way to dying. Why take a chance? Only before meals and at bedtime."

He kept smiling. "How much?"
I sighed. "Only the three house visits."
And in the drugstore he told it all again. Everybody heard him.

A week later, Papinku came in holding one of those black-rimmed notices that Gus Strauss prints and takes around. It always gives the age in years, months, and days. He handed it to me. "Frank Kubena's wife. She was getting well on your medicine. 'Throw it out. Bury it so don't let the chickens eat it.' "

He did not rub his head. He turned and walked out.

Looking at the closet door, I thought of the skull there. And its big grin, like it might be saying, *In their Card of Thanks,* x *one off for me.*

***

Even though it was Saturday afternoon, busy as all hell—and hot—they said I had to come. Said he was dead. Shot dead.

The body lay inside the door, an arm reaching out. Henry's Cafe: Bar-B-Q and Beer. Lay inside on the slippery floor, face down, with an arm reaching through the door, like trying to get out. Great big fellow. "Who is he?" I asked, pushing through the crowd.

"Otis Moore."

"Oh no! Not Otis!" The jukebox suddenly started playing by itself. Somebody gave it a flat slap and it stopped.

Ralph Voght, the deputy, said close to me, "Too bad they only killed one. They oughta kill a few these niggers every Sattiday. Wouldn't have so much trouble outa 'em."

"Oh, hello, Ralph. Say he got shot?"

"Six times. All in the back."

I acted through the motions of pronouncing him dead—all I could do. Couldn't think too clearly. It's as if I wanted to talk to him, like, Otis, get up off this dirty floor now, you hear? Get up! Or, What you mean getting shot? Right after you were all healed up! "Ralph? What was it . . . about?"

"Nothing. They do it for nothing! This one had a few these nickelodeon jukeboxes—here, Moulton, LaGrange, around. He wired 'em so they couldn't rob the boxes anymore without getting shocked. That's why they can't unplug that thing." It started again, loud, blaring, "Beer Bar-rel Po-ka!—" Slap!

Now I heard. A block down the street. From inside a house. "Oh Lord, they kilt my baby. My only baby. My boy. Oh Lord. They kilt him. Shot-im-in-the-back.

"Oh Lord. They kilt my baby dead. They kilt him. He gone—Oh Jesus Lord."

Through all the people I noticed a boy coming running fast. He peeked in between the people, came close up, and looked down on the big dead body. I thought he would burst into "It's my daddy!" or something like that. But he only looked.

"Oh Lord. No, Lord, I don't want this day. Take it off. I don't want it. Take this day away—don't make me keep it forever. Dead. Shot-im-in-the-back.

"My baby—done dead. No, Lord. My only baby. They kilt my baby. Shot 'im dead. Oh Lord—no!"

Ralph said, "Always takes the Cor'ner so long to get here—gotta come down from LaGrange."

"But this Otis was such a nice guy—a good fellow, I thought."

"Ain't none of 'em good, doc. Jest a lot of troublemakers."

"Roll out the bar-rel—" Slap!

"Kilt my baby over some silver nickels—oh Lord. They kilt my baby. My only baby. My boy. Shot-im-in-the-back. Shot dead. Oh my Jesus, no, no, take it away."

❋❋❋

On Sunday morning, I couldn't believe it myself—the change in young Frank Woytek. (Don't know why I thought of him as young. He's quite some years older than I am.) Came stomping in to shake hands, not waiting for his wife to come first. Pumped my arm up and down. Wearing coat, tie, hat—looked fine. "You fix it me gut. Look, no more the *berla*."

"You were supposed to come weeks ago. And bring a urine specimen. Remember?"

"I bring it *moc* now today," he pointed at his wife, who handed me the bottle, wrapped in a white cloth. "I vorking all day. No time for coming. Plowing and planting is now. Is late. Neighbor is going already vit cultiwaiter in corn so high—I am still vit planter. I plant me corn and hygeria and cotton. At Feed Store they ask it me, 'Where is it you *berla*?' and I say doktor make *berla* go avay vit vind. Is no needing sticks. And I yump up and down and show them knees and legs is strong. They are not believing the eyes. They say 'For three year already you are going and we thinking you vill be valking by *berla* always.' And I say 'I thinking same thing.' "

"But is doing too much," the wife added. "Always on tractor. At night, too, with the lights shining. I go to bed and I hear it going up and down and around and up and down—going."

He laughed.

"Come talk with me while I run the tests on this."

"Maybe he will make it come back by too much tractor?"

"That is one reason why we want to check the *moc* regularly. To watch if it starts again. This is not finished. We must check it regularly. You understand? Once every two weeks. I hope you understand." He kept grinning so big I knew he wasn't hearing me. "Otherwise he can do anything. How often now do you urinate during the night?"

"Go out? Nighttime? Vunce. Vun time only. Maybe two o'clock. But no more vit the fruit jar. I yump from the bed down and go outside."

"On rose bush. I tall him to go more outside."

"Outside is dirt on feets and shicken shit shmear between the toes. I go from the steps out."

"That all fits. But remember, this is not finished." I leaned, looking into the microscope. "No pus, no little round dots. Take a look. Get your eye close. Now. See? No dots like before."

"Is finish."

"No is not finished! We *must* keep checking. Once every two weeks. Understand?"

"But he should stay more from the tractor down, no? Makes it come back?"

"You all time tall me stay from tractor down! Doktor, don't tall me such kind thinks. I plow. I plant. Until is finish. Is late by me, but I still make crop. Then I cultiwaite on the tractor up, until is finish."

I smiled at him. "Remember. Two weeks."

❋❋❋

Was it Tuesday or Wednesday that he brought the boy? I can't remember days. The weeks go so fast. I think it was Wednesday—

Wednesday, about noon. But it doesn't matter at all what day. It only matters why.

Felix Kobza carried his nine-year-old Tony and dropped him on a chair in the waiting room. "Shop hisself the foot open," he pointed to the white cloth around the boy's foot. "Dumb kits."

"Is it hurting much?" I asked Tony. As the boy shook his head, tears flew both ways. "I'm sure it'll be all right. Don't be afraid."

"Costs me money. Costs more than the cotton makes it. Dumb kits. You should feed them and buy clothes and let them go to school, and vat you got from it? Now is doktor bills. And gasolina to town. And who should shop it now my cotton? And corn?"

"Let me carry you in, Tonik," I offered. But he stood up alone and hoped all the way on one foot.

"Dumb fools. What good is from school? Not to watch where shopping."

"Well let's see first; maybe it's not all that bad." I unwound the white cloth, smelled kerosene. The skin lay doubled back in a thick, convoluted layer with the tendons glistening bluish-white. "Move your toes, Tony, down and up. Good. Once more up as far as you can. Fine."

"It ain't for shits to have kits. Alvays vant to go school, school. And is learning vat? Vat you got from kits?"

The boy wiped tears off with a quick swish of his arm. I patted him on the back. "It'll only take a few stitches, that's all. Only the skin. No tendons are cut. Gretchen, get out the ST-37 first; it won't burn, doesn't sting—nothing. You'll see. Feels like nothing but water."

"In school should learn it something, no?"

"Just relax. Things will be all right."

"Is no good by shopping. Shop me sometimes the corn too, not only weeds. I say, Ven weed is *behind* corn, *push* vit hoe, not shop. You tink he learn it? Nodding. And he going school—alvays school. Vot they learning in school? Nodding. Vat this going cost—this . . . fixing?"

Tears fell near the cut.

"Is going, going gasolina, is take books, buy paper. And ven should help vit vork, right avay is making more vork, more gasolina, more . . . Vat you going get?"

I stared the man right straight in the eye—never talked to a grown man in that manner, ever: "Mr. Kobza. This boy was only *ask-*

ing. For you.'' I could see it—the results: nothing. I turned to the table, ''Lie flat down, Tonik. Don't worry. Soon it's over and you'll feel almost nothing. No bad pain. I promise.''

''Vat it going cost? You got to vait till picking time. Maybe make few bales. How much this dumbstock costing now?''

''Look. You seem worried about the money. Okay. I'll make you a deal: If you'll stop fussing at this boy—who was trying to help, I'm sure, and is trying to tell us something . . . by this accident—if you'll stop fussing at him and relax, I'll do it free.''

''Vat? You vork for nodding? No: nobody. But farmer, yes—he know. He know how many times he vork for nodding. Ven seed don't grow—replant and replant. And ven comes no rain. And ven comes planty rain and no price. Ven team mules is stomik big with colik—maybe die; but new ones—farmer knows. No, I pay. You not vork for nodding on my dumbhead kits. How much going charge?''

''Three dollars. In all. Includes the other visits and dressings. You will have to buy one medicine. A sulfa. And aspirin for soreness. You have aspirin at home?''

''Is Saint Yoseph aspirina gut?''

''Sure. Fine. Same thing. Aspirin is aspirin.''

The boy didn't cry anymore. Not that he had made any sound, but there were no more tears. And when Margaret asked him to, he stuck out his arm for the tetanus skin test. The father didn't say any more the whole time.

Tony, Tonik little son, is it a telling? Why the foot? What does it say in meaning? This slash into your own flesh, near your own foundation? Is it—are you saying something like that?

As I tied the knots, Margaret snipped them off even.

I can sew up the wound, Tonik, clean it against infection, and vaccinate a protection toward tetanus. Yes. But if I—we—could understand further this language of why. Why must we cut into ourselves? To tell what?

The last stitch, cleaned, bandaged. ''There you are,'' Margaret announced, ''all finished now.''

As the father came to lift him, the boy stepped quickly off the table alone, turned his back to the father, and walking only on his heel, led the way out.

***

Late Saturday night. I deliberately left Pete for last. (Saturday? Is the time going that fast? Has it been only one week or two since Otis Moore was killed. Only last Saturday? Yes. Yes, because the funeral's tomorrow. Everybody says they've been expecting a big crowd for this one, bigger than ever.) I wanted to talk to Pete. Not too much sewing this time on any of them—three small cuts on an Estrada, one longer one on a Salas. So the Salases were finished and they left.

Pete's cut was on his back; he lay on his stomach, and I sewed. (I like it better than their breathing sour alcohol in my face.) His blood on my hands, I knew—syphilitic. "You haven't come for your arsenic shots in a long time. Been away?"

"No."

"I realize it's no fun. You smell it—rather, taste it—soon as it goes into the blood, all that. Empty stomach, too. But you must get rid of it. Otherwise it's certain to cause bad things in you."

No answer. No response to anything. Never is. I'll bet I could sew him and the rest of the entire bunch up, without injecting a drop of local, and not a one would flinch. Pete's facial expression is always the same. Noncommittal, always.

"It's absolutely certain to cause bad things in you. It finally happens." I sewed, using a subcutaneous stitch. Tied knots, snipped the ends off. "Understand?"

"Yes, Mr. Shoes."

"It's only a matter of time and it will. Can even make you die. Kill you."

No answer.

"It's absolutely certain." Snip. "Only a matter of time. Know that?"

"How long it takes?"

"Before it begins to do damage—big damage? Ten years, five. Something like that. Fifteen to get into the brain. But it's for sure. It will."

Nothing.

"Will you come? For your shots? Any morning. Regular. Some morning?"

"Maybe so."

I sighed and pinched up the skin edge with the forceps.

"And another thing, the main thing—this stupid duel. I mean feud. Why take all these chances? Sooner or later it's certain to be something big. Bad." No answer. "Suppose you kill one of them? Then where will you be? You can't win either way—either if you kill them, or if they kill you. Neither way. Why not leave? Go somewhere else and forget it. Why do it? Is it for that machismo business? Is that what it is. That's adolescent. It's bound to be something more. Is it worth it—these chances? For what? Move your family somewhere else. California. I'll help you move."

No answer.

"Please."

No answer.

"What are you trying to prove? What are you looking for? You have to stop. My God, you must quit it. I keep preaching to you. I know it's very brave of you—macho—to fight other men with knives. I couldn't do it. But you must stop."

Nothing. No response whatever.

"I have something to show you." I laid the instruments down and opened the closet and reached high along the shelf and far back, bringing down the dusty skull with its wired jaw swinging. I set it on the desk so it faced him. "Now. What do you think of that? Huh? Look at it. What's it say?"

He looked. "Is smiling." And laid his head back down.

High Hope . . . and Despair

As I ran into the office—for once it's empty—slinging my hat to get the water off, Margaret greeted me with, "Such terrible rains."

"Oh, but it's beautiful! Coming down in blue curtains of water, splashing, cleaning. Washing all the trees—they're dancing around in it. And grasses along the road bowing and dripping . . . Middle Creek is a river!"

As near as I can remember, this became the first time we talked about it. Actually talked about starting a hospital. Maybe because, for once, we had a little time. Or maybe because it had always been too rare, too precious for me to even think about. Too dangerous if it became a hurt. Even so, we still didn't say much.

She sat at the typewriter with stacks of her new window type envelopes. "I need more stamps and can't get to the post office." She spoke loudly above the sounds of the hard rain.

"But sure comes in handy—got those hospital visits all done."

"To both hospitals? Dangerous for you to drive so far like that, in such rain. They're all doing all right? The patients? Do I charge Mladenka a hospital visit? He's Medical, isn't he?"

"Yes, intestinal and heart. We sure could use a hospital here."

"You should start one."

"I would indeed— That *would* be a dream! A fulfillment out of— I believe I'd be willing to give an arm. My own small hospital! Huh! One person. All alone start a hospital? Me?"

"You could do it."

"Me? That's too much to hope for."

I thought of the hospitals where I had trained—the corridors, the nurses, in one hospital the nuns with their "geese" starched heads. Saw again the perfect operating rooms, the exactness . . . The sedated patients being wheeled to surgery . . . The plate-glass windows of the nursery . . . And patients leaving, helped from the wheelchair into a car, restored to their families. These places were as temples to me. That's no exaggeration at all—temples, and of the right kind.

She answered in German, "If you'd put yourself to it." (In German it sounds like an obligation—more than *should*, beyond *have-to*, something you owe.)

"Yeah. But that's unrealistic. Beautiful dreaming."

She continued in German, "But the other one—your competitor—would—"

"My colleague. Another thing: I don't have the money."

"—would fight you on it."

"But why? Why should he? It would be for everybody."

"He did before. Fought it. And killed it. When the WPA wanted—"

"When? Who tried? Oh yes, yes. I remember. Thought you meant some person—persons—had tried . . ."

"I'm going to run out of stamps."

"I'll go."

"We should keep us extra raincoats here."

"Would be fine. Like when we go on OB's."

"Mike has those new plastic ones—they're not expensive."

"Who?"

"Mike Goldstein—clothing store. And once you're there, you could get yourself a few new shirts. On yours the collars aren't—"

"Okay. Okay."

"Take a look at your cuffs. They're frayed. That doesn't look nice and people see it."

I know she's telling me I shouldn't be so wishy-washy about it, about lots of things. But damn it all . . . I grabbed my hat and let the screen door slam. Her voice came through it into the drugstore, "Don't forget the stamps."

Going across the alley I wanted to stop—just stand around in the rain and think about starting a small country hospital. But that takes money, nerve, luck . . .

Mike Goldstein wrapped the package and tied the string around expertly. I had to ask, even though I didn't know him yet, "Do you think . . . the town here . . . would support a small hospital? Do you think . . . enough would?"

"Almost everybody except one."

"I guess it was a leading question. Shouldn't have asked."

"I'll ask around. And bring it up at Chamber of Comm—"

"Oh no! Please don't. It's only a passing idea—not ready. Only thinking. Shouldn't have asked." To make matters worse, I felt myself blushing. I turned quick, "Gotta hurry." And almost ran out.

❊❊❊

Although I tried to share my gasoline-buying with all the filling stations, I found myself automatically turning most often into M.J.'s station—M.J. Pulkrabek, called Mila by some. (His real name is Miloslave.) He stuck the nozzle in my tank and started washing the windshield. He checked the oil and water and battery and asked me, "Who you going? Who sick?"

"Going out to see old man Chupik."

"Vich von?"

"John."

"Vich Yon?"

"John."

"But vich Yon?"

"John. John Chupik. He's near Swiss Alp."

"Is different kind Yons."

"How do you mean different ones."

"Is Yon Xavier Chupik—is mine uncle. And is Yon Francis Chupik—is cousin. Twice. Twice is mine cousin, by mama-side and by papa, too. And is Yon Yosuf Chupik—is nudding by me—living close by Dubina. So ven is saying Yon Chupik is not telling. Say, too, how is in the middle."

"I don't know his middle name. I've been there once. Lives near Swiss—"

"Is no gut. You send bill to Yon Chupik—is nobody paying. Send it to him in the middle."

"Thanks, I'm glad you told me. Check the right rear tire please, M.J., looks low to me."

"M.J. checking all five. Spare too. You going mine uncle Yon Xavier. Is by Swiss Alp. He is sick, yes? Is maybe drinking too much Shiner, no?"

"It's his rupture again. She said he couldn't get it back in. We did it once before."

"Yes, yes. *Prutrz, prutrz.* He all time got it *prutrz.* And in attic got it plenty kinds trusses. All time order himself new kind truss. How is mans farming vit guts going out. Vy you don't fix him?"

"Operation? He's pretty old. It may not hold anymore—old. And he don't—doesn't—want an operation. I already told him. They're a pretty old couple."

"Is Ho-K. I put you vun kvart oil. Remember it vot I told you: Yon ain't plenty. You got to say vich Yon is it."

"Okay, thanks. *Spanna bohem*," I tried.

He waved good-by. "*Spanem bohem.*"

I couldn't see if the hernia might be strangulated, but you can't tell early for sure. Maminko had put the bricks under the foot of the bed, as I told her to on the phone, and started hot compresses. Everything ready and going, but she stayed out of sight now.

Well, I'll have to try to reduce it. And that will be hard to get done, especially since he's already tried it. You work and work at the hernia, squeezing and pushing and it won't go in. You try over and over. It becomes embarrassing. Finally you have made the patient sore and tender there; then he will tense up even more, which tightens everything into resistance. But you have to keep at it, trying, and it hurts him, and there's nothing else to do. And you apologize and keep at it again and again. If it gets to where he'll be too sore, I'll have to give him a hypo.

Had to begin. Couldn't stand there mulling it over forever.

So I cupped my hand around it. "John, you remember last time. This will hurt some at first." Shouldn't have mentioned last time—we worked for an hour before . . . I squeezed the thing flat and brought it up, pushing at the same time. Nothing happened. I grabbed it again and squeezed hard. He groaned. I squeezed *hard* and pushed all I could. It gurgled. He gasped. And it slid back up in. "There. Finished." I had won against it again. Such luck. But I knew it would only be temporary—soon the hernia would come out again.

"Ah," he breathed deep and rubbed his side. I hoped he wouldn't cough and pop it right back out. Now I noticed: He wore a fresh shirt, the sheets were fresh, he smelled bathed, and his white hair was still gray-wet. And on a chair beside the bed sat a pan of clear water and a new bar of soap still in its green wrapper—Palmolive, scented. And a fresh hand towel over the back of the chair. But Maminko had stayed out of the room, probably because this visit entailed a man's naked gonads where his hernia . . .

"Mama!" he called. "Bring me pants. Is fixed."

"Wait, let's see about a truss. Before you sit up."

"Is bust. I'm digging in garden with spade fork so Mama can put it more tomato plants—her cousin give yesterday. And comes such sneeze. And truss bust and—*ish ma yea*!—I think I bust me my guts out into the ground, like tomato plants. Is soon no more farming. Not with insides coming out. Mama likes farm, but . . . ven you can't no more?"

"If you want to quit farming, just quit. You don't have to hurt yourself first."

"How a man should go with guts outside?"

"M.J. said you had some trusses in the attic. I could go see."

"Mama. Show doktor vere is upstairs to attic." She answered but she still did not come into the room.

The attic was as clean as the downstairs, as if it had been swept and mopped yesterday. The big boxes, closed and tied with rope, seemed ready to be shipped.

And he did have every kind of truss you can imagine, all hanging from the rafters—"non-slip," "genuine leather," "no binding," "Real Steel." One even had an electric cord attached. Can't throw them away.

As I stood there alone in the attic with the locked trunks, like old remembrances past, and the neatly tied cardboard boxes, and all those trusses, I thought, At least some are brand new, but most have been worn, like days, like years past. He can't throw them away.

And mostly we, too, can't throw away old days and past years. We keep them, store them in the attic of the mind. Old days. Old rules. Old patterns. Even those we want to forget. As if we will use them over again. And maybe we do.

I heard a bird walking on the shingles, then heard it stop walking. Clean as everything was, I thought of the dusty odor of oleanders, pink oleanders—as if a bouquet of them were held in a skeleton's hand.

I turned quick, taking the nearest truss, and started back down the narrow stairs.

Outside, as I started to get into the car, I heard the distant sound of geese honking. I looked and looked and finally found the long wavering Vs, very high, moving, like writing something on the sky. Once you find them it is almost as if you are in contact, somehow connected, with them.

Good-by, good-by, have a nice trip to Canada. And come

again in the fall. You are such lovely creatures. We need to see you. We want to see you.

Their talking sounds seemed to say, *We shall come. We have always come.*

It's so far to Canada. It would be so far even to drive it in a car, and you do it one wing stroke at a time. All that way. And later, back again.

We always come. We were coming a thousand winters before you came.

I'm glad you come. You are like some fabulous promise, written in the clouds. You are lovely.

I stooped into the car and drove slowly back to town.

Only a few weeks later. The car lights showed the two tall brick gateposts. The iron gates stood fully open, with weeds and vines growing in them; the left side angled bent and hung crooked. The narrow driveway curved, and there on the steps of the huge, dark mansion stood John Chupik—John Xavier Chupik, who used to live at Swiss Alp—barefooted, wearing pants with suspenders and an undershirt.

"*Jak se mas*, John. Who's sick? Maminko?"

"Yass. Come down."

"Didn't know you moved here. When did you leave the farm? Because of the rupture? M.J. didn't tell me."

"Yo, and once more I fall from tractor, backwards over. Getting old. Mama she tell me to quit it the farming. Before, she always vant it the farming. And I tank so I quit. Son Frank—they got six kits—he leave his yob in Houston, gut yob. Say city is gut place for raising the money, not so gut place for raise kits. He come right avay home ven ve ask him."

We walked through the double entrance doors and into a large, long hall. "So you moved in here. When?"

"Only vun veek now. Is too long already. We stay here until Frank build us small house in yard in summer. Before picking time. Ve carpenter together."

Inside was a beautiful staircase, perfectly proportioned. I stopped and looked at it. Two of the banisters were missing and one hung loose.

"I tank mama she is sick from living here, from moving. She see so much veeds and vat needs fixing and I tell her not to do it—ve stay here only short time, in few months have our own little house.

"Everybody say I should sell farm. Sell farm, they tell me, and buy yourself in town a house. Other peoples do it. No. I should sit and look the vindow out? No. Is not me.''

I know the ''little houses'' of the farms, have made many calls to them. Many farm families, when the ''old ones'' can no longer work, build this small house in the yard, only a hundred feet or so from the main house. This becomes their ''years for resting'' yardhouse, and the son or son-in-law who takes over the farm looks after the old people. His wife brings them many things to eat—kolace or ''haefe kuchen''—but does not do their regular cooking except when they are sick. But maybe she always bakes an extra loaf regularly for them. And she always does their laundry. And although the young people look after their needs, they also leave the old parents alone as much as they wish. Finally, it becomes only one old person there. Then, it seems to me, the one always needs more attention, has more illnesses, than when it was the two. And when it becomes none, the little house stands empty. Sometimes it is used for pickers or choppers, but seldom so. If the family is large, the boys leave their attic and move into the yardhouse—it is a step in their leaving home. And the older girls, if there are many (and girls always stayed in the main house) take over the attic.

As we walked through the long hall, John Xavier kept saying, ''Vy you don't buy this big house—you got money—and make horspittle? Is gut house: upstairs in attic, yo, such fine strong lumbers—not like houses is today. And no knothole in whole house. Is not finding in whole lumber one knothole. And foundations—ya! Down to rock. Is gut. Needs plenty fixing but only all such little thinks. Yass, ve going in little house, mama and me.'' I saw again the little place, with its porch full of pot plants on benches and some hanging. ''Upstairs in attic I find crutch from old man Nordhausen. I forget me how little mans he is, not so big like my grandson Elo who comes fourteen in August.''

''Did Nordhausen break a leg?''

''No, no, vas cripple, always cripple. Little mans. Ven I am boy I remember his store—such big store. Ya, to the ceiling shelves and such ladders on rollers, and all such fine thinks: vagons, saddles, sugar, hats, coffee, sewing machinas—everythink. In back vas bank with cage in front like shicken coop. Is vere Nordhausen stay. Always sits hisself on high stool behind little cage vindow, looking out. Talk with you through the cage. Always in bank part.'' We passed through another set of double doors. "Vas rich. Made millionaire. Sometimes mean. Mean. Charge on bills vat peoples don't buy. In front room here is vere his son shoots hisself in head."

"God!"

"Sitting naked in empty bathtub, shoots head off vith shotgun. Is peoples living upstairs that side and vun family in back upstairs, and in here is mama. You should make it horspittle for sick peoples. Ve reading alvays every veek Thursday in paper, *LaGrange Yournal,* who is in horspittle. Make gut place. Needs not so much fixing like mama and me. You can fix it easy—is all best materials. Is solid, by gory. Is needing new life. Is vaiting. You make it. Horspittle. For sick peoples. Nize, on top of hill, cool in summer. Mama is in here."

I followed the silent bare feet and the clean-smelling breeches and undershirt.

Later I slowly walked in the full-moon light, noting the smooth gravel and perfect edges of grass and seeing the small lawns and monuments of my "private" place, where I had come to think. After a while I could see everything clearly, even read the inscriptions. *Should I risk it?* There was an aroma of different flowers blooming and the splashy colors of artificial ones in vases. Like a great formal garden, which it was. White-painted iron benches and a marble bench. Old plots with iron fences in squares or rectangles, roses, and tall tombstones with carvings and an urn on top with a cloth draping down. Often there were a pair.

A pair. . . .

One tall gray pair stood before a background of huge oleander bushes with pink blossoms. I turned away from them, the flowers symbols of failure that brought up again pained memories. The death of love. The death of a vision of what could be, what I wanted so much to be. *No, I will not let this be a premonition.*

Lots of big trees with great splotches of shadow and lots of streaks of droppings on the carved marble. I walked across the soft, even grass; when I felt it it was already damp.

This is like a park, a beautiful park. Why isn't it used more as a place of quiet celebration—as a park? If the dead had a choice, wouldn't they like it better? To see it used rather than set so aside?

I like to be alone here. If you walk along a country road, people always think you've had car trouble and stop and offer a ride and talk. Here it's quiet.

But hospitals lose money. No. I can't afford it.
That's too much to hope for.
I'm afraid . . . to risk it . . . yet.

Long green leaves of lilies fingered out over a walk of white marble chips. Trails of ivy meandered up a tree trunk.

⁂

Mr. Innocence Sobotik, a very large man, powerful, complained about pains and a constant soreness in the back and legs. Big man, great big man.

"And my vater, ven it vants to come, it goes—I can't hold it back. It goes, vithout me. I hate to make it so much vashing for Carrie, my son's vife—I living by them. But she say she vash from two babies now. She joke me. Pain is here." He too illustrated by punching me low in the back, but not hard. "And going this vay, oop." I held to the desk, prepared—Mr. Sobotik is a big man.

"The pains go anywhere else?"

"Yo, in here too." His broad stubby hands grabbed my neck. "And going oop in *hlava.*" I felt the strong hands smearing on my head—Mr. Sobotik was trying to be gentle.

"I have to examine you. Let's start from the top. Strip to the waist first."

"And sometimes my vater it is blood, *krev.*"

"What!"

He stripped himself of his shirt, showing a hairy physique with muscles bulging like a living Michelangelo statue. Yet he said, "I going too fast down, got to wear me soon the suspenders." By now I shouldn't be surprised anymore to see such a husky build for a man of seventy-two. But urinating blood! A gold crucifix hung nestled in the thick hair of his chest; it looked worn and smooth.

"Have you had it"—I pointed—"a long time?"

"Forty-one year. In August. My wife she give it me day after our vedding vas. I vear it every day, never miss once. I be buried vit in on me." He still wore his hat, with hair sticking out all around from under it. And hair grew curly out of his ears and nostrils, too, and long shoots of hair sprayed off his shoulders as if seeds of it had fallen there from his head and sprouted. And all over his big chest, a curly mat, reddish.

But urinating blood! Such a severe symptom!

What does it say?

That "I am wounded deep within?"

Surely it is a symptom of saints.

"Later we'll do the rectal." I first listened to his breath sounds, heard them clear and strong.

When I did the rectal, my finger felt suddenly the hard knotty surface, firmly adhered, unmovable.

Good God! I almost jerked my hand back.

Cancer! Of the prostate.

"Mr. Sobotik"—I stretched and snapped the rubber glove off—"we'll have to do several tests—blood tests and X rays. Take several days."

Cancer! And spread all through the gland! It was knotty all over.

On the second day I took blood tests and X rays of his pelvis. After he left the office I phoned to a specialist in Houston and sent the X rays. All this, I knew, was only a delay—so I wouldn't have to tell Mr. Sobotik yet: the diagnosis of cancer of the prostate with metastasis into all the pelvic bones. It would give me a few more days of not telling him. And him a few more of not having to know. On the black film, the cancer's splotchy deposits in the bone showed as bright radiant bursts surrounded by sprinkles.

I with my strange idea, feeling that people, unaware, choose their symptoms. Choose the illness that best tells their inner, unknown self-fears. Have the disease tell it on the surface and in the strange language that disease uses. So they can stay safely blind to their deeper fears. Disease is a disguise.

I sat, seeing his X rays in my mind, wondering why he chose a malignancy of those parts? Is he denying, even destroying, those parts of himself? Like "if thy right hand offend thee, cut it off"? He's a nice guy; everybody likes him; everybody is sorry for him being alone since his wife died five, six years ago. Looks much younger than his years—is younger. Has a good place with his son and daughter-in-law, Carrie, who are wonderful to him. Has a nice grandbaby boy for his name to go on. What's eating him so that he has to scream it, and yet whispers it in a cancer?

A few days later (and bolstered with the report from Houston) I put him in the hospital in LaGrange for more kidney-function tests and blood-protein studies. I know it was mainly because I still didn't want to tell him. Oh, it's all right to take such tests and repeat X rays, especially for preparation before an operation, even if it is a very small operation, but I hadn't told him about that yet either. These tests were not absolutely essential. I knew I was indulging myself—and at his expense. Delaying my duty of telling him. Of having to tell him.

His two daughters planned to stay with him while he was at the hospital, changing off so one would be with him all the time. One lived nearby at Ammonsville. And Carrie, the daughter-in-law, said she'd offer to stay, too, except for the baby, so she'd do all the laundry for him and for the sisters, too.

"Now, papa, I am going to the bus station." The oldest daughter spoke in Czech (Bohemian). "To meet Agnes. She is going to stay by you tomorrow and Sunday so I can do some baking and go to Mass. Now while I'm gone to the station, you will have to call the nurse. When you want to pass your water, push this button so, and the nurse she will come."

"Is Carrie coming?"

"Not today. Push the button so and the nurse is coming."

"She is speaking Bohemian?"

"No. So you must ask for the urinal. You know what is: It has the long neck—"

"I know. How you say?"

"Urinal. Say it."

"Yoinal."

"That's fine, papa. That's good. You see, you speak a nice English. Say it once more."

"Yoinal. Why can't Carrie come stay with me?"

"Karolina has you spoilt, papa. You live with her and she is only your daughter-in-law. She has the baby to look after, and you know how big that boy is growing. When you're well, you can go live with her again. And I will be right quick back, with Agnes."

Maybe because of thinking about it or maybe because of the secondary bladder infection—soon he punched the button urgently.

The nurse appeared in the door so quickly there seemed some direct electrical connection between the button and her. "Yes?"

"Get me yoinal. Quick. Yoinal."

"What?"

"Quick!"

She returned in a moment and hesitatingly offered him the week's issue of the *LaGrange Journal.*

He spluttered in English: ''Vat you tank? I'm a damn inside house dog?''

She was busily changing the soiled draw sheet when his two daughters entered carrying a suitcase.

I came into his room at the same time, too, with X-ray films. Agnes set her suitcase down and kissed him and I got the whole thing over with and done: I told him. And held the pictures up in front of the bedside lamp and the ceiling light and pointed to the metastases—to where it all had spread.

Strange, that he said nothing, asked nothing.

Is he hearing me? He's listening. Seems he is. I've explained it—shown him the pictures, pointing it all out.

He's looking. Does he see them? Hear me?

And at that moment Vestine and Carrie came, Carrie holding the baby. ''Only for a few minutes. To tell Grandpa good-night, and where is dirty clothes for wash? Say good-night, Tatinku.'' She waved the baby's hand. ''Say come home soon, Tat-tu. He's already too sleepy. We can't stay long.'' And Mr. Sobotik seemed to forget anything I had just told him—if he understood it at all—and forgot that I was still there, standing around useless. He talked to the baby, laughed, tried to take the baby—who wouldn't go. ''He's already tired, Grandpa.'' And he kissed Carrie and kept holding her hand.

For their benefit I held the pictures up again, gave my little speech all over, and I said for the third or fourth time, ''Definitely this is cancer. *Rakovina*.'' I had looked up the word to get it right.

And Mr. Sobotik patted Carrie's hand and smiled up at her.

I stood around a while longer, finally motioned Vestine to meet me in the hall. Mr. Sobotik didn't notice, still held Carrie's hand.

I told it plain to Vestine. ''It's cancer. He doesn't seem to understand. Proved it's cancer. He's going to die with it unless it's treated.''

''Treated? How can it be treated?''

''By castration. Taking a man's nuts off. It's the treatment. And inject ovary—female—hormones. It—in most cases—stops cancer of the prostate. That's been proved.''

''Cut his stones off? Out?''

''Off, yes.''

''Cures the cancer?''

''In most cases. It makes the cancer shrink down. Even disappear completely. And the urologist said so, too.''

"I don't think so he will do it."

"The operation? Why not?"

"I think he will stay—will keep it."

"I know it takes a lot of nerve for him to decide. But he'll die. For sure."

"I know it."

"How can I convince him? It *must* be."

"I can tell him so; you can tell him so. We telling other mans he should do it. I don't think so he will."

"He's in love with her, isn't he?"

"In love with? Who?"

"In love with Carrie."

"Oh, sure, sure. Carrie. Like his own daughter. Better."

"I know—"

"She good to him, too. Is lucky they get along so good in same house. He won't go to the others. Say he stay by Carrie."

"That's sorta what I mean."

"No, I do not think so he will do it."

I hated the thought picture of the X rays, with the cancer and its young offspring showing in silver-white bursts like skyrockets celebrating.

And I hated, too, to think of a man's testicles lying on a surgical tray, clamped with the big-teethed hemostats, the skin bluish . . .

On Saturday it was dark before I could get off to LaGrange. We talked alone in his room; he said, "No operations."

"I hate to insist on it, but we have to."

"Why cut them off."

"It's the only way. We'll expect good results. It retards the growth, even if its roots are spread. Many cases worse than yours have been reported in the medical journals and all have been improved—at least improved—and many were cured. I hate to cut them off. But it is necessary. It is the proper treatment. And why should you care? You are too old now. For using."

"Well, maybe . . . not so."

"They are of no more use to you."

"Not like young, no, but young mans like you not knowing what old mans—"

"'You have all the children you will ever have.'"

"'Could be yes. But— And they look nize and I am glad I have them and I cannot guess how it vould be for a man not to have. And how he thinking of himself. And when we take it hex-rays in your office, I think I see the nurse looking. Maybe not so. I think it.'"

"'You won't miss them half as much as you think. In any case—I hate to tell you—but with them you will die. A cancer death. Slow.'"

"'His death is something a man can do. And if the saints wish to test a man's strength of pain further . . . And many must do it. But a man-made misery staying alive—I don't know. And everybody will know it and think it. There goes Innocence, they will say. Innocence is a steer now. No stones. Or will say, Vestine is the only man in that house, the old one got cut out, and the baby boy in his small pouch is only two little nickels.

"'And it is nothing yet vat other mans thinking, but vat a man is thinking for himself. So even if it vorks to be well, it will not be well. It makes big question. Many go vit one leg or one eye or hand. But to say I give up my seed. Is more than only something from the body. Is from your kernel inside. Is even from before old country—is from beginning is given on down to you. To throw away like empty bottle the center seed from vich mans came all this long way? Only to stay a little vile longer? Maybe only to die longer?'"

If he can make a decision on such as this—evidently it's of great weight to him—if he can do it, surely I can decide about starting a hospital or not. If he can, surely I can, too.

"'Yes,'" I said it from nowhere, "'and cutting them off might be . . . like punishment, wouldn't it?'"

And strange that he should happen to be lying in the supine anatomical position, even the palms of his hands turned face up—as described in anatomy books, the body ready for dissection, for autopsy. He said, "'Who knows it exactly the answer.'"

I was silent too.

❊❊❊

There came the old woman Mrs. Bohuslav Bronecky, being led by her granddaughter, almost totally blind from pterygium, the skin that grows over the eye when it is exposed very much to dust and fine sand blowing, as can happen when a person works for years in the fields. In old England the condition was called Coachman's Disease for the men who were constantly in the dust from horses' hoofs.

A pterygium grows from the nasal corner outward, toward the ear. Hers were so bad they were grown over each pupil, covering it.

The eye is rounded two ways, and there is no knife that can cut rounded, curved corners. And there is certainly no way to cut a curve both vertically and horizontally at the same time. So how can I possibly cut these skin growths off and still leave her a smooth enough surface to see through? The cornea will be left rough—at least with ridges—and this will distort the light waves and everything she sees will have grooves in it like a bad mirror, big grooves. A case grown this bad cannot be corrected better than that, as far as I know. In this woman the disease enemy has already won.

I thumbed my mustache, thinking she probably expects it to turn out perfect. And it can't be. So she will blame me. She'll complain. She'll be telling all her relatives.

At this stage I am confused, uncertain. Should I dare try it? And if it fails? Maybe go broke—lawsuits, bankruptcy, disgrace. Would be ridiculed by Kotzebue for sure.

Doubt is a self-induced blindness.

Doubt is a self-induced achievement of purpose. The purpose of doubt is to avoid decision. And assertion.

Well, I mustn't let it stop me from trying to fix her eyes.

While she sat hunched on the examining table, I held my hand before her and asked if she could see it. She could, only when I moved it from side to side. She couldn't tell me how many fingers at all. With the ophthalmoscope you couldn't begin to see into the pupils. I wrapped the long gray cuff around her arm, tucking the tail in underneath, pumped the bulb, and listened to her blood pressure. One hundred eighty over ninety-two. And listened to her heart. No enlargement and no murmurs, but it was fast. So is mine now, I'm sure.

She'll blame me. But what can I do?

I asked her to lie down and pulled up the foot rest.

As it is, she is practically blind. Functionally she is blind. All she can actually see is light and dark. Why does she have this? And so severe? All farm women help with the field work, are in the dust and wind; they are in the smoke of wood-burning cook stoves and fires around wash kettles. Why should she have them more than anyone else, even right up to the very door of darkness?

And me? Why do I hold back, hesitate? Is it safer this way?—stay hidden in the dark, then you'll never have to face failure in the light.

"Maminko, I shall put these drops in your eyes. Do not have fear. This is to help deaden the feel." The old woman lay very still. "That was good. You are very helpful. Now again hold the eye still, for I must make a most small injection. This too is for the absence of pain." How am I to cut this thing? Those cases we were taught by in school had nothing grown over the pupil like this—they were never this far. Well, she is blind and, strangely, that helps me.

"Hold very very still now, Maminko." I aimed the pointed blade under the flap of conjunctival skin. It melted its way through. "You're doing fine. Keep it steady. Keep looking at the same place in the ceiling." Holding this freed tail tip with forceps I pointed the cutting edge toward the other end of the wing-shaped skin, sliding along under it, moving it outward. There was no feeling of pressure or of cutting—whatever the steel edge touched dissolved away. My hand did not pause nor stop to begin again. It was one continuous movement. The whole flap lay loose. Holding this by the forceps I now cut back toward the base of the growth. There! So that much is done. It's not perfect but it's done. Now for the other eye.

With the other eye finished too, she sat up and looked around. Looked at her granddaughter and said, "You have lost a baby tooth in the front." And looked at me and began to cry, "Holy Mother of God, now I can see again. I did not know it you had a nose beard. I can see everything. It is as if coming alive again."

She talked almost in a chanting, perhaps in a rhythm, and looked at her own hands, examining them closely as she continued to cry and talk. The little blond granddaughter also had tears but she made no sound. The old woman talked. Now, she said, she could pour the cream into the churn without spilling. Now she would again set out the cabbage plants and onions and—with her happy crying—she said now she would not lose her way to the toilet and have to go out by the peach trees. (The little granddaughter blushed.) She kept looking at my hands while she spoke rapidly, continuing a chanting, almost like a litany. "Again I can pick the eggs, and vipe them vit a vet cloth. And set me a cluck and peel the string beans—and—and again I can be. And chop in the garden.

"Oh, *Pane* Doktor," she kept crying, "you have made it me to live again. Now I shall see again the rock steps of the church, worn by vear into little bowls vere is the vinter vater standing ice. And in spring the little vite leaves from plum trees is blowing and makes nests and nobody steps. I vill see it again. Vat wonders can that man do. Surely he has been touched by the sunlight of saints; he has the hands of shining gold.'' And she kissed my hands, dripping pink tears on them.

I didn't know what to do.

No, it's impossible. Fifty years ago—like Albert Schweitzer—yes, start on a shoestring, but now it takes money. Or a group like a whole church congregation, a large one. Or an entire town. Or an extremely wealthy man.

No, I have to stop dreaming and wishing.

I wouldn't have the nerve.

❊❊❊

Every time I see Aurelius the thought comes back—Did Aurelius abdicate his rectum?

He has none. No rectum.

Met him as I came in the drugstore—he was going out. ''Hi, Aurelius. Everything all right with you?'' But I don't stand and talk with him. Everybody knows he has no rectum—there's no secret. It was removed surgically. Not by me—several years ago. And everybody knows it was some kind of disease, not cancer. So they know he's not going to die from it, has to live with it. And everywhere they see him—at the post office, driving his pickup, or going into the bank—they know he's wearing a little rubber bag (actually, it's plastic—James told me—but people call it rubber) on his side. And that his bowels move into it anytime. That he's got no control of it, can't make it wait. When you stop and talk with him on the street and ask how his hogs are doing, you can't keep your mind off the little bag. You listen and wonder if something's in it and will he have to wash it out when he gets home and things like that, and it's hard to listen to him about his hogs. You think, maybe it's happening right now, right here in front of the drugstore.

There was another thing about Aurelius that everybody knew—that he and his wife couldn't have children. They had been married twelve years and had no kids. In this area, that could mean only one thing: They couldn't have any.

Men would say it to him, right out on the streets, ''And vy not, Aurelius? Vy not no kits? You shoot it only blank shots? Vy no kits?

Maybe you cut. Like you cut it from the peks the nuts out? You shoot it only blanks? Like bully calf with his eggs cut out? No bull, only steer. Yust blanks?" It must have hurt his feelings, but he never let on. Acted friendly and like it was all in jest. Which it was, but cruel.

So Aurelius and his wife, Hilda, had been making quiet trips—not telling anybody where they were going—toward Austin. Must have been to Austin because they headed out toward Smithville.

There's nothing in Smithville. It's one of "those American places" where you find no German or Bohemian names on the mailboxes; where it is "dry" so you can't even get a glass of beer unless you go the back roads and buy it from a bootlegger at twice the price and then have to ice it down yourself. And there are no big churches on any hill. And at their dances they get wild drunk and fight and cut each other up like Mexicans, and go out to their cars and get pistols and shoot people. And the courthouse is always full of people listening to murder trials, and everybody gets a life sentence, which means they're back seven years later and shoot somebody else. Where black people have to get off the sidewalks and stand aside for whites to pass—have to "stay in their place." Where the men wouldn't think of having any business but cattle. They "run cattle" and sit around and talk and claim the auction barns are crooked, and disputes and fights over stray calves or unmended boundary fences start feuds. It's one of "those American places." You don't go. If anybody sees you going that direction, they know you're headed *through* Smithville, toward Austin.

So when people saw Aurelius and Hilda head out that way and come back later and do the milking and feeding-up by flashlight—but they hadn't asked any neighbor to keep an eye on the place—well, that showed it was some big secret-mystery, and it had to be Austin.

And then it came out: Aurelius and Hilda had adopted two children. Through the state adoption agency. Everyone said with surprise, "Two yet!" But they were relieved to know now what the trips had been about—were satisfied on that. "Adopt two kits. How much you got to pay for kits when you adopt?"

"Nothing," Aurelius had said.

"Nothing? You paying nothing? Get kits free when you adopt? No doktors, horspittle, no labor pains? Free?"

"But they did make me pay to the United Fund Drive. Donate."

"How much?"

"Nine hundred."

"Dol-lars? That's lots of peks."

"Apiece."

"Apiece! *Yish Ma-yea,* that is *hogs*! Vy you pay so much? Huh? For kits? Vy not you say, Keep kits yourself, sell to somebody else vat got more money—somebody big vit cattles. Vy you let them make you pay? Is state Taxhass selling you kits?"

"Oh no. Well, Hilda—she wanted them. So . . ."

And the talk went around that Aurelius had bought himself two children—for a price that would have bought dozens of registered Duroc sows. Registered yet. Durocs.

And he has no rectum.

And the land. Everybody knows about that, too. It happened when the parents went on "Old Age." When you go on the Old Age you can't get the pension unless you have only three hundred dollars in the bank (allowed for funeral) and no more than ten acres each. So they divided the farm and gave each child a part and left themselves with twenty acres total, including the house and well. The agency lady said it could be accepted like that on the grounds that the children had worked and paid for their part, even after they left home. Therefore it did belong to them and they were only letting the parents live on it. And so she put them on the pension, and they got their first check two months later—thirty-nine dollars for him and nineteen for her.

But this dividing up and the agency worker's statement that the children had in fact owned the farm by paying it off started Julius, the oldest, to thinking and figuring. And he figured and thought and figured that he had paid the most, more than the rest. Aurelius had paid nothing but the taxes and had only brought his tractor and implements over and worked the farm for the old people, and farming doesn't pay anything, so Aurelius hadn't paid in much. And the sister—well, she had that child when she was sixteen and she always worked out and had to spend the little she made supporting the kid, so she had paid in hardly anything. And the folks kept the girl for her so she could have a job in Houston, and now the girl is finishing high school and that took a lot, so what she gave the folks, well, that went for keeping the girl, not paying for the farm. And the youngest boy, Loddie, now he had sent the folks more than any. He had a good job in Houston and had worked himself up, but, after all, it was Julius who had got him his first job in Houston. It wasn't a good one, and the boy didn't stay with it anytime before he found himself a much better job, but by rights—since Julius had got him to Houston in the first place so he *could* do better—by rights everything he made in Houston really belonged to Julius. So he went to the younger brother and told him and Loddie told him back, "You come once more here with such crazy talk and I kick you some sense between the eyes—knock some sense *in* your head. Can't knock none *out*." And Julius decided maybe that brother had paid his part.

So he went next to his sister, who worked in a big house in the rich River Oaks section of Houston and he told her. She said, "No, I don't give you nothing." But he knew she liked working for these people, and he said if she didn't sign her part over to him, he'd tell them she had a child but no husband—ever—and what would they think then? She answered, "I work already eleven year here for them. They gut peoples. I tell them many year back about mine little Natasia. I show picture. They tall me she pretty. They give me clothes for her. Like new. And gut shoes, coats—plenty clothes. Save me money. And Christmas they give presents—new, wrapped with ribbons in fine stores—for me to take her. So you go tall them. They vill think you vun big fool. You go tell him—I give you address from his office. Go tall. Make big fool-ass from youself."

Well . . . but there still was Aurelius to try. And Aurelius thought that yes, he hadn't paid in much money except the taxes every year regular, but he had plowed and hauled manure and planted and paid for all that with his own money, and put the corn in their barn so they had feed for pigs and chickens, and plowed their garden spring and fall every year and that's mainly what the folks lived on all these years. And Hilda did the washing and ironing for them every week. But Julius said that wasn't money, and it was the money that paid the place off, and Aurelius said, yes, he guessed that was right and Julius said that's the way it should be. He had Aurelius and Hilda sign at the bank. And they kept on plowing the farm and doing the wash.

Everybody knows how it is with Aurelius.

"Everything all right with you, Aurelius? Family okay?" But I didn't stop—walked right on in through the drugstore.

And saw a mental picture of a man's rectum, on a blood-dripped surgical tray, lying there alone . . .

I hurried on through the screen door. "Howdy, folks, be right with you." And went into the examining room and washed my hands.

❋❋❋

As I came into the house, the woman held the lamp before her; the fine tremble of its flame echoed the slight quiver in her words. "So late, we did not wish to call you out. But doktor, very sick he is," she spoke German. It kept raining steady.

Leaning over the bed—now she brought the lamp closer—I looked down into the wrinkled red face with long strands of white hair almost like a woman's. His face was flushed with fever and his breathing short and fast. "Forgive the . . . disturbance of your . . . good sleep, kind doktor. But an old one . . . is afraid—since he does not know . . . if it is the time. Is this . . . the time?"

We bundled him up good and put pillows in the back seat. I carried him—the little father weighed almost nothing—through the rain and drove twenty miles to the hospital in Hallettsville, where we started him on oxygen right away. Put the hissing mask over his red face . . .

It's simply a fact: there are certain things that only a hospital can do.

Almost immediately his breathing came easier—and he slept.

❋❋❋

"When is pulling pick sack, is hurting worser."

"You've had it how long in all?"

"Eleven year. Now is from garden. I set me out cabbage plants and tomato and onions, and it comes again. Always from garden comes. Shop veeds makes it. And carry milk buckets to house. And cotton-picking. And always going and going to doktor and different medicines and pay and pay and always same."

Again I pushed deep into the abdomen and it always lay exactly over the right tube and ovary. Vaginal exam also localized the tenderness. No doubt about it, same place. And the cervix is tender. So what else could I say? "This is a low-grade tumor of some kind. A growth. Hard. I can feel it between my hands when I examine inside and push here.

"With all the trouble you've had with it—so long—it should come out."

"I tal Alfonse. Always. Vat it is, it should come out. I tal him many years and he take me Kotzebue and more medicine. I tal Alfonse many years but he no listen. Never listen me nossing."

The surgery went well, no trouble. I did it at LaGrange Hospital and Dr. Frank Guenther—assisted. We found lots of adhesions knotted around the tube. Protected inside it, wrapped again and again in adhesions (fibrous connective tissue), lay this calcified small tubal pregnancy. Never saw that before. A calcified foetus.

About two inches long. Calcified. Swaddled in scar tissue, adhesions. A perfect specimen. I skinned and cut the tube and connective tissue off and washed it. Should go to a path lab at a medical school for teaching purposes. Perfectly formed. Even tiny fingers. "It's a pregnancy—in the tube—from at least eleven years ago. Turned to stone."

Why should a woman unknowingly carry in her abdomen a stone image of infertility? Like a stone wall against fertility? Is it a fear? A monument to the fear of becoming a mother? Or does the stone in her pelvis make her more like a man—give her more authority? And aggravated by "women's work." A calcified foetus. Like a rock wall, a fortress against . . . Or some remote, blind reason to "marble-ize" a pregnancy, a possible offspring, almost into a very tombstone?

After the operation I showed the specimen to Alfonse and his sister and sister-in-law. "It's unusual, rare. Very seldom happens. Hysterolith, I think it's called, if I remember. Most unusual. This part is turned to bone—she had it that long. Nature tried to seal it off—did—calcified it. Into bone. So it wouldn't rot and poison her."

"Extra bones," Alfonzo said. "I hear it extra ribs, but never before growing bones in stomach. Is gut think you cut it off." He spoke of it like pruning a fruit tree.

The hospital. Will I too not dare—not dare start the hospital? Carry it, too, within me forever dead? Keep it forever inside, safely unborn until it is a dead weight, a tombstone?

That night, at Margaret's yard gate, I turned the car engine off. "Gretchen, I'm going to see what I can do about beginning a hospital."

"It certainly is a big undertaking, as you said so yourself. Tremendous."

"You . . . think I shouldn't?"

"You should do whatever *you* want to do. Not ask *me*."

As I drove off I said aloud, "I've decided." And I had.

⁂

A *pri-mip,* their first. Special people, too—noticeable families and well-to-do. That's why, thank God, it happened in a hospital. Both he and she—the young couple—are from locally outstanding town families, the Herziks and the Knabels, owners of reliable businesses, well thought of. And this baby, not only the first for the couple, but also the first grandchild of both families. Not a bad situation for a young doctor starting out.

Everything is going fine. The mother's in top condition. There have been no prenatal complications, her pains are coming along, the nurses are efficient, pleasant. The two prospective grandmothers are here somewhere, waiting, probably chitchatting about such matters as whether the coverlets should be pink or blue. The baby's heart is fine. It's going to be a breech. So what. I've delivered breech before—during internship—even *pri-mips.*

And with her pain—there, first—came the feet. That the little toes pointed downward didn't interest me much—I was more aware of whose darling little grandtoes they were.

A baby's head is its largest part. That's why in a normal delivery, once the head is born—almost always—the baby comes sliding out. Almost always. The shoulders are smaller than the head and the hips are smaller than the shoulders. But in a breech, it's all reversed. A breech becomes three deliveries in one. First there is the delivery of the hips, then of the shoulders, then the head. And the first two came along just lovely. Why not? This is all going to be finished in a few more seconds, and the baby will be crying and—

I had to tug a little on the baby's head—it has to be delivered quickly because the oxygen supply is cut off after the navel is born. A little more tug. Gently tug still more. Mustn't let the little fellow get bluish—we wouldn't want that now would we? Tug. Pull. This has to come—what's holding it? Pull firmly, a mite hard. What is this? Come out of there! If you pull too hard you can tear the brachial plexus, and the child will grow up with a paralyzed arm. We certainly have to avoid anything like that. I pull. Bluish. The seconds are ticking away! I can't get it out—it won't come! Bluish.

I tell the mother to push, push hard; she's too drunk from the gas. "Keep her under." Tell the nurses to push on the uterus, the abdomen. Bluish. Seconds ticking away. They push, I pull. By this time I would settle for a torn brachial plexus, because by now it might be brain damaged. I pull hard. Past bluish—*blue*. Come out! Damn it!

Mustn't break its neck. It's said as long as you pull *straight,* it can't happen. Terribly blue. Finally I'm twisting, turning, pulling, even pushing. The seconds have done their ticking—they're gone. This limp thing in my hands, hanging by its neck, must be dead, and I'm still working. Sweat has blinded me. Pull. Pulling. And now I would have sworn away anything just to get the dead thing out. Exhausted, I let it dangle there a moment, hanging by its head. Then I resumed the desperate pulling.

I'm still at it, pulling like hell. Have a foot against the delivery table, because I've been pulling it around, too. I have probably by now damaged the mother's bladder and rectum. An old head nurse, a hard Mean-Mama type, comes in. She has just come on duty—the shifts have changed, that's how long I've been at this—and in one glance she sees the whole thing. Maybe she's seen other young doctors, maybe it isn't just me.

Somehow she knew, and seeing the whole thing gone, she, without sterile hands and not a word spoken, simply reached in, took the flaccid dead thing, and bent it up, backwards, over onto the mother's abdomen, *all* the way up, like a *U*. And the head peeled right out. She turned and left. Not a word. I'll always see it lying there, limp on the tray, a purple-blue heap—it would have been a boy—before a nurse laid a towel over it.

I remember, as it lay on that tray, saying to it, I'm sorry, baby, so terribly sorry. Believe me, I'm sorry.

It did not get to live. But because of it, later, some others did. Maybe I gave its life to others.

A facedown breech. My ignorance. It becomes a simple thing once you know it. Simply bend the child up—it won't break, the bend is in the neck—bend it back *onto* the mother's abdomen, way up, its heels on her navel, and the head rolls out. And if it doesn't right away, simply put a finger in the baby's mouth—the chin makes a perfect lever for up. You don't even have to tug. Just lift, and there it is.

Not that this child was my only failure. God no. But this one is always with me. And always will be.

I never mentioned it to anyone, not even to Margaret. But every OB we went on—and every case now yet—that dead baby went along too, in my mind.

I do not remember driving back to Schulenburg that morning. But, coming into the office, I knew instantly the news had preceded me. Because Margaret asked nothing—no "How did it go?" "Is it a girl?" "What do I charge—is the episiotomy extra?" Nothing. Showed she'd already heard all about it—at least heard the baby was born dead. I felt my unshaved chin, told her that I had "abdominal flu" and would stay in bed today. She asked if James should fix up some milk of bismuth or something.

"Thanks no. I know what's causing it. Best if I simply—"

"You mustn't blame yourself for everything that doesn't turn out perfect."

"Yes. Thank you. But . . ."

Mrs. Smorksky was one of the first who came in; Margaret told her I was sick in bed. And Mrs. Smorksky—bless her heart—went straight home, cooked some chicken soup with homemade noodles and brought it to the hotel. And it was the greasiest-looking, slimiest, wormiest . . . and with dumplings, too. If a person could have held it down, it would have given him the "running-off something f'urce," as the timber people say it, which I already had. I thanked her kindly, and she glowed all abeam with goodness-of-heart and helping-others, and I told her how very much I appreciated it (and actually I did), letting her have all the goodness-of-heart she damned pleased, but I wasn't about to eat any of that stuff.

I couldn't put it in the hotel garbage, because Rudolph, who collects garbage for the city twice a week, is her brother-in-law (James tells me these things). He might see it and tell her I didn't eat it. So I poured it in the commode in my bathroom and that stopped it up. When the plumber came—I hoped he wasn't kin to Mrs. Smorksky, but in a small town anybody can be somebody else's cousin—and had unplugged it, he came into my room and said, "Doc, you got that stomach flu real bad. Sick. Because nothing of what you ate got digested—none of it."

And Frank Sobotik brought me a half-gallon fruit jar full of a pink liquid. "Cactus juice. Make it myself. Squeeze it from the pears out. You take one cupful every three hours. Watch it by the clock—you got clock? It cured my aunt from her art-tritis."

They're good people, all. They're wonderful people—yes, I know. But I wish for now they'd leave me alone. They're kind and good and I'm sure they've heard about the baby—everybody certainly has by now, especially about such important people. And these gifts are, I'm sure, saying "It's all right, we're not blaming you." I know it and it's wonderful of them. But I wish they'd stay out of my bedroom and let me be sick in peace.

Then Mrs. Zapalac brought me a poppy-seed cake and sat and talked and talked an hour, telling me her troubles. It became all I could do to keep from using the bathroom. When she finally left, I layered a bunch of toilet tissue around my hand, just in case I did need a little more of that kind of expression, slid it into a pocket, went down to my car, and drove out into the timber country. (I don't have to worry about gas stamps, because M.J. says farmers don't use half of theirs and he takes extras out of their books.) Far out in the beautiful woods, far, toward Colony. I stopped beside an old iron bridge, high up over the small creek below.

I came down and sat under the bridge and watched the slow water. The trees gradually became alive, and the little grasses, and the tiny blossoms of plants right flat against the soil. *Nobody ever notices us,* they said.

It is their loss—you are lovely. But I confess I never knew you were there either.

We've always been here.

I'm sick, I said to them.

We know.

I don't mean the nausea and the stomach—

We know.

The next morning, at Pavlicek's Cozy Cafe, I sat down on one of the blue plastic-covered stools along the counter, next to Bohus Bartek. I'm sure he's heard about the baby. Sure everybody has—Kotzebue will see to that. Well, nothing for me to do but keep going, one foot in front of the other. Is there any other choice? I pretended not to see the small bowl of chili Bohus was spooning up. "Morning, Bohus." It's the cheapest thing you can order, twenty cents. The large bowl is thirty. "Nice cool morning. What brings you to town so early?"

"Peks," he said between slurps. He had both elbows on the counter and, leaning low with quick wrist movements, spooned food to his mouth. The left hand stuffed torn bread into his mouth with the same mechanical motion. The elbows never came off the counter.

"Pigs?"

Gulp. "Today is auction."

"Oh yes, Thursday. Guess there'll be a lot of people in town." To the waitress, "Usual." She smiled. Little Marie Darilek—no, Mrs. Kubenka. Now wears her wedding ring and is greatly pregnant. She'll have to quit here soon. Wonder if they'll be afraid to have me deliver it?

She leaned toward the kitchen between the plastic curtains, "Doctor's breakfast."

A loud voice answered—Cecelia's, she's always so loud, like she might be partially deaf—"I timed it yust right. Here it is."

Marie placed the large platter before me: four eggs, medium-fried bacon. She returned in a moment with a saucer stacked with toast and a cup of coffee with a small jug of cream perched against the cup. I felt embarrassed. This was the largest breakfast on the menu, and the most expensive—sixty-five cents.

I might have blushed, because I've been to Bohus's house—a cold night, one of the children sick, a high fever. They called me to come, explaining they feared taking him out in the cold could add pneumonia. (The word *pneumonia* often is almost synonymous with *die*.) And their house had no furniture—only beds, one table with two long benches, and a chair at each end. No icebox, no REA electricity. But everything perfectly clean.

But Bohus did not seem to notice as he tilted his bowl to scoop up the last spoonful, then took bread and mopped the bowl, wiping first around one way, then around the other. "So, I go auction." He belched.

"Lots of good luck, Boaty. Hope you get a good price."

"Is nize fat pek—I give planty corn."

"That's good."

Bohus just stood. I wondered what I could say to get him out and on his way.

"Ven I get home I must change me the shoes."

"What do you mean?" He's got farm shoes on now, big clodhoppers.

"Ven is valking around by auction barn, shoes pick op sickness from ground vere sick peks has been. From pek shits. Go home and no change shoes and go by pekpen and all peks get sick—die. Is cholera. Is sure bad think. All die. Ven get home, I change me the shoes to odder ones."

"I'll be dern. It's really picked up that easy and carried?"

"Yo. Is from ground from hog shits. Peoples is selling sick hogs. Maybe sometimes don't know hogs is sick. Maybe know."

He sucked air through his teeth, picked in his mouth with a finger, and told it all over again about walking at the auction barn and picking it up and carrying it home to his hogs and how he was going to change shoes.

He still stood there, like he was going to tell it again, so I said, "Well, thanks for telling me that—about how hog cholera is spread." And with real finality I added, "And also, Boaty, lots of good luck."

I avoided looking directly but saw Bohus at the cash register waiting for his change, taking a toothpick and letting it stick out of his mouth. Marie counted out silver into his stubby hand. He reached for the toothpick box and took another—maybe he forgot he already had one. But as Bohus went out the door, he tilted his head and began to dig the second one into his ear.

Cecelia Vinklarek, who cooks and scrubs and owns the place, came from the kitchen wiping her hands on a dish towel and tucked one corner of her apron into its belt. In that way it made a clean triangle instead of a spotty square—she always did this automatically when she came through the plastic curtains. She ran her hands through her hair and wiped them again and stood before me. "Mama she don't do so good on those tablets. Still don't eat good and her bowels—is all time same. Is two days now. Should she the blue capsule—on one end is blue, odder end white—she should keep taking?"

At the cash register, when I reached for my wallet Maria said, "Mr. Bartek already paid for yours."

"Bohus?"

"Yes."

"What?"

"He paid."

"Mine? For me?"

"Yes."

"Did he say why or anything?"

"No. He just paid."

In my mind the blue baby lay still on the tray. Maybe starting a hospital would help vindicate . . . Maybe a hospital where baby after baby would be delivered, born all right—hundreds of them—to make up— No, I must not always think about it. Guilt leads to more guilt, as if hatching its young. But what other things am I ignorant of?

❊❊❊

John's wife, Rosalita, phoned from a neighbor's. John's full name, by the way, is John Holy Word Estrada. They all have names like that: Jesus (Hay-sus) Holy Trinity, Xavier Blessed Mother . . . All the Estradas.

She asked could I come to the house. She has no way in because John's in jail—she had had to get the sheriff again. (Ralph Voght is called the sheriff, but he's only the local deputy.)

"Did he hurt you much this time? Is that it?"

"No, not so much. But it's the boy. Has a fever. He's too sick to take him out and lifting him and all. Will you come?"

It's a shack. The porch sags far on one corner like it will soon fall down. Can't John fix these things? It's theirs; they own it. But I doubt that it's paid for. And paint the place? I noticed there are no pots of flowers in old cans, as one sees at other Mexicans' houses—no matter how shanty or temporary the place may be, there are flowers, planted neatly in discarded cans and blooming. And strings up around the porch with morning glories twisting up. Here nothing—an old tire and trash.

Her left eye was purple and swollen almost shut. "Let me see." I pressed the lids open. "The eye itself is not damaged—be all right."

The boy—you know he's been this way since birth: the mouth always open, the drooling. (Birth defect it's called now, but the defect comes before birth, congenital.) He seemed about four, peered cross-eyed between the slats of a big homemade box of crate lumber. "Can he walk? Oh, I shouldn't have asked—not in front of him. I'm sorry."

"No, I lift him out, when I have time to watch. He crawls with the hands, the legs slide behind."

"Howdy, young fellow."

He turned his head away.

"Fever you say?"

"Always gets fever. Everytime when John beats me and he sees it"—I suppose I looked at her curiously—"next day fever. And coughing."

I reached into my bag. "John's such a handsome man. Ought to be in the movies."

"He's in jail. And that's where he ought to be."

The boy coughed and whined. I tousled his hair; his head felt hot. "Always after a . . . family fight, you say, he's sick?"

"He cry and trembling, shaking, and hides his face from it. And next day sick. At first I didn'tknow it. But now I see. After every time. Like he take the blame himself—on himself."

I turned to her so quickly she started. "Why? What's it?"

***

Rain. For two days. Steady. A good time to catch up: letters to answer, a few insurance claims to fill, lab reports to file, books and reprints to order if I get that far along. Margaret cleaned, sterilized, and rearranged. We could always stop anywhere in all this to see a patient. Or to talk a little. And we talked about and enjoyed things we hadn't had time really to notice when they happened. Like the day we had given each other our flu shots and then Thelma Ohnheiser went into labor. We leaned over her bed checking the foetal heart when Margaret happened to touch my arm and said, "You're warm," and stuck the thermometer in my mouth and I had a hundred and four temperature. "Only a reaction to the injection, you didn't feel badly you said. But you teased her, 'Move over, Thelma, I'm sicker than you are.' And it was such a pretty little boy."

I wondered if Margaret was trying to be nice to me . . . feeling sorry for me? Aw, I simply have to stop it. Make myself quit it.

She clattered things and had the water running. "And the porter from the railroad who insisted on tipping you a whole dollar right after you did the hysterectomy on his wife—and never paid a dime on the operation itself?" We laughed, probably some from fatigue.

"Listen to that lovely sound of rain . . ." Rain on the roof. Heavy rain. Washes the old dust away. Cleans. Renews. Thank you, rain.

She came back in the door again, hands dripping. "Hope Auntie Callie's roof's not leaking. I had never been in one of those . . . shantys. Not until you delivered the Jackson baby—Henry Jackson's, remember?"

"Certainly. But *we* delivered the Jackson baby."

She smiled more. "That had such a nice feeling there. *Heimish.* You took off your boots and went in your socks. The old uneven floors, covered with rugs—old worn rugs. Surely other people had thrown them away.

"The grandmother was there, keeping the children. And they say Auntie, like you call Auntie Callie; it sounds almost like *Tante. Tante,* but with more more . . . 'fireplace' in it. And the father kept playing with the three-year-old to keep her busy, otherwise she'd have been right in the middle, she was so curious of what was going on. And no screaming or putting-on through all the pains. All so nice. Such a warmhearted home."

"I enjoyed it, too—usually do. In fact I've often felt we should thank people. For letting us share in—" I answered the phone.

The operator, Mrs. Harmann, said somebody from High Hill had tried to call in. She could hear the party clearly but something must be wrong with the line again because they could not hear her. So they never gave her the number they wanted. However, the last time the party tried they said something to another person there about having to get the doctor right away. So she'd ask us first.

"High Hill? Margaret, who might be calling us from High Hill?"

"Let's think. Maybe the Frank Kobzas . . . baby. Yes, it's due." I took the regular bag and Margaret brought the second, the OB one that she keeps always perfectly ready.

The road was slippery soft, the car slid, and I tried to stay in the middle. It was still raining. Within sight of the Kobza's old rock house on the hill, the car slid into the right ditch. I buzzed and buzzed. We were stuck. I tried forward and tried reverse—and buzzed.

The rain let up a bit and Margaret said, "They're waving a sheet out of the attic window."

There it waved, a white sheet flapping fast. We jerked off our shoes and socks, and I rolled my pants up to the knees. I snatched a bag under each arm and with white bare feet began to run through the rain and the oozy black earth and rows of knee-high pale green corn. Margaret, barefoot, held her white shirt high. "We'll be so muddy, and they always have everything so scrubbed clean," she breathed.

We sprinted through the knee-high meadow grass, which cleaned all the black mud off perfectly, and into the house. A woman held the door open, saying "Hurry. In there." We were only minutes ahead of the baby. By holding the head back and up, I probably did keep the mother from tearing. It was a lusty boy.

As we were finishing and cleaning up, Margaret said close to my ear in German, "This must be the first time you delivered barefoot and with the hat still on."

Two large men came in from the barn, covered with white dust, for shucking corn is rainy-weather work. "We hear it. You sitting too much by the axle and turning too much by the wheels, so we hitched you up the mules."

"It's a boy," I said to the solidly built men. Their heavy shoes klumped the floor like giants walking. Remembering my rolled-up pants and soft, white, naked feet, I stood closer to the bed.

"Yass, yass, is good. Now, how many is it, mama?" The patient wiped sweat off her upper lip by pulling a finger across it and opened her mouth to speak. "Six boys now and seven girls," he continued. "Next year is maybe even."

Both men looked down at my feet. I wished they'd stop it. I stood closer against the bed and said quickly, "The baby weighs eight pounds and nine ounces." Both big fellows—husky, rough men—still looked at my feet.

"Yass, yass. Is good. You through now? Is all finished?"

"Yes. Everything all packed. When you have a name for him, come tell me because I must put it on the birth certificate."

"Yass, we do. When raining stop. Now you rady?"

"Yes. That's every— Hey, whatcha doing! Put me down! Hey!" The big men had stooped down and, each hugging a leg, lifted me up on their shoulders.

"We carry you to wagon. Is rady. Wagon go to car. Carry you to car. Is dry feets."

"Oh, that's all right. I don't mind a little mud—hey—" I had to duck way down as they, laughing, carried me through the door not realizing they almost knocked my head off. I felt ridiculous being carried and Margaret walking behind, barefoot, with both cases. They set me up on the wagon seat where another big man, also covered with corn dust, held the reins. They climbed into the wagon, behind us.

"Gidd-op! Ho!" The reins slapped the mules' fat backs. They switched their tails, farted enormously, and the wagon rolled forward.

At the car they carried me again while the third man unhitched the mules from the wagon, tied them to the bumper of the car, and pulled it out of the ditch and all the way back to the gravel road.

Driving slowly along the highway with the wiper going swish-swish, swish-swish, I simply had to relive it: "See Margaret? I tal you: Is nuddin. We yoost laft you oop and carry. Then sit you in car down. See? Is dry feets." We laughed and laughed. "Oh, those wonderful, goodhearted, knuckleheaded, clabberbrained Bohunks. I'm glad . . . grateful . . ." I became suddenly serious. "So glad I've become part of them. I'm thankful to them." They know about the baby—the other one. Surely everybody knows about it. Won't I ever forget it?

A few days later the same three Kobza men stood in a row in the office, wearing old-fashioned suits with vests, which smelled of moth balls, and hats too small which sat tall on top of their heads. This time I stayed suspicious of that jubilant good cheer radiating from all three. Have they been drinking? No, because they don't do things by small degrees: If they had been drinking, they'd be really drunk—hollering, singing, staggering, loving everybody, or fighting.

"We pick it name for baby and ask priest is all right and he say is Ho-K."

"Fine. I'll write it in."

"Xavier Gene Kobza. After you."

***

I doubted Margaret would ever bring it up, so I asked, "What is Kotzebue saying about the baby?"

"Which baby?"

"Oh, come on."

"Him! He tried everything he could. Said all kinds of ugly things, tried to find out more at the hospital and—I have this straight from the anesthetist—nobody'd talk about it. He tried to act like something was wrong."

"Well . . ."

"Even went to the Herziks'."

"Oh, God."

"Not the young couple—the older ones. Said it served them right for using such an unexperienced doctor. They said it could have happened anywhere."

"Such a wonderful people—"

"But when he went to Knabels', she told him theirs was sadness enough without his making it more for them, and Mr. Knabel threatened to put the shotgun on him if he didn't leave."

I shook my head.

"Kotzebue stopped taking the daily paper from one of the Herzik boys."

"It's so terrible. Hurts everybody. I'm so sorry."

"Threatened to get his shotgun if he didn't leave. He left, saying they should never call him in the night. Mr. Knabel said he wouldn't call him in the night nor daytime either."

"Gosh, I'm sorry."

"He's impossible."

"What about Mrs.—there must be a Mrs. Kotzebue, isn't there? I never see or hear of her."

"That poor thing. No one sees her. They keep her in all the time. Sometimes they let her walk around under the pecan trees on sunny days, but they watch her. They seldom let her out. She's insane."

"What?"

"For years. He won't send her to the asylum; keeps people with her around the clock. She did get away twice—once with no clothes on, nothing. They never leave her alone. Ever."

"Gosh. How'd it happen?"

"Oh it's too terrible to talk about. Nobody does. Poor thing. I don't want to talk about it." Her eyes became very shiny. She went into the examining room and blew her nose.

That evening late, I asked James.

"Began right after she had the baby, a girl. A few days later, they found her in the kitchen "cleaning" the baby with the butcher knife. They never left her alone with the baby again. He built a house next door and his mother moved there and she sort of raised the baby. A girl—she and Margaret went to school together. Lives in San Antonio, if you can call it living. She's a drunkard. He still pays her bad checks, fines, has lawyers get her out of jail. I think the girl hates her father, blames him somehow for her mother, and would do anything to hurt him, even kill herself if she thought it would hurt him bad enough. Well, that's what she is doing slowly."

❋❋❋

One of those waiting was Mrs. Bronecky. I wanted to watch that the pterygia were not growing back over her eyes yet. She sat alone, no granddaughter to lead her around. She entered smiling and held out a package in a crinkled paper sack, probably saved over from the grocery store. I took out something in a white cloth, unfolded that, and saw a glass dish. A yellow cooked cheese, sprinkled throughout with tiny canoe-shaped caraway seeds (reminding me of microscopic enlargements of Doderlein's bacillus). "Um," I inhaled. "Koch Kaese. I haven't had any since I'm—since boyhood. Thank you, Maminko, so very much."

"I tell the young ones: The doktor no having the cheese, eating always by cafe in town. I take it him. Is all right?"

"Is wonderful. I don't know how to thank you."

"But no. Is me. I so belonging to you that I can see to make it, and do not burn the fingers for feeling, and can see ven stirring in the pan and not slop out. Yes. *Pani doktor.* I now do all the things I did ven my husband be alive. Gone many years. Ven he dies, my seeing is dying same time. Now I go see his grave and plant roses—he like it always roses, pink ones."

As soon as she left, Margaret stuck a strip of adhesive to the bowl and wrote "Bohuslav Bronecky" on it. "So we can keep some of these plates and bowls straight." She placed it in the icebox, with the smallpox vaccines and typhoid and tetanus . . .

***

And there come again the days when it seems nothing is happening, but happening fast and routinely. Busy, uninterestingly empty days. Moments and days of nothing but fibrous tissue, connecting the last important time to some future one. "Connective tissue" days, simply nothing but fibrous connective tissue, unmemorable as a drink of water. Days of little color, mostly gray. And yet one knows how valuable each day is, each a heartbeat of life—the very pulse of it.

"One tablet before each meal. One, three times a day. For three days. On the third day the infection should be better. And you will feel all right again."

I seem to be saying that so often.

Even when I'm not sure what they've got, I'm saying it—like with a mere slight sore throat, which could, after all, be the onset of polio or acute leukemia or Hodgkin's or some such hideous all-out choice. So there I am saying it with pontifical certainty: "And on the third day you [like the heavens are going to open and shine down] will be well again." All the while hoping to hell I'm right.

And, a strange thing, sometimes they answer, "Yes, father." But they don't seem to be aware that they call me that.

I do remember one who certainly did not. Her boy had a sore throat and runny nose and red eyes, and in his mouth I saw the "diagnostic sign of measles." It's a tiny white dot surrounded by bright red, just above the first lower molar. It's called a Koplik's spot. They're described in every textbook on medicine. They're not always there, hard to see if they are, and when you do see one, is it a Koplik's spot? And if so, how can you tell? Like so many things in medicine.

So in all my professional wisdom I pronounced, "This boy has measles. In three days he will break out in the rash and you'll see it. In the meantime give him this sulfathiozole and he'll have less chance of the complications—pneumonia or ear infections or 'brain-fever' or any of those."

"In three days? Yes? He get the measles?"

"Definitely." I know it's a Koplik's spot, a real beauty. I think it is.

"You vun gut doktor ven you can tell it measles is coming in three days. You can tell it measles already before it comes measles. Vat vunderful news."

And they gave him the tablets—too big to swallow—ground up and mixed with jelly or honey as I suggested and kept him out of school and the room always dark, to protect the eyes.

And on the third day he did not break out with measles. Nothing. Still had a sore throat, coughing, red eyes . . .

If a disease could have laughed at me, this one would have.

Really, I could have sworn that actually was a Koplik's spot.

They bundled that kid up in blankets against the cool spring day—a slight norther—got the car heater going good first, and gave him hot tea to drink so he wouldn't get chilled on the trip. They were "taking him to horspittle and gut doktor vat don't talk foolish about Koplik measles in the mouth. Is measles and three-day measles and German measles and all is outside. Now measles vat is only in mouth? No." And they got in the car and drove; and past the edge of town the boy's forehead spotted red; and at County Line his whole face and neck; and near Mettlebach's Store it broke out over his chest and they turned around then at the store and drove back and phoned me again. "Now is measles outside. How doktor knowing it is measles inside for three days first? Is new kind? Koplik?"

❋❋❋

It was late. I dropped Margaret at her gate, and now I wanted to get to bed and sleep and sleep for at least one whole day. As I snapped the light on in my room the phone rang simultaneously. Them again: those Salases and Estradas. So I had to go back.

Blood. My God, how do they keep from killing each other? You sew and sew, although I've never yet seen an opening into a lung cavity or into the abdomen, or a biceps cut in two, or tendons sliced across. Nor a real-sized artery cut. It's all skin and subcutaneous. It's almost impossible to do this much cutting on each other and never get into something vital. Sometimes I think there's a fine art involved here—don't cut deep, cut often and plentifully, but keep your opponent alive. Don't really hurt him, aggravate him. Make him bleed. "Damn I wish you fellows didn't have to fight all the time."

There was so much of it all, I got to where I could recognize the different techniques. For example, Felipe Estrada always made several small cuts in a row. I could clean a Salas chest and say, "Oh, Felipe cut you." Whereas Julio Estrada, Felipe's cousin, used long single sweeps, sometimes forty-two or forty-five stitches in a row. But his best work was done on Eulogio Salas one Saturday night—or rather Easter Sunday morning—with the longest single cut of them all: It began under Eulogio's left armpit, crossed the chest, went around the right kidney, the back, over the left kidney, left hip, back to the lower left abdomen almost at the navel. One hundred eighteen stitches. And I could have put lots more in, closer, but I got tired. If it had been deep enough, it would have cut his top half off from his bottom half. "Whatever were you doing, Eulogio? Looks like he stuck a knife in you while you were twirling, doing a ballet." Pete's signature is short stabs, deeper than cuts. They worry me—someday it's going to be such a stab in somebody's heart, and I'll be having to crack ribs loose and open pericardium and be trying to put a stitch in somebody's beating heart, not only to save him but to keep Pete's life out of prison.

God! I hope . . .

I didn't say a word to Pete, and he didn't say anything to me.

Just took his shirt off.

Small cut under right scapula. I put in a short running subcutaneous; two and a half, three inches long. Bandaged.

Not much this time, but what will it be next time?

He put his ripped shirt on, and left.

We hadn't said a word.

***

"Clarice, why hello, haven't seen you in so long. How are you? And how is the little daughter in San Antonio?"

"Up to Sunday—last Sunday they come—up to then I'm studyin' I ain't never goin' go see my girl again. Just knowed it so. They writin' nice and sendin' checks and money orders, sho' nice, but up to Sunday I'm cryin' and wishin' I ought'nta done it and all. Oh, she so pretty. And they so nice too—good people. They ain't gonna let her forget I her mama and birthed her. I couldn't wish for 'em to be no nicer folks." Tears suddenly came dripping fast. She nodded her head up and down and I waited, decided I should be saying something.

"I'm so happy for you, Clarice. I think you did the very best thing. Proud of you. Ain't easy, I'm sure."

"This last Sunday I'm thinkin' everything bad. For long time. Everythin' I do, Dr. Shoots, come somethin' bad. Everythin' turned bad on me. And I do a little bleedin'—irreg'lar. My friend he say I gotta go see. He say he don't think it him doin' it. He made me come see."

"Oh? How long you been knowing him?"

"Only a week."

"And the bleeding? How long?"

"Noticed that first maybe las' month. Wasn't much. I think maybe it war a little somethin' and he doin' it more—make it bleed more. A little somethin'; ain't nothin'. But he say we oughta be sure."

"He sounds sensible."

"Oh he sho' nice. Nicest man I ever knowed. Reg'lar job, too. Work at Eastern Seed—long time—do they haulin'. But I jest knowed him 'bout a week but he said it. For me to come git myself examined. Yes suh, nicest man I ever knowed yet. Maybe onliest man I ever did know."

"Sounds almost too good to be true, afraid to believe it."

And it was exactly as I feared: I inserted the duckbill speculum and simply by opening it caused a bleeding of the cancerous nodules. There on the cervix. In an old tear that had not been repaired. Cancer!

How am I ever going to tell her this?

"Looks like a little something growing here. Here is a little piece I can burn off easy. I'll send it to the lab in Galveston."

"What is it? Kinda somethin' like proud flesh?"

"Yes, you might say it's kinda like that." Margaret held the biopsy tube ready. Even with the small cutting and the cautery—and only one of the cluster of nodules—yet the bleeding seemed to insist and insist, determined to have its say. Finally I packed the vagina with gauze, telling her to leave it in overnight. I wanted to add: Don't let the new boy friend, Gordon, take it out tonight, but couldn't say it in the face of this malignancy.

I can't tell her. Taking this biopsy will give me a little time—that's all the good it's doing—so obviously malignant. Maybe I can think up the best way to do it—gotta tell her someday, somehow. The small piece of tissue, pea sized, floated in the tube. With so much clustered already, it's probably far past deep X-ray therapy and surgery. Too metastasized inside.

Margaret, who keeps all empty boxes—has one every size—while packing the biopsy tube said, "I'll bet it's the same as poor Mrs. Koricanek."

Mrs. Koricanek—her husband owns the lumber yard—also had started the same way, but she came early, with the first unusual sign of bleeding. I sent her on to Galveston for the biopsy, which proved malignant (scirrhous carcinoma, grade I). They immediately used deep X ray, then performed a total hysterectomy, and felt almost absolutely assured they had caught it all.

Less than a month later she noticed a "knot" in her left breast. I feared it would prove to be a metastasis from the original cancer—unless it proved to be nothing more than a benign cyst. It was a malignancy, but an entirely new one, with *no* relationship to the first—uterine—cancer at all! From entirely different tissue. A second original malignancy! (Adenocarcinoma, grade II.)

So they removed the breast. Did a radical, just to make certain they had it all. And they felt convinced they did and told her so in very certain terms.

Amazing. To have two separate malignancies all in a short time practically made medical history.

About a month after she's home from the hospital, she's walking across the living room and falls. A broken leg. Did not trip or stumble—nothing. Just fell flat with a broken-R leg, femur, above the knee.

We X-rayed it at the hospital, Mr. Koricanek again saying he wanted "the best of everything for my wife—don't spare no expenses," and I'm holding the wet, black pictures, ready to tell him she has to go back to Galveston. A bone cancer, which is the most vicious and the fastest of all, osteosarcoma, grade III.

Three new, entirely different separate sources of cancer. All in a short time. The last the most virulent known.

I read the report on Clarice from Galveston—malignancy, cervical tissue epithelium, (adenocarcinoma grade III)—and dropped it on the desk. I phoned Eastern Seed Company, asked them to send Gordon to my office after work. He came right on over and I told him, thinking he could prepare her for it best. Or he could bring her to the office and I'd tell her with him present.

How I dread all this. Poor woman's had nothing in her life, and now that's going to be taken too. And taken slowly and despairingly, and the children will have to watch her slowly die . . . God! And I've got to tell her.

They came. But instead of a shy troubled Clarice being told she had "a bad thing, I'm sorry to say," a different Clarice said, "You mean cancer. You told Gordon that and he told me, but I know it ain't. Ain't no disrespectin' you, Dr. Shoots, you been nice to me. But ain't nothing like that in me. I ain't saying it's not a little somethin' there—sho', bound to be. Maybe a little proud flesh cause it bleed a little. Like you say, from a torn place birthin' the children. He say you want me to go to Galveston and they cut my womb out and all that, but ain't no need—nothing like that."

"Clarice, you have to. There still might be time."

"No, Dr. Shoots, ain't nothin' like that. Not to cut you off, but I ain't goin'." She wrapped both arms around one of Gordon's. I knew it to be hopeless, that I needn't even try anymore. She wasn't going to leave Gordon even for a week, much less for months. The whole thing was hopeless anyway, so maybe it was best: Let her have a month or two of total happiness, and then . . . At least that's better than sending her on now and her having nothing at all.

And that's the way it became.

They lived together—so we heard. She came for no checkup of any kind. It's not something I cared to remember anyway, and I must confess I forgot about it after some time and some hundreds—thousands—of other people. And would probably never have seen or thought about it again. Except:

How many months had it been—two?—since we sent the biopsy in? Four? Six? And here's Clarice, stouter, nicely dressed, all her children in neat school clothes, shoes, and one with a fishhook through his ear.

"Ear?"

"From playin'. Like boys, careless. Gordon gonna strop a few when he come. No use boys actin' childish and careless. He don't want 'em gettin' theyself hurt actin' foolish."

It was here that I remembered. And Clarice, looking healthier than I had ever known her, simply did not look like a cancer patient. I told her I had to examine her.

"I didn't come for no examinin' on me. You done fixed his ear—cut the hook out."

"No, have to give tetanus yet and test him for it first. Examine you while we're waiting for the skin test to show."

"Don't wanna make no big bills for Gordon. He don't say nothin', but dat's enough 'bout the ear."

"Won't charge a thing. I'm curious. Margaret, get her up for a vaginal."

And there is her cervix, pink and healthy. And there is the old tear and not a nodule nor pimple anywhere, and not a drop of blood. On exam I could feel nothing but normal tissue in normal positions. "It's gone," I said.

"Sho, it heal up fine."

❋❋❋

I had never been to their house before. A neighbor, August Bohac, phoned and gave the directions. I had heard of them. Two old sisters who lived alone way out there. With their dogs. Out on the prairie past Freyburg—the open, windy prairie.

I drove along to their place—fence falling down, beautiful high wild pasture grass (means no cattle have grazed here for years), abandoned fields growing thick with dry-land willows. Even from a distance the house and barns seemed deserted, sequestered. No paint, a shed half-fallen, barn doors hanging, tin roofs rusty, some sheets of roof missing and laying crinkled against a fence, dead hackberry trees full of dry mistletoe wilted straight down . . . As I drove up to the house, the lines and proportions of it said it had once been a beautiful place. Now it was tumbledown, neglected. And here came the dogs. Many, maybe fifty. More kept coming. All barking. Never saw so many.

I drove up to the back door—one always goes in the back or side door. No yard fence here. Front doors are seldom used—only funerals, before there were funeral parlors. Long ago they were also used for weddings and their formal receptions. One could see it had once been a magnificent house. I stepped out of the car, but the dogs made clear I wasn't to go any further. I slammed the car door, using it as a signal or call over the barking.

A voice somewhere in the kitchen part of the house called, "*Aht!*" and the dogs quieted—except two or three. "*Aht!*" again, and these quieted, too.

See, stupids? I'm supposed to be here.

I thought it to a big white beast who had been one of the snarliest. Now his hair gradually began going back down on his neck, but he did something with his lips. Not exactly a snarl, more a *Necht*! Two little black puppies came up cowering, crawling, wiggling themselves like silly, looking up, blinking. I patted both and they fell all over themselves and squirted urine without control.

I stepped up the shaky kitchen steps, ducked around some things hanging on the porch—dingy things, like they had been washed without soap—walked around a hole of missing boards, called "Hello?" through the rusty screen door, which had no screen left in the bottom half. "Hello?" I walked into the cool dark room with half of the dogs following. An old woman with straggly white hair that looked unwashed and uncombed, wearing an overcoat—in this hot weather—sat beside a wood stove, no fire, holding a can with a spoon in it.

"*Guten Tag,*" I came with my hand out.

"*Aht!*" she screamed, and the dogs scratched the linoleum all getting out at once. I noticed opened cans setting on the stove, on the floor, on the table, on chairs—everything filthy. She ignored my hand, waved toward the other end of the kitchen, and spooned something out of the can into her mouth.

I looked toward the other part of the room, not expecting to see a bed there and especially not expecting to see what looked like the sister, dead—except the skinny chest kept breathing. I found almost no pressure, the heart fluttering in irregular fibrillation. Edema—pitting—puffed the skin over the bony hips and up her back. The gown she wore had brown smears, and the bed had not been changed in days or weeks. Her lips, ears, fingers, and feet—dirty—had that blue-ashes color. The woman lay not fully conscious, but she looked at me, her mouth open, dry.

"She needs to be in a hospital—oxygen, nurses—"

The sitting woman shook her head no and continued eating out of the can.

"But she dies," I continued in German.

She kept spooning—looked like canned applesauce.

"Her heart—it is tired. Very weak."

No response. Does she hear me. I spoke louder. "The heart. Worn. Weak. It gives away. Soon."

I know she heard me.

"Is she Catholic?"

"Ha?" asked the toothless mouth.

"She dies. Is she Catholic?—the last sacraments?" Germans here are usually Lutheran, but not always. I saw no crucifixes on the dark walls.

She dropped the spoon into the can long enough to wave a finger No.

"Is there someone I should call? Relatives? Pastor?"

She kept on eating.

"There's not much I can do. Here. I gave her an injection. But it's only a temporary stimulant."

She set the can aside. I knew she heard me, but she didn't answer.

"*Wie lange?*" she asked.

"How long? Will she live? She dies before morning."

This didn't seem to be any sort of news to her. She reached down under her chair and brought up a fat, bulgy handbag, black, worn at the corners. "*Wieviel?*"

"Make it twelve dollars." I had seen when she reached down that her legs bulged, wrapped in old rags. Probably varicose ulcers, open. "Is there something you'd like for me to do? For your legs?"

She shook no and unsnapped the bag open. It gapped, stuffed full of rolls of money. I saw fifties and twenties on some rolls. She carefully handed me two fives and two ones, shaking the curl out of them.

"*Danke*. But your legs—wouldn't you like for me to do something? I have plenty new bandage. And check *your* heart?"

She turned the white hair no.

"Should I ask the neighbor—the one who phoned—to sit tonight?"

She ran her tongue around in her mouth, swallowed something, and said in precise German, "I shall call—when there is need," and looked at me like, Well what are you hanging around for, you've been paid, haven't you?

As I started out the door all the dogs charged at me, led by the big white one.

"*Aht!*"

They cowered back and let me walk to the car. But the moment I was inside it they charged and jumped and barked and snarled at me to get the hell out and never come back. A black one kept bouncing straight up, as if he couldn't see enough from back there.

The funeral started up a lot of stories again—about the family's deterioration; about the old sisters having huge amounts of money in many banks; how they never wrote a check and probably had even forgotten they had "five thousand" in this bank, "ten thousand" in that one, "twenty thousand" in another; how the old house would someday be like an Easter-egg hunt with cans full of money hidden everywhere. And now just the one crazy old girl out there with all those dogs. It was said that people ought never to live like that, with so much money in the house. It was asking to get murdered for it, but that's why they had kept so many dogs—nobody could get close to that house. And not going to her sister's funeral! Now that was more than . . . Living together all those years and then not go to her own sister's funeral—and such a pretty funeral, so expensive. And they said Marvin had to soak the body overnight to get the filth off it. But not going to her own sister's funeral! And all that money!

The time seemed so short, like a few days, but it must have been at least a month. The neighbor phoned:

"This is Oou-gust."

"Which August?"

"Bo-hac. By the old vomans? Vere you vas? Vit all the dogs?"

"Oh yes, yes. August. Are you with sickness now?"

"No. Is not for us I'm calling. Don't put me down in books. Is old voman."

"Yes, yes. Is she sick?" I remembered the legs wrapped thick with rags.

"Ve don't know. Her vindmill—it don't run now for four days."

"Oh. Can you go see? Ask her?"

"No. Is dogs. Like crazy is dogs."

"Oh yes. Well look, August: I'll get the deputy, Voght, and we'll go. He can manage dogs—he'll do it. We'll take care of it. Thank you for—"

"Ve go to house yesterday, my vife and me in pickup. But dogs von't let us get down. Ve call Hello but no answer."

"Okay, August, I'll call Voght and we'll—"

"And again ve go this morning and still is nobody saying something to dogs and ve Hello and blow the horn and is nothing."

"Okay. I'll get Voght—"

"Today is fourt. My vife she had it some fresh bread and eggs-noodles soup, but can't get down from the dogs."

"Yes, I know. Okay now. Thank you and good-by." I hung up quick. That old woman sick, probably too weak to answer. Or unconscious. I'll take Coramine ampules, intravenous aminophylline. Or broke a hip? Morphine. Let's see—what else? And Ralph will be the very man for this dog situation. Everybody knows he always takes strays home and feeds them (and any boy in town who wants a dog can come take his pick). Always does. Maybe he's reliving his own boyhood with it. And stray dogs almost seem to seek him out, let him see them. And the next thing he's feeding them and they're starting to trust him.

Ralph did have to shoot in the air, twice. Gentle as he is with dogs, he's killed at least two people over the years—both times while trying to arrest a person. They were drunk, crazed, and attacked him and he shot them. Once he shot a "timber" man under the same situation—while arresting—and the bullet hit the sternum, veered around a rib all under the skin, and came out the back. The man lay in a hospital for weeks. Someone in the sheriff's office then gave Ralph hollow-nosed bullets, saying, "Next time you shoot some sonnovabitch in the belly, he ain't gonna make the county no hospital bills and tell everybody he wasn't drunk and . . ." And that's what Ralph uses now all the time.

He shot into the air. Twice. And it did the trick. We went up the rickety steps, and we knew before we got into the house.

That odor!

"She must be dead for days—whew! Let's look in the kitchen first. I think they lived entirely in there." As we came in, some dogs—three or four—jumped down off the bed and, slinking, circled us widely. She lay in the bed—God!

The flesh lay torn, eaten off her face; her scalp hung pulled loose to one side and lay like a dirty white wig, her skull bald. The muscle, tissues, scratched, eaten, all off one arm and one leg—the bone exposed. And the quilt torn, blood-smeared and muddy-dirty.

"Good God!"

Ralph, looking closely at the skull face, throat, chest, said nothing.

"This is sickening." She lay looking at the ceiling and sort of as if laughing. "Terrible."

"Yes," he answered. "And they haven't had any water or food."

He's not always that considerate of people. James told me the last time John Estrada and his wife had a big fight, she ran to the deputy's house and woke him calling from the gate, the dogs all barking. He said, "Oh, it's you again. I wish he *would* kill you—then I'd be rid of you both! Wait there till I get dressed."

"But what are you going to do with all these dogs?"

"I'll come feed them every day; they'll keep prowlers off. Till they locate heirs. I'll call the sheriff. Need the cor'ner for this." Don't know why he never learned to say *coroner.*

The stench, the filth, a bloated dead black puppy . . .

To the big white one, I said, I'm disgusted with you! Didn't know you dogs would eat on your own masters—mistress.

He walked around big like he wasn't ashamed of anything. "It's disgusting."

"Were used to being fed by 'em," Ralph said. He closed the porch window and the door. As we came down the shaky steps we could see the Bohac pickup coming, far off.

Ralph unhooked the windmill brake, and right away the tail swung around with the breeze, the fan wheel began turning, and we heard water falling down into the empty cistern. Under a faucet lay an old iron oven door for a bowl. He opened the faucet and it began to drip, and dogs came, licking at the falling drops but watching up at him. And more came, and they crowded ever closer to him. Except Big White. Acted disdainful, as if not thirsty at all.

❋❋❋

Timber people often said it of themselves, and it did seem true.

"Us sand folk don't take to sickness much as black-landers do."

But the Tatums called. The Nicely Tatums. Mr. Tatum himself had spoken over the phone. It's usually the neighbor who owns the phone who does the talking, secondhand. So maybe this would be different.

The fence and the gate and the shanty all said no, it's the same. I saw no phone wire and, of course, no other wires—never are. But actually there did appear to be some small differences. Among the usual trash strewn about the house lay more shining new cans—ah, a sign of sheer prosperity. Maybe I will be paid a dollar or two. And what struck me more: a hog pen *fenced*. Not what any German or Bohemian would call a fence—just old boards nailed unevenly and tied together. But timber people's hogs are not kept in pens at all. They are marked with certain ear cuts and left to roam the timber for acorns and roots. These boards connected the house and an outdoor privy (with no door) to make them part of the hog fence. A privy! The first privy I'd seen anywhere in timber country. Oh. Now I saw the hogs rooting behind the privy, into the human— Do hogs *eat* that? Apparently they do. Eat anything.

The man himself stood in the door.

"Good morning, Mr. Tatum. Who's sick?"

"Grandpa. Only doing tolerable. Thought you'd best take a look 'fore hit's anything bad." Limping up behind Mr. Nicely stood a young man with an enormous open harelip, the cleft extending up into his left nostril. "Burt here been taking care of 'im day and night." Burt, a rag in one hand and a worn bar of soap in the other, grinned widely, showing the cleft with missing teeth and gums—a classic case. (Later, when I described the condition to James—how there's simply a missing cleavage there with no gum, teeth, lip—simply an open division—James said, "Burt's an inbreed. From the old man and his oldest daughter. Feebleminded. They also had an albino one, but he died.") "Burt, show the doctor."

I followed Burt's limp into the second room, but couldn't understand what he said—maybe "I'm giving him a bath." On a cot lay a skeletoned old man with white matted hair and beard, naked, sores all over him—no, only over pressure points: heels, ankles, elbows, shoulder blades, hipbones . . . Seeing me, his eyes flared wide. He struggled up on one elbow, reaching out toward me, grabbing. "Don't let them do it. Please help me, don't let them."

"Do what, grandpa?" His hand—a bundle of bones—had wormed and fastened itself onto my shirt. I noticed that all the sores were secondarily infected.

"No, please, don't let 'em. Not that."

"Sometimes he talks a little outa his head," Mr. Tatum spoke from the first room, watching.

"I ain't neither talking outa my head. You said you'd do it. Say it alla time. Don't let them do that to me." His arm trembled with weakness.

"Do what, grandpa? Here, lie back down." I took his pressure and listened to heart and lungs. He smelled ugly. Not like the odor of a disease, no single particular disease, but an odor of ugly—the infected sores, the filthy mattress. Maybe it is an odor of fear.

"Is his sores festered? Burt washes 'em most every day."

"Very infected."

"Don't let 'im. They gonna feed me to the hogs!"

"Goodness, grandpa. No one would do anything like that. Please calm your—" The bony hand dug deeper into my stomach.

"Oh they would too. Say it alla time. They gonna throw me to the hogs."

The hogs grunted, standing just below the window looking up, as if waiting. Burt kept dabbing the rag at the sores.

"No they wouldn't."

"Oh yes they will. Don't let 'em," his voice quavered.

"We have to clean up these sores and *keep* them clean. Plain rubbing alcohol—it'll burn a bit—but that'll keep them okay in the future. Put it on every day, Burt. Once or oftener every day."

He answered something. "He'll drink it up."

"Well, simply keep it out of his reach. He's too weak to get up and find it."

Burt said nothing, but his eyes turned to Mr. Tatum.

"Oh. Oh. I see," Not as feebleminded as they said. "Well then, Merthiolate. That'll do it. Cost a little more, but *nobody* can drink that."

"Don't let 'im do it. They will. They did it afore. With the other one—"

"Shut up! Such crazy talk! You know it ain't so."

"Is so too. I seen it—seen a leg and foot. War it awright."

"Shut up!"

His beardy voice turned toward me, "Heard 'em crunchin' on the bones for two whole days."

"He talks crazy sometimes, doctor. Don't pay him no mind."

"Tain't crazy. They want you to keep me alive so as they get my check."

"You can refuse to sign it," I said, for some reason.

"They put the *x* on it theirselves and take it to town. They'll do it. The hogs'll eat me."

"I don't believe that, grandpa. Maybe they're just trying to scare you into staying alive. He needs vitamins and more foods, bananas and cooked cereals and thick broths. He must have these things."

"If nobody'd know I'm dead, they'll keep cashing the checks. And won't hafta do with me neither. They'll do it."

"Grandpa, you've worked yourself into thinking that. From your weakness. Nobody'd do such a thing."

"See? The doctor knows. Now jest shut up."

"I seed it. Leg and foot. Heard the bones."

"Grandpa, try to be relaxed, restful. Your eyesight's not too good—you saw *something*. And hogs do eat bones, any bones. Try not to worry yourself with disturbing thoughts. You need rest. I'll prescribe you a medicine to relax you."

The old man closed his eyes.

Mr. Tatum's voice. "How much that gonna cost?"

"With the Merthiolate and vitamins, only a few dollars."

Mr. Tatum grunted.

Grandpa opened his eyes; he did not look at me.

"You can live a long time yet, grandpa. Your heart is still strong."

His face lay relaxed, more smooth, less wrinkly around the eyes. The look of fear seemed to be gone. Maybe he's responding to my words already.

The eyes looked right into mine. "Make 'em wait." Even his voice sounded a bit stronger.

"Wait for what?"

"Don't let 'em do it. Make 'em wait until I'm dead."

***

"To be gone three days? Friday, Saturday and Sunday? You know how crowded Saturdays are."

I did not reply.

"*Aber* what shall I say? What will I tell them?"

"The truth. They can't object to me going to a medical convention—might learn something that's good for them. Besides, I have to go. Want to get away. Now that's the real truth."

The train schedule is very convenient—catch the ten-thirty night train Thursday and be checking into the Saint Charles in New Orleans at ten-thirty Friday morning. Registration, get your name pad. Lectures had already begun—easy to follow, lots of slides, a few tinted in colors. All fascinating. And except for main speakers, always a choice of two lectures—but you really wanted to hear both—into Friday night. And beginning at nine again, after breakfast.

At lunch. Talking back and forth across the long table—always beautiful service with silver containers, rich table cloths, huge linen napkins, waiters in tuxedo with a napkin on their arm, quietly efficient. One great lecture to discuss after another. This is a different world.

But I kept looking each man over, almost searching for something, someone. No, that one wouldn't do, and that one talked too much about cars, and that one's too young, too—looks a little scared or shy . . .

"Why does he call it Rh?"

"After the rhesus monkeys. First found it in them."

"I don't know. How does it sound to you?"

"They seem to have proved it," I answered. "Of course, now others will have to, too." No, I don't think he's the one I want. Wonder what I really do want? I keep looking . . . No, he's too elderly—respectable, nice, but too elderly . . .

"Well, I for one am going to use it from now on," said a young man probably my age but very direct and outspoken in his manner who sat directly across from me. I didn't want to stare at the name card on his lapel. I thought the stripes in his suit a little too wide—liked my pinstripe better. "I'm not going to give a transfusion in my hospital again without it, especially not to a woman—young woman." I can tell by how he holds his knife and fork—fistlike, Bohemian style—that he grew up poor. Did he say? . . .

"You have a hospital? That's great! Just too great! I think that's the finest thing a person can do, start a hospital. I wanted to. It's what Albert Schweitzer did. Only do it where it's needed, at home. But I sure can't afford that expense. Is there any chance . . . that one would pay its own way?"

Before I had finished asking he pointed at me with his knife. "Don't! Not unless you've got"—he peered at my card—"oil wells in Texas to support it. It'll soak up money faster."

His makeup is that of a real go-getter. Wish I could be like that, but I'm not. "Gosh."

"I'll sell mine right now, if I could get back what I've poured into the place, provided they'd let me use it. Then they'd have all the headaches plus the loss. I tell you straight, don't!"

Oh I wouldn't—no—no, not after the way he said it. Everybody hushed quiet, so quiet. A complete silence. "Well . . . And at one time I had seriously thought—considered . . . That's too bad. But thank you."

"I've got two rich old women who live in the place. All year round. They have nobody, no family. Without them—huh—I'd have to fold up. It's easy to bite off, start something, then you're stuck with it—have to work and work a lifetime to finish it."

"Thanks again. But congratulations—that you *did* it. That is the . . . greatest. I wish I could have . . ." I turned away, but now looked right at the fellow beside me. I added quickly, "But I have also thought about going into a residency."

"Now that's it." And several others nodded. "Specialty is the thing. More going into specializing all the time."

Yes, but a hospital would have . . .

A man farther down who had said nothing while we talked about the Rh factor now spoke up. "Know a surgeon who is pulling down fifty thousand a year." No, he's certainly not the friend I'd like to find. One I could confide to—confess to. Nobody answered him.

A fellow near me said, "Then we ought to test every OB. Test her and the husband both."

"Right. And I'm going to."

"What do you do if one is negative?"

There was half a moment of quiet. A lone voice said, "You anticipate." And we all laughed.

. . . one I could simply say to, I didn't know how to deliver a facedown breech—about bending the child up over the abdomen. How did I miss learning it in school? How? Did you learn it?

The words came without my thinking about them. "You could give the infant a transfusion, I believe, right after birth, couldn't you?"

"I never gave a newborn a transfusion."

"Me neither," I added.

"That would be through the ventricles," another said, touching the top of his head. Some nodded.

I guess it's good I came. This is another world. But I have lost my hospital. And to think I actually wanted, planned to start one. A man was saying, "Everything began going so nicely, the intestines all so relaxed and I'm cutting and sewing away. I did notice there wasn't much bleeding. I kept happily working away there for several minutes before it finally dawned on me I was operating on a dead man." The way everyone laughed—the burst release of anxiety in it all—told how each had worried over his surgery patients, too, how each had worried about his patient dying on the operating table. It's good to hear their talk and to hear of others' mistakes. Somehow it helps. Helps the listener and the one telling it. Maybe it is a confessional. It is good to hear the others, but my small hospital—gone.

I wiped my mouth with the rich napkin, and almost held it over my eyes. Dared not—I'd really start crying. In leaving, I walked beside the young hospital man and I had to say it—how I would have liked to start a small country hospital. Sometimes they grow—generations later—into a great hospital. All the big ones began small. It'd be a start—a seed—and then maybe it'd grow through the years, generations. Become big and host a research department. Maybe find a cure for polio and blood poisoning, save the arms and legs that have to be amputated today. Maybe a cure for cancer—why not? And in the meantime think of all the persons it could help.

"And yet . . . those small hospitals I know of—a few—owned by a doctor. He's buying farms, so even though the hospital is costing, it isn't breaking him." We came into the lecture hall now. "Well anyway," I sighed, "dreams do die, this one on the operating table. *X* off one more beautiful dream. But—gosh!"

Sunday morning, as I was going from one booth to the next, getting free samples and literature and seeing displays of artificial legs and arms with mannequins and with a live model—young woman with only one arm, smiling and slipping the arm on and moving the thumb, closed, open, slipping it off, smiling—someone tapped my shoulder. The man with the hospital who said "Don't start it," motioned me aside, alone. Not the kind of friend I had hoped to find.

"I've been looking everywhere for you. I couldn't tell you in front of them—two of them use my hospital and I don't want them to start their own. You go right ahead. A hospital will not only pay its way, it'll make more money than your practice. People today *believe* in hospitals when they don't believe in anything else. More than in their churches. Maybe it is today's church. Anyway, today people believe in colleges and hospitals. So do it. But now remember one thing: The expenses are exactly the same whether you have two patients in it or twenty-two. The same. That's the secret to make it pay: Keep it filled to capacity. Good luck, I know you'll do all right."

I stood there with both hands full of free samples. "Huh?" He was gone.

A Hospital–
Birth or Miscarriage?

"Who's going to run her rest home while you operate on her?"

"No idea. I told her she can't lift for six weeks after. I'm sure she's made arrangements."

I can't help but smile these days. Haven't told Margaret yet, but she suspects something the way she watches me. And she asked, "What happened in New Orleans? You're so cheerful since you're back. Did you meet a girl?"

All my thoughts seem to be happy ones since New Orleans. Even the thoughts while removing Mrs. Hodanek's gallbladder.

Fair, female, fat, forty. Fertile and flatulent.

It's a little rule of thumb.

About who is most likely to get gallbladder disease. They fitted Mrs. Hodanek perfectly. But it doesn't tell *why* this type of patient has tendencies to get this kind of disease, instead of kidney stones or pneumonia or some other pathosis. Only helps make the organic diagnosis. Mrs. Hodanek had said she had three children (fertile) and had complained of gas (flatulent) and belched big as if to prove it.

I hummed as I operated.

The scrub nurse held the retractors perfectly, giving me a constant view of the underside of the smooth dark-blue liver—a good field—and I peeled the gallbladder loose easily.

The nurses here at LaGrange Hospital are nice, as are those at Renger Hospital in Hallettsville. Twenty miles each in opposite directions from Schulenburg. Nurses from the country make excellent personnel. They are devoted, hard-working, consistent, reliable; and they stay with the same job, don't move around. And all of them are trusted with the keys to any drugs—couldn't do that in a big city. Will some nurses like that come work in our hospital? Surely they will.

Both hospitals were begun in an old home, a big house, and added to. It's good to have them. But it's forty miles round trip to either hospital. And sometimes I have patients in both places. Eighty miles takes so long to be out of the office, so I go in the evenings. Only trouble with that is, it gets too late. The patient usually has already had his bedtime medication, often sedatives, and is asleep or half-drowsy.

But with our own hospital . . .

That is, *if* I can buy the old Nordhausen mansion.

She'll be showing these stones to her friends and relatives. Roll them out on the dining room table like small dice and count them.

I slid the silver probe into the common duct—Okay, no stones there. All right, ready for covering the bed and closing. I whistled away through my mask.

Wonder what this symptom says? What is she saying about herself by growing her gallbladder full of small-faceted stones? If we could only translate this odd disease-condition language! Stones could connote—pure guessing—strength? Like, I need more strength to withstand my person-position?

Or is it saying anything at all.

I can remove the stones, but not the why-she-selected-to-have-them. If she did.

In any case, she should get nice results from this. If I can now keep her from overeating and away from fattening foods and worry and unsureness about herself and . . .

"How'd it go?" Margaret asked.

"Lovely, just lovely."

"You are walking on clouds. Hope you don't fall through."

She simply doesn't know. I ought to tell her, poor girl.

He said his hospital *made* money. But he's talking about himself and his ability. And he *is* a salesman—I'm not. Maybe it means mine could break even or not lose much. Okay, so here goes. "Doctor, you're whistling."

I did tell Margaret a short while later. And started making plans.

"But don't tell anybody—say I'm at one of the hospitals."

"Everybody'll know it's a lie," she said. "Everybody'll know where you'll be."

"How would they know? I've told absolutely nobody but you. You don't . . . do you?"

"Tell things? Don't you worry. And does it kill them at our card night. They know I know something and won't say a word; they could simply die."

"You sure? Then how would people know?"

"Oh, good heavens! John Cupik knows and told everybody; the tax assessor you asked there for Waldman's name and address—"

"How do *you* know these things?"

"You phoned long distance, and that Mrs. Harmann is the biggest gossip of them all. Why, everyone knows."

On Highway 90 to San Antonio, long army convoys, olive green, rolled along almost endless. One passed and got in between, and passed and got in between, and passed . . . All new. New uniforms, new trucks, new shoes, new thick black tires with heavy deep treads—what mighty moneys are spent on wars. And along the railroad, clacking sounds of boxcars beside you, faster, with the iron wheels under them.

There must be mountains of money spent on hate. Almost seems the world runs on it.

I watched boxcar after boxcar, endlessly flitting past. For a while could see neither the engines nor the caboose. Did it somehow remind me of something? Each passing, each carrying, one after the other, each from a different place, each with different markings, each in line with the others—endless.

Mr. Waldman's white mustache was sharply trimmed, his pink loose cheeks were smooth, barber shaved, and his soft handshake said the way has always been gentle. " . . . but will you be able to get the things you need there? New plumbing? And electrical?"

"All I can do is try and keep trying."

"Hospital beds? Surely they contain much steel."

"Have those things all pretty well located. Through salesmen. The hardest will be nurses. There are no registered nurses living around there. I hope I can persuade some convent of nuns to take it over and run it."

"I understand that here, at Santa Rosa, they never have enough Sisters—have to hire much help, can never get enough nurses."

"Oh!"

"Will you have to go into service?"

"The draft board—" my eyes went down, as if studying the oriental rug. "I don't know. So far I've always been deferred. Automatically. I never asked to be—don't even know who's on the board. But even if I do have to go, the war will end someday—hopefully soon—and I could go on from there. But there is the Procurement Assignment Board, too."

"What's that? Don't think I—"

"It's among the doctors themselves. Looks better if they decide among themselves and don't have to be drafted. It's in Fort Worth."

"They can draft you?"

"Can, yes. But so far they have left me alone, too."

"I sincerely hope you don't—hope you can continue."

We were slowly walking toward the front hall. Everything had all gone so easily. He had agreed on my offer of twelve hundred dollars—I think he would have agreed on any amount, even less—and he would have the deed drawn up. "You understand, I assume, that the place actually belongs to my wife's sister, in Houston."

"But I got your name from the tax office—"

"Yes. I manage the estate—what odds and ends are left there yet. But I know she'll sell it—I'll urge her to, especially for such a purpose."

"Should I go talk to her?"

"She's not always . . . too well. And quite old. It might confuse her. She takes my advice usually, so there should be no objection. I only mentioned her so you won't be confused by the names on the deed."

"I thank you. My, what an interesting mirror—and so tall. Beautiful gold-leaf frame." And a marble shelf beneath it.

"That's from the old house, too. That's why we had to build this house with high ceilings—so my wife could use some of the old things. Everything had large proportions in those days." Our images seemed small and clear in the great deep glass. "We wish you luck with you hospital. If it works, the old house will have an entirely new life, the most useful it has ever had. We're delighted. We're especially pleased to see a small, personal institution—so much more serviceable to the individual than the great monopolistic organizations. Of course, they surround us, are essential to our world—the big railroads, the military, the banking, religions also—essential to our way of living. And all striving to become ever larger operations and larger—the 'bigger-the-better' rule. But in practice, the larger an institution—of any kind becomes, the smaller and smaller the consumer shrinks in importance—almost into nothing. In direct proportion to the size.

"My wife and I are especially pleased with your idea and efforts at a small hospital."

"Well, at this point it seems mighty large to me, Mr. Waldman."

"Certainly. I understand. Please come visit us anytime you are in San Antonio."

Driving home I saw the dark green convoys again, drove parallel to the railroad, where long, long freight trains passed, fast, almost endless. Box cars and open flatcars loaded with miles of great large guns and tanks, all with their muzzles pointing up at the same angle. Mile after mile of the trucks and fast freights, of tanks and towering guns moving past, thundering their weight over the roads and steel rails.

I have fifteen hundred in the bank—leaves three hundred. How will I ever get the place fixed up, repaired, painted, furnished, equipped? An autoclave—the right kind—is six hundred; operating table alone is three hundred; resuscitation unit . . . I'll have to have an X ray there for fractures. Then operating costs, salaries, sheets. God. Even if I do it little by little, can I ever get it done? Maybe I shouldn't have started this.

Two days later Ignac Cernosek stood in the office door, sliding his stubby hands over his melon-shaped stomach, and said his wife ordered a new cookstove—an electric—and the old one, gas, was in perfect condition, like new. He asked could I use it in the hospital. I said yes and we'd need one more, too. How much?

"Nuzzing. She vant to give it you for nuzzing, for ven you start horspittle."

"Thank you so very much. But the deal isn't closed yet."

"Yes, sometimes thinks go wrong. It's like vit veather.

***

The fences along the Hodanek farm sag; the posts have weathered into thin stems and lean loosely forward or backward. The drooping barbed wire is sometimes held to the skinny posts with baling wire. The fence (which is man's work entirely—women never "make fence"), this fence is saying it to everyone along the road. The man of this place is sick, has been sick for a long, long time—or is dead. In the case of Alfonz Hodanek, it is alcoholism, which is an extremely rare disease condition among these people. Months ago, before Mrs. Hodanek even mentioned gallbladder and gas, she came and asked for something to put in his coffee, so he'd quit. She said he'd been drinking for fifteen years.

"I'm sorry, but nothing works like that on it—no medicine. He'll have to want to change, to quit, himself, for it to succeed. Can't sneak up on it—has to do it himself. It's a different level of living. He *can* change himself—we all can, but it is difficult."

"Vouldn't it be—no?—such little pills to put it in his coffee? Make it him to throw up when he drinks?"

"Antabuse? Be too dangerous without his knowing it. Never reject him no matter what. If you can do that, it's about all you can do. It is very difficult—"

"Make it taste bad to him ven he drinks?"

"If anything will work—it's not easy—it will have to be acceptance. Rejection makes us hate. Either others or ourselves."

"I alvays hoping he quits someday yet. For fifteen years." She belched. "He drinks it milk. Maybe so I could put it something in milk. Milk is better? To make him womit?"

At that time I did not know—nor did she mention it, not even while she lay in the hospital—that they had a nine-year-old boy who was born brain damaged, that he still couldn't walk and only made sounds instead of words. She kept him in the kitchen, on a bed with high sideboards, so she could tend him and cook for her six rest home patients at the same time. The first time I saw him in his boxed-in bed I thought, Good God, another one? Just like John's boy. And there is a grown one, George Taylor, a black, who was raised by Miss Emily. So many? And maybe others I don't know about.

That first time, as I went toward him, he began a whining that clearly said, Fear, fear. Stay away from me, I'm afraid. And he cowered in a corner. "He's like that vit strangers," Mrs. Hodanek had said.

"Then he needs strangers," I had answered from some unknown idea, "so he'll learn not to hate them." But for the moment, I backed away, telling him, "It's all right. Don't be scared, we are friends."

"He used to throw it things. Throw me everyvere in the kitchen things down. I had to stop him."

Ever since then, I give him—his name is Clyde—a small gift every time: tiny toy cars, balloons, gum, a cheap little metal marked "Hero." Margaret keeps a supply in the office and in my bag. She orders them from a doctors' supply house. "It's good business," she said.

The thing with him is like with John's boy: His realities are different than the rest. His realities were *born* different, so naturally they *are.* His language—he's speaking from a different world compared to everyone else. If we could only understand his language, then we'd know his level, his world, and could reach it, touch it.

This day again I turned in at the homemade sign—"Mrs. Hodanek Rest Home." Four senile old ladies lived crowded together in one room, but two other women had a room each to herself and were not senile at all. And Mrs. Hodanek's old mother also lived with her, upstairs, also not senile.

I have never yet attended a senile patient who seemed worried, scared, anxious, or angry. No matter what they say or do, it's always in a pleasant mood with an untroubled attitude. Except when our reality is forced on them—that always irritates, actually disturbs them. It angers them. As if they did not want to be called back to this place, like children who do not want to be called in from play. If they choose to think I'm their son John, or a brother, or the preacher, it's best to simply agree, make no objection, and go right ahead with examining—palpating the abdomen, listening to the lungs, looking in the throat . . . Once, while doing a vaginal exam (the woman had begun an odorous discharge, no blood), the little lady seriously remarked, "I didn't know the preacher had to do such as that."

"Well," I answered ordinarily, "sometimes we have to."

"I suppose so," she answered agreeing.

They are darlings, if you let them be—these old men—old women. As long as you let them stay in their contented place ("their happy place" Bertha Moore used to call it) and did not insist on the sharp corners and metal edges of our own rigid reality, like, "Oh no, you're mistaken: I'm the doctor, come to examine you."

Immediately the door would have been closed. "I don't need examining."

Reentry into this—our—world always seemed to call for irritation, obstructionism, anger.

Usually it's Mrs. Hodanek who opens the door (It's latched from the inside, taking no chances about one of the seniles wandering off), but today it's the large, bosomy Bertha Moore (mother of Otis Moore. "I'se cut." "Otis, I do believe you have a hundred yards of intestines." ". . . no need to carry me home." "They kilt my baby—oh Lord—they shot my baby boy dead."). "Hello, Bertha. So good to see you back at working. Best for everybody. For you."

"Yes, sir, thank you. Always enjoyed others—takin' care of them, helpin' out. And it helps to forget too, some.

"Mrs. Hodanek's upstairs. Doin' well it seems—gets about right smartly. Givin' her mother an enema just now. It's Mrs. Kolticek again. She wanted you to see. Come this way, please." I followed her voice and her rolypoly walk. "Yes, it sho' come a hard thing to do—try to forgive somebody who done it like that to your only child—leaves you all alone. With the Lord's hep maybe I can finally forgive him. I figure it weren't the man, but somethin' else come up in him to make him do it—had to. They knowed each other for years and years—grew up together. Wasn't him. Was somethin' else come up in him. It's this room, doctor." All four. "Not a one of these knows her own name, poor dears."

In our hospital, should we later add a nursing home wing? Add twenty, thirty beds?

Three lay bedridden, and the fourth stood at the dresser opening the drawers like she always does. Opening, closing, opening, fooling around in a drawer. "There's that old bastard again," and she laughs with high cackling glee and closes the drawer only to open it again.

"Ssshh. Mustn't say that, grandma. That's all she says all day long. Never says anything else."

"I know."

"Her family can't imagine where she ever learned it—they say she never said anything like that before in her life. Here, it's this bed. Mrs. Kolticek, here's the doctor to see you." She whispered, "Doesn't know anything; we have to spoon-feed her and she wouldn't eat this morning, poor soul."

I examined, feeling her neck, looking in her throat—a small abscess. Deadened the throat—and the swallowing and gag reflexes—with a spray topical anesthetic, Bertha helping by holding her hands and saying encouraging words—soothing and security sounds. I quickly lanced the abscess. And caught, on the tongue-depressor blade yellow pus, pink blood, and a small bone.

Bertha said, "Now looka there—a bone. Reckon it come from Friday?"

"I think it's fish. Doesn't look like chicken bone. She should do all right now."

"Musta had it a long time. Comin' ripe and couldn't say it—never says nothin'."

"There's that old bastard again," and the gleeful laugh.

I laughed too. So loud, so good that the little woman stopped opening a drawer and turned to look, like Have you joined us? "Yes, I'm in a happy place, too."

Bertha's smile was automatically warm. "She feelin' better already. Looka, swallowin'."

But my smile was about the hospital.

I played with Clyde, but only for a short time—never have enough time. He needs someone to be with him for hours, until he's exhausted. "I'm sorry I have to go. Sorry I have to hurry back to the office," and I put my head against his for a moment.

I examined—quickly, I'm afraid—the two who were not senile, who apparently do not need it yet. And Mrs. Busky, the one who has diabetes, said, "You seem frisky, happier than usual."

"Just in a hurry this morning, I suppose." Couldn't tell her about the hospital yet.

"How's your son?" Don't know why I asked. He's always so grouchy, always complaining about everybody. Says I charge too much, says Mrs. Hodanek charges too much. His sister said he's been like that all his life.

"Who?"

"Your son, Frank. Do you have more sons? I thought only Frank. The one who lives in Houston."

"Yes. Frank's the only boy. Oldest of them. Oh, he's doing all right, I'm sure."

Every time I've seen him he's complaining. About something. Even tells his mother to not take "a lot of medicine," always figuring up the cost. And Mrs. Busky never says an unkind thing about him, nor about anybody. I've never once heard her complain. Even Bertha said, "She always sweet and nice to ever'body."

"He works long hours." She smoothed the skirt over her knee and rocked. "They visited me again last Sunday. It's such a long, hot drive to come here and go back."

She passes sugar in her urine.

***

The telephone rang.

"It's Mr. Waldman in San Antonio." Margaret smiled, handed me the phone with her hand over it, whispering, "Calling long distance."

"Doctor, I hate to have to tell you this. It could well be my fault, too, because I didn't call my sister the same day you were here—we went out and it was late when we returned. But I did phone her the next evening—last night—to tell her you had bought the old home place. She said it just so happened that she had agreed to sell it that day herself. Yesterday.

"I asked her to whom? She said a doctor from our old home town. I thought it must be you, but she said it was not a young man and had a peculiar name—she couldn't remember it. And he offered her more than four times as much. Insisted she take something down and sign a receipt he brought with him. I think that man knew you wanted it. He's no gentleman."

"Yes, I'm sure I know what happened. And who. Mr. Waldman, may I call you back, say in an hour?"

"Yes . . . if you wish to. But you do remember I told you it actually is her house?"

"I know. May I call you back? Okay?"

"Certainly."

As I hung up, Margaret asked, "It's something bad. They won't sell?"

I told her as I turned a blank sheet into the typewriter.

As I left, with the paper in my hand, she asked, "Where you going?"

"Kotzebue!"

"*Aber!* You're not going to get into any trouble! Are you?"

I wasn't aware of it but I yanked the screen door of his office full wide, and as it slammed behind me—so mad I could kill—the receptionist jumped up, "Did you wish to see the doctor?" She stepped directly before me in the narrow passage. Everyone sat staring. With one slow sweep of my arm I backed her aside, against the wall. "You can't go in there." She called, "Doctor! Doctor!" but I'd already opened the door.

He sat at his desk, asking an old man across from him, "Is it water-white or milk-white?" and in the same sentence, looking up at me, "I'm with my patient."

I slapped the paper before him. "You went to see old Mrs. Koehler in Houston! Sign this! It says you are no longer interested in buying the Waldman place—Nordhausen place, I mean. Sign it!"

"But I paid her twenty dollars down."

"That's ridiculous. Here's twenty." I threw the bill, remembering even at the instant that I'm amazed at having a twenty-dollar bill, like some fortunate prearrangement by Fate.

He signed the page and turned back to the old man. "First, is it milk-white?"

The receptionist, Mrs. Biermann, standing right outside the door, said pleasantly, "You came in mad as an old bear."

"Mad enough to tear *this* damn place apart." And slammed the screen shut.

I called Mr. Waldman and again he apologized and said, "That man's no gentleman." He said he'd call his sister right away, and he'd have the deed written up soon as the lawyers could do it.

"Congratulations," Margaret smiled. "You won."

"Won what? I'm only back where I was." My cigarette trembled.

"No. That business of acting like he didn't care. And her—I know that Susie Biermann—they were trying to *schmeicheln* it over, sprinkle with sugar over the top."

"Gretchen, I acted like a . . . a bastard. Unreasonable, I'm afraid."

"No, you won."

"I would have—would actually have started wrecking that office. God."

"You wouldn't have, not you. You won and everybody will know it."

" . . . like a big fool. And got myself sued in jail, too. He'da claimed he got hurt, injured—"

"No you wouldn't. And I'm glad it's over."

"Me. Me of all people. Couldn't I have done it by talking? Civilized? Me!"

She smiled like she might still be saying "You won."

"Sorry I acted like that."

"Ready to see them? They're standing—so many." She opened the doors. "Who's next out here now?"

Seeing my cigarette tremble I smashed it out.

***

There are back streets, small ones, which most people of the town never see. There is one behind the feed and produce store that doesn't go anywhere, stops down at the draw, where people used to unload their trash before the city dump opened. A person would hardly be on this narrow street unless going to see Miss Emily and Miss Sophia about buying a pair of parakeets. Or going to see Theo Krejci, and nobody ever goes to see Theo Krejci for anything unless you're his doctor and he's drunk again or sometimes has fallen down steps or beat up his skinny wife.

And there's George. George Taylor, the crippled black man. He's a saint—and doesn't know it. Hobbling, jerking along down the middle of the deserted street, with one thick shoe, swinging his good arm wide with each step as if that helps. He lives back here with Miss Emily and Miss Sophia, lives in their basement. I never stop to pick him up—unless it's raining and he's without a coat. Because it's more trouble for him to get into a car and out of it again than it is for him to crook along the short distance home—and less embarrassing to him. It's kinder not to stop and make him crawl in with the one big shoe and pull himself in with the one hand—it's better to wave and go on. Jerking, swaying along home on his bent short leg with the short stiff *z*'ed arm tight against his chest—it stays there.

But when people are feeling low, depressed, worried, they'll automatically stop and make the poor guy go through all that stooping and clomping in and trying to hold his hernia up without that you should notice (he also has a hydrocele on that side, which gets as big as a small melon if we don't drain it)—all that under the self-delusion of being "nice" to him.

He is saintly in that people (without knowing they are doing it) go to him, taking little gifts; old clothes neatly cleaned and folded, freshly baked loaf of bread or kolace, or an old necktie. But these are like candles before a saint's statue—they're an asking, somewhat of a prayer. And the people receive from George. Not that he knows he's giving them anything, but from him you do get a strange something. Maybe call it grace, maybe forgiveness. Maybe it's a mental capsule of rebirth, a self refilling—God, it's something. I can't say what causes it, other than no matter what your troubles may be, George's troubles are so overwhelmingly more and so visually obvious that maybe by comparison it shrinks your own difficulties down to a size you feel is more manageable. Maybe it works something like that.

Margaret says his own mother couldn't raise him. When he was born, all crippled up like that, his mother told everybody right off that she couldn't stay home and take care of him—she had to work and feed the other children, and none of them were big enough yet to look after a baby brother during the day—that she'd have to give him up to the state institution to keep. She couldn't do it, had no other way. And she went to Mr. Freytag, who was just beginning at being the new justice of the peace, and told him so. And he said there wasn't any blank forms for something like that, that the closest thing he had was an application to Austin State Hospital for the insane, and you couldn't send a ten-day-old child there because he wasn't old enough yet. He'd have to ask the county judge. The people of the town said wasn't it just too awful that a mother wouldn't keep her own child and everybody talked about it. Finally Mr. Pulkrabek, a great-uncle or something to M. J. who has the filling station, who was Miss Emily's father and Sophia's too—but Sophia was married—who had retired at that time from the feed grain and poultry business and later imported parakeets—but they were called love birds in those days—talked with his wife and they told Mr. Freytag that they'd take the boy and raise him. People were completely surprised and said to him, "But you and your wife are too old for a baby; when you die he'll still be a boy." And Mr. Pulkrabek said Emily never married and she'd probably be around to look after George and it'd be good for Emily to have somebody to see after. And Sophia never had children either, so the boy, God willing, would be left some estate, enough to get by on in his old age.

When they went to get the child—word scattered along ahead was the only way the mother knew they were coming—other townspeople went along. This they had to see. Most of them had never seen inside a Negro shack at all. When you went to pick one up for work or for ironing on a rainy day, you drove up in front, and if they weren't waiting on the porch or with the door open, you just honked and they came out. So the townspeople were crowding in behind Mr. and Mrs. Pulkrabek and Miss Emily and they couldn't all get in, but as many as possible stretched to look in. Mrs. Pulkrabek asked if they could have the baby to raise. "We'll look after him as well as we can." The mother—they said later she hadn't changed her dress for their coming, as far as anyone could make out—said, "You can take him." The people stood real quiet and later they said it was simply terrible that a mother would give up her child like that, without a tear or a thank-you or a smile—nothing. One of the other little ones came to her skirt and asked, "Are they gonna take my baby?" and the mother didn't say a word to that child. Mr. Pulkrabek slipped her a big wad of bills and she never looked at it nor said thank you or cried. People eyed it there in her hand loose against her skirt and tried to calculate how much it amounted to.

And people said when they left that woman, instead of buying something those children needed with that money, she went straight to that place—what they call it now? the Blue Flame?—and got drunk. Or almost drunk. That place where they are always cutting each other up and it has all the ground in front so covered with beer caps that it's like a sidewalk, that's how much they drink in that place. And she sat and drank so all the day that you'd think they'd tell her to go home, but they didn't. Probably wanted her to spend all the money.

The story was told back and forth, her giving up the child without a tear and spending money on drink. The little girl asking again into her mother's skirt, "Ain't we gonna see my baby no more?" Mrs. Pulkrabek had said she'd heard it and wished that she could have answered something like "You come and see your little brother anytime you wish," but you can't have that sort of thing. Can't have your yard and maybe even front porch full of black children any time of the day and maybe picking up things. So right there George lost his black family and community and he was never again a part of it. So he didn't have that. And he never really belonged to the white community either, except they all "looked after" him.

And this all happened in the days before most people heard of corrective orthopedic surgery and Shrine hospitals for crippled children, and before the March of Dimes, so he didn't have the benefit of any of those.

Since he walked too crippled to go to school, George never received an education. He signs his Old Age Assistance check with *x* and Margaret, who has known him all her life, witnesses it. (It struck me as odd at first, that a man receiving Old Age Assistance should still be someone else's ward, especially someone as really old and feeble as Miss Emily.) When he pays for his visits (he has diabetic checkups frequently), it takes him twenty minutes to unbutton on down through all the layers of clothes to a bag with a big safety pin on his last layer of underclothes—Miss Emily taught him that. "He'll never be robbed," Margaret said in German the first time she waited. "So much time to wait has no thief."

After he finally left, Margaret said, "He has just about nothing. With his speech, hardly no one can understand him; he has no close friend. He's not part of the black people. Nor of the white. And his diabetes, and his hernia, and his hydrocele, and his foot, and his arm, and— He does enjoy taking care of the birds—does have his birds—and they don't belong to him.

"He does have his pipe. That's about all he does have. Big, cheap, stinky old pipe."

One morning while he was in the office, Miss Emily phoned. "George is coming down there this morning."

"He's already here. And he'll be here another hour too; taking off his four pairs of britches so I can get to his hydrocele."

"He's already gone home?"

"Oh no. I said he's here now. What is it?"

"It's about that old pipe of his. It's not good for him. For his health. Please. Would you tell him to throw that thing away."

"Why don't you tell him?"

"I did. I do. Doesn't act like he even hears me. So aggravating."

"So you think I can."

"Yes, he listens to you."

"But what makes you think I will?" I could almost see her; always in white blouses with high collar and a little ruffle around the neck.

"But it's not good for him. And it smells."

"How do you know that it's not good for him? How can you tell? You ever smoke a pipe? Why, Miss Emily, you never told me."

"Oh—oh, you're just as . . . as stubborn as George. Good-by!" You could almost see her stamp her little foot.

So he does have his pipe. Wouldn't have that if he didn't get "Old Age," because Miss Emily actually would cut off his spending money until he'd have to quit. But I did tell him, "Try not to smoke much around Miss Emily: She's getting so old, and it might be irritating to her lungs—you know she had the flu."

George answered with a jabber of words that I couldn't understand at all, except it ended with "I'oo 'at."

People stop him on the street, tell him their troubles. They don't do this to any other people, only to George. Practically pin him against the wall, in front of the bakery, the bank, Migl's Grocery, and he stays and listens. I don't think he knows how to get away from them, nor dares to. Wouldn't ever ignore or walk away. Even if he had to go urinate, he wouldn't—he'd hold it back. And he'd never say, or try to say, "I don't have time," or "I must go now to feed my birds." No, he'd stay. Maybe that's why he has diabetes—maybe it's a choice. Because all the other things—the leg, arm, speech deformity, hydrocele—all those were installed in him before birth. Before. He had no choice with them. But the diabetes came later. And it's the one that doesn't show. People see all the rest, and maybe that helps them be sympathetic, sensing he did not choose them. And the drool. Saliva gathers in his lower lip and sometimes suddenly spills over, and he has to catch it quick with his good arm.

They bring him things, clothes, "do things" for him. And without knowing it, he helps give them back themselves. He doesn't know it, and they don't seem to either, but he's a saint, the town saint.

It doesn't work for me. No one starving helps my hunger. No one can be cripple for me. No one can die for my doings. The blue baby died, but not for me—for my ignorance. And all it gives me is guilt. Guilt to carry and keep carrying inside me forever. I ask no one to do it for me—they can't.

On my way to Krejci's, I drive slowly and see him, hobbling, jerking along. Hear the klomp-slide of the thick shoe; see him swing the good arm each step.

Other people give us our life, yes; but living it is ours to do. We still have to live it.

And you, George, are doing it beautifully. But why must there be the diabetes?

"Hello, George," I wave.

A week later I made a rush call to Krejci's—you never know if she actually is hurt or not, so you go quick—and while driving back there's George, the one thick-soled shoe going klomp-slide, klomp-slide. He can't be going to town. It's too late. Wonder . . . I stopped alongside of him. "Going as far as town, George?"

"Only to the branch." Sometimes I get what he means right off.

"Why the branch? What for?"

He wiped his good arm across his nose. "Gotta bu'n 'f my buds."

"Bury? One of your birds?" I think that's what he said.

With his good hand he pried the other's stiff fingers open, and there, held against his stomach, lay the green-yellow form, almost as in a nest.

Wish I hadn't stopped. I've broken in on his . . . I didn't know what to say. What can you give him at a time like this? "It's such a pretty bird."

He said nothing, and when he turned the fingers loose they sprang shut, traplike.

"I'm sorry the bird died." He didn't answer. Rubbed his good wrist up under his nose. "Other living things give us our lives, George . . .

in small pieces. Or take it away from us. In pieces. All living things. We are parts of them. They are pieces of us."

I didn't really know what to say. So I muttered a self-conscious farewell, eased on, and left.

⁂

At about five o'clock Margaret handed me the phone, smiling big. "It's Mr. Waldman again," and she closed the door because of a patient on the table.

"Again I must say how extremely sorry I am—"

"Why, sir—Mr. Waldman—that's quite all right. Please don't feel badly, it's all straightened out."

"But I'm afraid it isn't."

"Oh? What . . . what do you mean?"

"My sister will sell to you, but she insists if it was worth five thousand to the . . . other person, then that is what she wants for it. She's adamant. She gets like that. She's old, the oldest of us. I'm sorry. I tried everything. I talked for almost an hour—and called her back. I'm exhausted. That man caused it. I know she believes what she's saying. I'm indeed very sorry."

"I . . . I . . . So'm I. Well . . . I simply don't have the money. That's all. Not that much. I see. I'll have to . . . let it go. There is no other building in town large enough—not one with rooms. There's no choice. I do thank you for your efforts, Mr. Waldman. I think you're a very kind man. But I'll simply . . . have to drop it.

"Well, thank you very much, sir. For all your effort. Good-by." I could have cried.

The instant I hung up, Margaret opened the door. "What's wrong? I couldn't hear everything—she kept talking." She was referring to the patient.

"Five thousand dollars. She might as well have wanted a hundred thousand."

"That Kotzebue!"

"Yes. He knew he had won. He knew my bank balance—what I'm making. I see now. I've lost. I give up. It was great while it lasted. Still think it is the finest thing a person can ever do. Oh, forget it. Have to. I give up. In a way I'm glad the strain is off. What am I examining her for?" *I could kill that bastard.* "Well, we can stop worrying about a hospital now. Let's see, I guess you've got her ready? What am I examining her about?"

"Pains lower left. I believe you were thinking ovary. Here's the glove. Heavens, it's a left—my mind has gone *fusch*."

I didn't listen too well, kept thinking of the skull in the closet. Got to get rid of that thing. I'll take it to the cemetery some night and bury it. In some new, deep, fresh grave—no one will notice the diggings. If Kotzebue died, in his grave. Wouldn't that be perfect!

While I did the vaginal, Margaret said quietly, "I hope you're not too disappointed."

I ought to kill that sonnovabitch!

I kept feeling and pressing, "This might hurt some, Mrs. Kutac, but we have to find out."

Later, when I stopped at the post office, Henry Eilers said they had two refrigerators at home, one upstairs and one downstairs. When we were ready I should let him know, and he'd have the upstairs one hauled to the hospital, as a gift.

I didn't tell him. I couldn't.

❋❋❋

Margaret said toward the end of the waiting room that had gradually become the black section, "Well, come in now," and she didn't sound friendly at all.

Three well-dressed black women came. Fine tailoring, expensive looking. Long red fingernails perfectly manicured. Two of the faces looked out from brownish wigs that did not look like wigs; the third head was styled straight down all around like a thatched-roof African hut, and the tip of the roof bunched into a tuft like a small umbrella with a pink ribbon tied around the stalk. It was especially the little spurt of hair that set you into a smiling mood. The same woman also wore great circles of gold earrings that gave almost a savage flair. Another wore a short gold necklace of bear claws or tusks. Ora Tar was the big fat one, in a perfectly tailored coat suit accented with only one gold clasp near the left shoulder; she carried only a matching scarf and a small pocketbook. "Hello, Ora, nice to see you back from California; hope you stay awhile. Which one of you handsome girls is it? None of you look sick."

Margaret did not say Humpf!, but some jerk in her quick action did.

"Susan's the one," Ora pointed. "About her stomach."

"What's with your stomach, Susan?"

She slipped her hand over her eyes and peeked at me through long fingers.

"Stomach trouble, doctor. She can't keep nothin' down. Ate some Bohemian sassage, few days back."

"But I ate it, too," said the one wearing the little thatch roof. Large circular braclets jangled down her arm.

"And big me—umm, was it good."

Susan said nothing, only smiled down at her pink pointed shoes.

"Musta et half a yard of it myself." Then seriously, "Sometimes I wish things did upset my stomach—just a little anyway. I eats anything." She wrinkled her nose and felt of her full hips.

I asked Susan a few more questions, which she answered by nodding or shaking her head. Found the vomiting occurred mostly in the mornings. "Margaret, get her ready for a vaginal, please."

"Come in here!" and Susan followed her into the examining room. Margaret almost slammed the door.

I asked Ora, "Are you liking California?"

"Just fine—it's nice. Weather so much easier than here. My husband's a carpenter. Works nearly every day of the year. Weather so fine and lots of work—they buildin' everything." She changed tone to ask, "How come it didn't upset us none? She can't hold nothing on her stomach. Not even water this morning. I told her, this gettin' worse stead of—" The door opened; Margaret held out a sterile glove on its sterile towel.

With her high heels into the iron stirrups and the sheet over her knees, Susan looked toward her friends, "I didn't come here for no such pokin' around."

"I won't hurt you, Susan, just be easy." I held out my gloved hand while Margaret squeezed Vaseline on the fingers.

"Y'all made me. No, wait." She clamped her knees together.

"Just relax," I encouraged.

The one with the roof said, "You gotta let the doctor zamine you," and giggled.

"No wait."

"I wouldn't hurt you. Now loosen up. Take a deep breath and let—"

"No," her knees stayed clamped tight shut. "Wait."

"Let the doctor examine you!" Margaret ordered.

"Y'all wait. Made me do this."

Margaret's tone was not kind, "Why are you so bashful?"

"Susan, child, I can't examine you like this. Don't be afraid."

"No wait."

"Here, honey, take this," Ora handed her the scarf. Susan laid it over her face, covering her eyes, and then spread her knees wide open.

With the left hand I pushed down against her abdomen slowly and up into her with the right, and in a moment I said, "You're a good two months, Susan. That's—"

"Pregnant?"asked Ora. "Pregnant! You don't say. Hah-he!"

"Why yes, certainly. What's so—?"

"Hah! Look what she done to us!"

"Ummhuh!"

"What'd she do?"

"Sho' did. Hah!"

"Did what?" I still wanted to know.

"Didn't tell us nothin' about it."

"I wasn't sure. Not yet."

"Pregnant!" laughed Ora. "And never—!"

"And I did eat that sassage."

"Hah-he!" and she slapped her fat thighs. "Pregnant!"

As I skinned off the glove, "What's so . . . much about that—so funny?"

"Hah! Oh ain't it! She ain't got no husband! Hah!"

"Ain't right. Made me come."

The thatched hut, too, bowed in laughing and laughing.

Suddenly Ora's laughing stopped. "Why is it, doctor, these skinny girls get pregnant so easy and a big person like me can't get pregnatized no matter what I tries. Doctors examine me in Portland and in L.A. and they says I'm all right."

"Maybe it's not you: Men can be sterile, too. Has your husband ever been tested?"

Susan smiled. "She don't always depend entirely on him."

"Oh you shush up!"

Margaret grunted.

"Well you the one made me come to the doctor. Just had to come, had to get here, couldn't—"

"Course I was, honey, and see: It wasn't no sassage atall."

The one with the earrings added, "Least ways not no Bohemian sassage." Her bracelets twinkled as she bowed laughing again.

"Hah-he," Ora bent over and slapped her thigh. "Sho' never hearda no black Bohemian."

Margaret ordered, "Get up!"

"By the way, honey, you ain't promised this to nobody has you? I'm the first to ask." She looked to the other woman. "You heard me, Vera."

"I don't know. You been mighty snippish to me all the morning."

"Aw now, honey, I had to get you to the doctor. And you see? Was important too. You gotta know early and take good care of yourself, don't she, doctor? And remember I asked first."

"I'll have to be thinkin' about it."

"Sure, honey, sure. How much is it doctor?" Ora laid the small pocketbook down and reached into her bosom.

Margaret said "Three dollars!"—we usually charged two—and almost snatched the five dollar bill and stomped off toward the desk where change is kept.

"Oh don't jump down so, honey. Gotta take it easy. You gotta remember you got my baby in there."

"Maybe yours."

"Sure, honey, sure."

Vera laughed. Her bracelets jangled.

"You come back once a month now, Susan. Or sooner if you have any questions. And"—handing her one of our specimen jars—"this each time."

When they were gone, Margaret, folding the sheet, said in German, "*Solche schloppie*—"

"It's all right, Gretchen. Different people, different ways . . . on the outside. They're not breaking their rules. Only ours."

Like it still wasn't all right, she brought in the next person, and said nothing.

He came in limping and saying in Czech, "Now is coming slowly Stary Emilisko [which means "old worn-out Emil"], who is walking with the legs too many miles."

Somebody left but before Margaret could fold the sheet away, the door opened, and a woman stood there hugging a large black handbag to her chest. "Heard you took right nice care of my niece."

"Oh? Thank you."

"Thank you nothin'."

"Er—well—" I didn't know what to say, and Margaret was no help either.

"Seems you didn't refuse her."

"Well—I'm glad."

"Glad nothin'. Done your due."

I said nothing.

"Seems you come there each time she send for you. She got along nicely—doin' right tolerable now."

"Glad to hear it," I ventured.

"Glad nothin'. Was expected, wasn't it?"

"I—I suppose so."

"No use you standin' here supposin'. Others is awaitin'. Tell me what she owe you."

"All right. I mean, who is your niece?"

"You don't know?"

"I—I'm afraid not."

"No use bein' afraid. Liza Crawford."

I remembered. A shack in the timber, an old car body out front in the weeds with chickens roosting on it, streaking it white.

"You come to her house. Married that no-good Travis. Run off and married him—had to. And he's treated her like a dog ever since."

I closed the door.

"I don't care. Everybody know it. Give her nothin'. Can't hold no job, drinks. Never a dress or pair of shoes. Nothin' but work. Work. She might as well amarried one of 'em Bohemians or Germans. Washin', milkin', churnin', sellin' a little butter. Nothin' but a cow pen full of kids. And when she called you, you come. How much she owe?"

"I'll look it up, Miss Clara." Margaret fingered through her card index while Miss Clara scratched in her bag and laid out a checkbook. "Twelve-fifty. Shall I write it for you?"

"Why? Think I can't write more'n my name?"

"Er—and his name is Travis?" I asked. "Don't think I've ever seen him."

She wrote slowly, laboriously. It looked like the handwriting of a fourth-grader. "Him? Never been sick a day in his life. Wasn't to home, war he oughta been, with a sick and ailin' wife. War asittin' one way in the saloon or tother way in jail. Crazy in the haid." She replaced the checkbook, snapped the bag closed, hugged it. "He oughta be shot—needs killin' hisself.'' She handed the check to Margaret as if it were some official document.

''Thank you, Miss Clara,'' I said.

''Thank you nothin','' and she left.

I shrugged. ''Who was that? Or what?''

''Clara Kincaid. One of the richest people in the county—and the stingiest. Oil under her little forty acres, and won't spend a nickel. Doesn't even eat enough.'' She kept smiling big.

''What now? You look like you're itching with something.''

''I fixed that old penny pincher. I hadn't sent Liza's bill—they don't have anything, waste of postage. So Liza didn't know how much it was. And this Clara didn't. So I added a little. It was nine.''

''Margaret! We're not supposed to be . . . bandits.''

''You got plenty others to put it on. And she'll never miss it. Stingy old tacky thing.''

''Gosh. And she came, paying a bill that wasn't even hers.''

❋❋❋

As I returned from the call, Margaret took the bag. ''What did you use? The small syringe?''

''Yes, gave her a sedative.''

''Was it all so much of a rush as they said.''

''Well yes. Church full of people waiting.''

''But she didn't have a heart attack?''

''No. Just fainted. But I gave the sedative anyway, for whatever had—''

''Fainted? During the wedding? I've heard of them being nervous!''

''Fainted because she had on a corset that was too tight. At least—''

''Oh, yes. After all, six months pregnant.''

''Four.''

''I heard six—bet it's six—that's why the corset. We'll see. Four would barely show. Why do they wait so long?''

''Or at least the corset was the surface reason. But I wonder . . . Faint. Is it possibly fainthearted? . . . a fear? a guilt? Oh, I don't know.''

''When the Zapalac girl married, she took her shoes off before the ceremony, it being such a hot morning. And couldn't get them back on! That swollen already. She was married barefoot. Barefoot and pregnant." She changed to German. "*Schloppie.* Totally stupid. Why do they wait? So they can still have the big wedding?" Back into English. "But she wore a most beautiful veil, handmade, something her grandmother brought from the old country. Seems anything that was brought . . . always such fine material—they'll last forever. Without the corset, did she look big?"

I stretched my arms into the stiffly starched jacket. "I think they'd simply say, 'It's the season for it, it's natural.' "

"What did Father Puziovsky say?"

"Nothing. He never says anything."

"Do I send the bill to Marie Darilek or to Mrs. Frank Kubenka. She wasn't married to him yet, was she?"

"Why don't we just send it 'Mr. and Mrs.', marked, 'Paid. Happy congratulations on your wedding'?"

"A Mrs. Weston called." Her hands scrambled through the bag until she found the used syringe. "They're the Houston family bought the old Krhovjak place. She has poison ivy, wanted an 'appointment.' I told her I'd call her when you come back. Mr. Pesek is first—prostate, you remember. You'll need a rectal glove—use one of the sterile ones; he brought his urine. You're to circumcise the Hanzlik baby this morning; it's all ready when they come."

"I think it's going to be a beautiful wedding after all."

"Who?" In German she said sternly, "O those! *Schrecklich.* I'm autoclaving over the noon hour. If you need a syringe before then, I'll take one out of the office."

⁂

We drove again over the spring-covered land—a rounded hill of blue bonnets, another of red Indian paintbrushes, a swipe of pink buttercups down an entire valley, and scatterings of small yellows.

"Ohhh, look there, doctor. A baby calf, just born. What's the cow doing? She's not eating her calf is she? She's eating something!"

"The afterbirth. She's eating it. They do that."

"That's terrible!"

"Didn't you know cows do that?"

"If I ever did, I forgot it completely. But why?"

"Primitive instinct. Some say it destroys—conceals—the blood scent, which could attract a predator."

"That's terrible."

The young corn leaves wave hello and the cotton bushes bow. We are on our way to deliver the Kobza baby—*a* Kobza baby. There are so many all over. These are out near Dubina. Like a whole clan—it must have included thirty people or more, and everybody had brought food. We entered through the kitchen and walked past the long white-covered dining table crowded with plates of kolace, frosty pies, a pink cake sprinkled with poppy seed, sweaty glass bowls of cold salads, and meats: roast beef, fried chicken, stewed chicken, sausage . . .

The cloth hung down the sides of the long table almost to the floor; its sharp creases marked out silent squares. These tablecloths—you saw them on special occasions: rich heavy material brought along from Europe in strong, plain wooden chests, hanging down almost to the floor and so exactly creased—always reminded me of pictures of the Last Supper.

People were laughing and eating as we entered. The men stood talking outside, where it would be understood they passed a jug. I looked over the roomful of fat women as if puzzled, "But which one of you is having a baby?" They laughed and pointed on into a bedroom where a handsome young woman in a frilly gown with real lace lay covered to her neck by a crisp new sheet. A gold necklace lay loosely about her throat, and a blond young man sat holding her hand.

"My!" Margaret burst out spontaneously, "what a lovely picture you two young ones do make! Really. Ought to have a picture of you two right there. You don't look like more than children yourselves."

"Young papa, you'll have to step out while I examine her."

Margaret took the pan of warm water that one of the women offered and laid a safety razor beside it. After the door closed behind the broad young shoulders, I pulled the sheet up and Margaret began instructing. "Now bring your knees up, honey—so."

We were each on a side of the bed, each angling a leg up, and spreading— Something strange there: a bluish coil of thin shiny rope. It lay snug between her legs, coming down out of the vagina and returning there. The umbilical cord! Quickly I felt it. Cold. No pulse thumping through it. No life. Prolapsed cord. It had slipped out, been born first. I pressed the stethoscope tight against the big abdomen to shut out the sounds of laughing from the other room, but there came no tu-tu-tu-tu- of the tiny heart. The baby had strangled from the pressure on the prolapsed cord. Its life had been squeezed off.

"Honey, did the baby kick a whole lot today?"

"Oh yes. Early this morning. My, it never acted like that before."

"Was there . . . water coming, last night?"

"Yes, I couldn't hold it. Even in the bed."

"Did you tell anybody?"

"They were all sleeping. Why? Is something wrong?"

"Oh honey, it's only that doctors have to ask a lot of questions—that's part of the job. Otherwise I don't earn my pay." Margaret kept looking. "Now for a little shaving. Oh—I don't think this water is quite warm enough."

"Here, I'll go add some hot." Margaret's voice was subdued.

"No, you stay with her. I'll get it." I closed the door firmly, slowly. Now I would have to tell them—and him—that this child about to be born was already dead.

I had to tell it to the young man with the strong thick neck and wavy hair—told him there in the kitchen, with the others listening. He turned to go to his wife, but I stopped him. "Keep him out here, for she will see it in his face. Keep him for a little while. He should not let her know yet." He sat down there beside the pink cake with poppy seed and covered his face with both hands. "And turn the radio up—she'll hear you're too quiet."

"Oh," said one woman looking down at a half-eaten kolace in her hand, "and they so young." She held the kolace in midair, looked at it, and laid it back on the plate.

"Will she be all right?" he asked, mumbling through his hands.

"Yes."

I took the same pan I came out with and reentered her room, noticing all the shining new bedroom furniture. "Now for that shaving. Did you know I am an expert barber, too? Sure, you'll see. Expert. So don't be scared about it now." Margaret usually did the shaving.

When the baby lay there on the mattress between her feet, on its face, its knees up under it, lying there so cozy dead, I couldn't resist the impulse—and that was horrible—to feel of it. I held my hand flat on its cold back. Cold. I wanted to pull my hand off, back away, but my fingers cupped the cold buttocks. And moved over its cold scalp, as if blessing or baptizing it. I felt Margaret watching me, so I asked, "How can it be cold," muttering in German, "when it has just come out of her warm body?" I liked feeling that dead cold flesh. I hated it—but I liked it. I kept feeling the cold back, cold small buttocks, cold soft abdomen.

"Shall I give her the Pit now?"

"Yes," I answered and took up the limp cold cord still leading up into the mother. I wanted to feel the dead baby some more, but Margaret might notice.

You're dead, but I did not kill you.

Baby, you cannot do my dying for me. Let's don't even think it. Nobody can do it for me. Each has to do his own. Each must hold his own hostility and choose the using of it. Each man holds the handle of this, his own dagger, and turns it out—kills—or in—dies.

I wanted to feel the baby again, but Margaret'll see me.

Gosh. Giving lectures to a dead baby. How utterly absurd. And on philosophy yet. Good gosh, how absurd can you get? I'm sorry, baby, I did not mean to bore you with—

Sorry? You're dead? But of course I'm sorry you're dead. That you died. Yes, certainly I am—of course. But you'll come again, probably in some other way. Yes, of course.

Oh certainly they're sorry. Certainly. Especially him. He was ready for a baby, especially for a little baby son.

Well . . . yes, I will tell you truly what I think. I think they weren't ready—she wasn't ready. To have a baby. She's been pampered, had everything, everything perfect. She not fully ready to try raising a baby. She wants to do a perfect job at that, too, but she's been too sheltered. Is still too tender afraid.

No, of course she'd deny it all to high heaven. Of course. No, she doesn't see it. Wouldn't dare—ever. No.

The next morning, before the funeral for the baby, they had the photographer come in. The older ones wanted it. It is a custom, brought along from the old country. He took pictures of the baby in its small coffin. The coffin had a pale blue lining.

***

Washing my hands, I looked up and saw Margaret ushering in a skinny woman wearing dark glasses. "No. Not again!"

"You remember Mrs. Schneider's eyes, of course."

"Look, Mrs. Schneider—"

She ignored me and asked Margaret, "Wasn't that Mrs. Burns who just left?"

"Yes, that's her."

"Always dresses so nicely," touching her bobbed hair at the naked neck. "Takes money to dress like that."

Maybe I should see about taking a culture of the pus pimples and send it to a special lab. There they could identify it and grow it in a vaccine. And from that I could give her increasing doses—it would take a long, slow time—and gradually desensitize her to this infection, whatever it's coming from. That might be the way to save her from blindness, which I'm scared to death might be coming.

"I guess she'll be marrying again one of these days," Mrs. Schneider almost sighed. "Everybody says she collected fifteen thousand dollars from that electric company in Houston." She again touched her stringy-looking hair delicately and smiled, showing some lipstick smeared on a tooth. "I suppose some women never know how lucky they are."

"Lucky?" I practically shouted. "Mrs. Schneider, don't you realize her husband died? Got killed?"

She made no movement whatsoever.

"Well— How bad are the eyes this time?"

With the little finger raised and without speaking, she lifted the dark glasses to show me; her lips wrinkled together, I thought, in a suppressed smile.

❋❋❋

She walked slowly up and down the fragrant paths of bordered blossoms, which went around and to the left and to the right and up and down and led nowhere. The moon shone full.

"A pain?" Margaret asked.

"No." She looked toward the round moon. "Only aches."

Hilda walked the geometric designs of her mother's flower garden, her long nightgown touching each heel in turn. Back and forth slowly between the square-shaped flower beds and the diamond-shaped, each edged with brick, both bulging over with blossoms of all colors. The aromas floated up onto the porch and through the house.

The old couple had each said their "Dobra nuch" and gone to bed upstairs, she carrying the night jar squeaky on its wire handle. "Is plenty grand-kits," the old man had smiled, "thirty-three. Four," he pointed his curved pipe at Hilda stopping to put her hands on her back, closed the door behind them and clumped his way up the tall narrow stairs.

"They're sleeping upstairs tonight. So we don't disturb them," Hilda said from among the flowers. "Upstairs was always for brothers."

From on the porch I looked down on the blooming small yard, at the walks that made patterns but went nowhere, ending at circular beds or at outside borders. The snowball bush, a hump of solid white—*Schneeweiss.* The road ran beside the garden, close, narrow, past the house on to the barns. The ground sloped steeply down under tall pecans to the brook, which now meandered white in the moonlight. "Hilda, this is the loveliest spot imaginable to be having a baby."

"Yes—if only Bill could be here."

None of us mentioned where he was. In Germany. She stood still with a pain.

"Tell me when it goes away," said Margaret with the watch in her hand.

The moon bright over this tiny garden of central European origin. "In these old gardens, notice, they planted the balsamine along the edges. The scent—when women swept by, their long skirts stirred up the scent. And there it is, along the edges." The sound of a calf calling, asking, and a cow answering, reassuring.

"It's starting again," Hilda said, leaning forward, her hands on her back.

Holding the watch in the moonlight, Margaret answered, "Still five minutes apart. Tell me when it quits."

What is the moon like over a battlefield? It is still winter there. Snow.

Perhaps it shines on a silent field of white, with scattered humps—the snow softly covering the dead. Tomorrow the haulers will come, vans with heavy chains across their tires tracking through the snow. And men will shovel the humps and pickax the hard ice, breaking loose, levering and lifting the stiff strange shapes, tearing them out from under the quiet snow—

"It's gone now," she sighed.

Margaret looked at the watch. "Keep walking again."

"If it's a boy"—Hilda slid her hands over the large abdomen and said toward the moon—"his name will be Bill. Little Bill."

She walked slowly between the fragrant blossoms, like my mind going up and down geometric paths that led nowhere.

❋❋❋

The geese have flown north, far, far north, one stroke at a time. Thousands of miles, one wing stroke at a time.

Day after day. One moment at a time. You continue. You examine one person after another—

"Okay, Wenzel, I'll have to examine your wife." Wenzel Foitik or Vatzlav Foitik? Whichever you choose, it's the same man. Most call him Wenzel. Big, big talker. Talk, talk, talk. They say through the domino games it's so much you can't think what your partner played. Talk, talk—big braggart. How he fixed his '37 Chevy with a piece of baling wire, how he nailed the entire barn roof on in one afternoon. And maybe these things are true, maybe he did. But always big talk, talk. "Vaginal," I said to Margaret and began to leave the room.

"Inside? You hexamine her up inside?"

"Yes, have to," and I went into the office.

"Step here behind the screen, Mrs. Foitik, and take off your panties—"

"No. Wait!" says Wenzel. "Wait a few minutes. I go quick and come back. Wait for me—don't hexamine—I be quick back," and he's out the door. Margaret and I looked at each other.

"Mr. Blankenberg is next. Blood sugar check. You could be seeing him in the office; card's on your desk. Urine's okay. I'll bring a syringe."

As Margaret held the tourniquet and I drew the blood, I said, "You won't have to wait today, Adolph"—always spoke German to him—"I or Gretchen will phone you, probably in the morning." We heard Wenzel return and go directly into the examining room and heard paper crushed together into a ball. Margaret's eyes and forehead went *?* again. I reviewed a few other things with Adolph: diet, soft shoes, no excitement, no worry (but how can you tell a man not to worry when he has lost his only son in diabetic coma, for surely worry and grief are the same emotion, only different in being before or after), no strenuous work but steady activity. And if this test shows high, return in one week; if fairly normal, one month; but we'll discuss that on the phone.

Ever since his boy—nice blond teen-age kid—died in a coma, breathing harder and harder . . . I got him to the hospital that night in the high hard winds of a storm. The hospital lights went out and we had candles on plates—in the hall, because we kept giving him oxygen.

And I had to tell Adolph and his wife together, while the boy's breathing came louder and harder, that their son would not live—would never again regain consciousness. And ever since that night I have always wanted to give Adolph something—I don't know what. Always feel like I want to give him something . . .

Back with Mrs. Foitik, Wenzel was saying, "Now can hexamine." And he talked away about how the weather "she will shange" because now his Chevy starts better—from the first try—and this always means it will rain, and how we need the rain, and . . .

While I'm examining, Margaret, standing behind Wenzel so neither of them saw, glanced behind the screen. Then her eyes arched over that way, telling me to look, too.

So as I stripped the glove off, I turned slightly. The screen was not in the way and I could see it too:

On the chair, a new pair of panties—peach colored. A small tag on a string—the price tag—dangling.

❋❋❋

I hear myself saying it again and again, like a priest: "One capsule three times a day. Before meals. On the third day, you should feel the difference, should know that you are getting well."

It sounds like some kind of benediction.

❋❋❋

On an early morning call out through Freyburg . . . The roads already dragged smooth by the road-commission crew spreading the soil while it's still damp. Makes for smooth driving—no hard-crusted ruts.

This beautiful day.

This is a "heart-muscle" day, a day made of the heart-muscle tissue. This special tissue responds all the way or not at all. Each tissue in its own function is special; this tissue has the characteristic—and no other has it—of contracting all the way or not at all. Total contraction or nothing. Heart tissue is the only tissue in the entire body that performs in this manner. One hundred percent. Or zero.

All other muscle-tissue can contract partway, or partway and hold it, or sometimes all the way. Totally variable. But heart tissue responds only the one way.

And each beat of the heart of every heart on earth—each contraction—is the simultaneous contraction of all muscle fibers in that cup of the heart.

Today with its sunshine, its green fluttering, its bird songs sown on the winds, its reds, pinks, and blues splashing in their bath of sunlight, its fragrance wandering off and greeting— Today is a total day, a "heart-tissue" time.

Everyone loves the country roads when they're smoothed. After the rains pass and the ruts harden into small mountain ranges and valleys, the road commissioners have their men come with teams and drag large wooden sleds, smoothing. Or if that district owns one of the new big "Maintainers" with its great blade across the front, that cuts the roadbed level, smooth as pavement. It's almost like floating along—up a hill, down, curves, rumbling across the culverts and small bridges, with doves scattered along the fences and in a straight row on the telephone wire. A jackrabbit racing along before you for a mile before ducking into tall weeds.

A car is coming down the hill before me. It should begin moving over to its side, but it's staying in the middle. That's strangely obstinate—it's simply not like these prairie people. I begin to pull far over, giving more than my half. I recognize the car: Kotzebue. A white glove waves out on one side, a black hand out the other, to call me to stop.

I pull up even and Raymond and I are looking at each other, and the other white glove beckons me to come into his car. I can't imagine what this is all about. Kotzebue waves at the ignition key; Raymond turns it off. And as I come up I hear: "Now go walk up this road one hundred steps into the wind. Don't want nobody hearing what I have to say to this . . . doctor."

He waited until Raymond walked far down the road. "You're treating Rose Psencik. They used to be my patients. Whole family. Always were my patients."

What's he want me to say? Actually they had little choice. He looked off into the fat white clouds, bulgy, pregnant-looking white blobs against a flat, blue distance. "Before she married she was a Mrnustik. I knew all of them."

I waited.

"I remember from her symptoms and reading up on it a few nights ago—weeks ago—months—I believe her symptoms fit sickle-cell anemia."

That's impossible. She's white. Doesn't he know it occurs only in Negro blood? Should I say it? Tell him? It occurs only in persons of Negro blood, just as Reynold's Disease occurs only in Russian Jews or their bloodline descendents. Should I say so? Explain it to him? No.

"I didn't want to tell you that over the phone. If you'll check into it, I think you'll find that's the case."

"Hmm. Well, I—"

"She's a mix, if you know what I mean. It's on her father's mother's side. Rose is a one-sixteenth . . . of that blood. Nobody knows it. Even Margaret—your Margaret—doesn't know that, so she couldn't tell you." The white glove reached over, blew the horn, and waved Raymond to come.

Why is he telling me this?

"Rose herself does not know it. Her father does." He looked at me. Is he asking me a question?

"I won't tell her."

Why is he doing this?

He's not doing it for any love of me—he hates me.

He despises patients who leave him.

Raymond climbed in, asking, "Ready?"

"Get going."

But why tell me?

They drove off. He didn't even glance back.

Yes, the symptoms do fit with sickle-cell. Was he thinking I'd miss the diagnosis? Sure would have, since she's white. I would not have made a blood smear—wouldn't have had any reason to think of it—and so would not have had a chance to see the sickle shapes of some of the blood cells. If that is what she's got. And it just might be the case. It fits.

But why? Why him telling me?

Could it be that old, old thing that you help the patient at any cost? That all that counts is: What is good for the patient? What is best.

And that's what he did?

I stood frowning. His car rumbled across the culvert and sped up the other hill, a trail of dust following it.

And if he'd do that for one—and one who has left him—what has he done for how many others?

His car, boiling the dust out from underneath it, rose smoothly up and over the hill and sank behind it. But I still heard it and saw the dust gradually disappearing.

***

"There's a whole delegation—*alle Schwarze*—out here to see you."

"What about? Bring them in."

"Too many. Can't all get in here."

I went out to the alley and the black man standing in front, Jasper Jones,—Jass—spoke. "Good mornin', doctor. We all don't want to bother you none, and we do want to thank you. You the first doctor who treated us like white folks. You treat us like human bein's."

"Well, certainly. And what can I do for you?"

"We all don't want to be no bother. But if it ain't too much trouble—and we 'preciate what you done, we do . . . You done more—"

"Oh, Jass, now stop."

"Oh man, yes. It's true." Other voices murmured approval; some laughed. "All right, I gonna ask it: we'd like our own waitin' room. Now wait, we don't say it ain't nice you have us in the same room with the white folks. You been so nice—that why we feel we can speak up. The reason bein', we can't talk amongst ourselves there in front of them. It jest don't do. Amongst us, you understand.

"If Mr. Hajovsky allow you to use that storage room off the side there—ain't nothing in it nohow—we got plenty carpenters; we'll cut the door through. And we can hear when Miss Margaret call us next; won't be no extra trouble to her. We would like for us to have our own room—no disrespect, mind you. We—"

"Come on, let's ask him."

Mr. Hajovsky rubbed both hands over his bald head.

"I'd like it, Papinku. Give us more room on crowded days."

He continued to feel over his head. "I don't know. Some of them don't get their prescriptions filled here. Go out the side door."

"I'll pay all the expense of doing it and pay five dollars a month rent on it—sixty dollars a year."

"All right."

We started right away—cut a wide doorway and sealed the walls and ceiling with Sheetrock. Margaret checked on the work every hour or so. She chose the room's color, pink. And made out the checks.

"Let's try to have it all done before the Juneteenth celebration, Margaret." This is reference to the June nineteenth, Emancipation Day, observance. "Also, I wish you'd order new furniture."

When they brought it from Knabel's Furniture, "But, Margaret, let's have *all* new furniture, not just for the white part. Let's have all the same."

"The old is good enough."

"Then give it away to somebody. To Pete. Or Clarice. We don't have to be saving . . . now. And get *all* the same."

"All right. But that's a waste and people will talk. I know what that Mrs. Greely is going to say."

After it came into use—they began using it before the carpenters finished—the noise that came out of that room! Happy noise. Loud laughing. Like everybody became drunk in there. Aunt Jodie'd go in with her hearing aid squawking and spluttering, and in there you couldn't hear it for all the loud talking and movement and slapping their own knees in laughter. The sounds would come syncopating in to you, almost tickling, and you'd smile. Couldn't help but smile, it was all that contagious.

I whispered to Margaret, "Don't see how anybody comes out of there still sick."

But the Germans and Czechs sat rigid and silent like saying "Them!" or spoke to each other about rain and early Mass. Except on Saturdays, when they all came crowding, they too took on louder sounds of visiting, as if by osmosis. I told Margaret, "They're curing each other without knowing it."

Laughing and laughing until they had tears. Talking—telling and asking. Their hearts sharing, touching. That is the greatest cure, the hearts touching, sharing laughter.

❋❋❋

The line sounded clear, clearer than my head, which was still half asleep. I could hear him distinctly. "You come to my house? Is time for baby."

"Yes. Give me directions."

"You have to wait for you money, until I sell it peks."

"Yes. We'd better hurry. How do I find to your house?"

"I got no money, just kits. Got nodding but kits—is nine."

"Yes. Yes." If she'd had nine—eight—we'd better get there or she'll have it without me. "Where are you?"

"Is calling you from Vrana's Gin. I wait here. Then you follow me. Is too many gates and lanes to tell. And is everything dark."

At the farmhouse, the mother lay down in a clean bed just as we came in. She had made it herself, for there was no other woman around to help. There are almost always other women. The man didn't know where anything was kept, and Margaret and I had to ask the patient everything. She'd answer, "In the closet. The shelf. On the right-hand side, under a shoe box." Or: "A big pot? Look under the cabinet below the shelf of pickles." She gave instructions and had pains alternately.

Three lamps, all with sparkling polished chimneys, radiated plenty light. Children size ten and smaller stood wide eyed all around, and some still lay sleeping, their nightgowns frayed almost into rags, but clean. I knew such worn clothes were only for home use. When it came to going to school or church, each child would be well dressed and wearing shoes, and the shoes would be shining. After looking us all over good, the children went back to bed.

"The baby things? In the basket behind the door. Belly bands is on top—first."

"All ready, freshly washed and ironed," Margaret said, smoothing her hand over them as she laid it all out. "But," she added in soft German, "Bohemian colors again," and her eyes rolled up the bright red walls, and across the ceiling of bright blue, and down the bright yellow woodwork. All newly painted or kept washed totally clean. I felt the oilcloth under the sheet, it would protect the mattress when the water broke. The man made sounds on the porch, pumping water into the large pot.

"We'll need some rags later to clean you up."

"In the chifforobe, third drawer from top down." Margaret pulled a drawer open— "No. No. Not that—"

Margaret screamed! I went. The man came running from the porch. In the drawer lay a baby, sleeping soundly and hardly more than a year old. "Oh, that gave me a surprise. Cute little baby. I've heard of children sleeping in dresser drawers— But shouldn't it be left open? Like this?"

The mother clutched the sides of the mattress and pulled down. Her head strained backwards and the chin came up as if she were looking at the pictures of the saints on the wall above her, but her eyes squeezed shut as she tried to answer, "When closed . . . kits can't fall out."

Wiggling my fingers into gloves I nodded, "Now that's what I call being practical."

It was a hearty baby girl, nine pounds two (by my scale). With the delivery finished, we busily washed, cleaned, and oiled the baby and packed final things away. And the patient got up out of bed. I thought she meant to go on the pot or fix the Kotex on herself better. She did, but next I heard things in the kitchen and she's there in her nightgown making breakfast and talking with an eight-year-old. "You glad is baby sister? You glad is?"

"But you should stay in bed!" And I was practically ready to carry her back, frying pan and all.

"*Ish,* no. Having baby is nodding. Come sit yourself down to table, is almost ready. Eat."

I led the way, sat at the long table. A child climbed up on the bench, snuggled beside me. Here in the kitchen the walls were bright yellow, the woodwork a terminal-cyanotic blue, the ceiling a bowel-movement brown, and the linoleum patterned squares of ivory and gall green. Margaret shook her head slightly in a no!

"You vait? I bake it kolace if you vait." She pointed the ladle to the counter—large tin trays of kolace, puffy rising. "Today is Friday." She pointed again to the unbaked kolace. She served us coffee in big blue-white enamel cups, and sliced fried potatoes with piles of watery sauerkraut on top, and dumplings. "Eat. Eat." And a large plateful before the child, too.

Margaret looked at me as if to say, You got us into this. I looked back saying, I don't care, I'm hungry. The child ate, apparently unaware that it rubbed its bare feet on my thigh and knees while it chewed. Felt good.

"More? I fix more. Eat. The peks get it anyway. Eat."

Actually it was delicious. But under the circumstances, I thought it did smell faintly of afterbirth.

"Eat. Vot you don't eat, peks get it anyway."

As we were driving home, the sky grayed open before us gradually into light. "Since you're always trying to figure them out—see people—see into them—what did you see in her?"

"But wonderful. Absolutely. She's using it. *Doing* it." I laughed.

She breathed a sound like, Humpf.

"She's a creative joy. Well . . . it's hard to explain."

"Nine children."

"I know. I don't mean giving birth to kids, like sausage links. I mean contented and *doing.* She radiates it—like a saint's halo. Like it should be. She's saying such a beautiful thing."

"Neither your 'in' nor 'out'?"

I laughed. "She's . . . she's using it. All of it. In. Out. And balanced. With the big middle—the stalk—being the balance. Like the hospital would have been." I should never have said it—there was no use saying it. And so help me, I said it again, "Like I think the hospital would have been."

A house cat slunk across the road before us, visible clearly in my headlights, a bird hanging from its mouth, the wings dragging down flopping loosely.

"Oh that's horrible!" Margaret exclaimed. "It gives me chill bumps to see it. They ought to feed their cats or drown them." She almost screamed it. "Not throw them out to run wild. That's terrible. When something isn't cared for, it turns wild." She put a handkerchief to her nose.

We drove silently for miles, driving into the early dawning day. Margaret asked, "What are you thinking? You seem so serious."

"Oh, nothing. Nothing especially."

I guess she knew I was lying.

We drove.

***

You couldn't get to everybody, no matter how fast. The phone rang constantly, people knocked on the doors. It was hot. I had all the fans buzzing. Calls were waiting to be made, and who would have thought a big six-foot guy would faint from a typhoid shot? Big beefy fellow, going to start welding in a shipyard in Orange, and needed a typhoid vaccine. I gave it quick and answered the phone and there he came, falling over like "Tim-ber!" The way he hit made the house shake. I hoped he didn't break something. He fell through the doorway so that his head and chest lay in the examining room.

And Aunt Jodie sat on the examining table saying in the middle of everything, as if this body weren't lying on the floor, "Believe I'se gettin' a touch of inward fever," but with her hearing aid snapping and squealing and popping loud electrical sounds, and Margaret trying . . .

"Turn that thing off." She stepped over the big guy's body, where I knelt waiting for him to come to.

"What?" It whined like long steel wires dragged against each other.

"Turn—it—off."

I pulled his chin up and felt for his pulse.

"Fern? Don't recollect nobody name of Fern."

"Off!"

His pulse felt good, he'd be coming around in a minute.

The sounds came like static zinged from outer space.

"What? I don't hear so well."

"No wonder."

"What say?" The man opened his eyes.

"We can't hear with that thing going."

The sounds were like code messages from Mars.

The man closed his eyes.

Aunt Jodie fumbled at her bosom. "Maybe if I turn this up a little."

Margaret pushed Aunt Jodie's hands aside, unbuttoned her dress, found the small black case and the wires and the switch, and it was suddenly silent.

"What you say, Miss Margaret?"

Margaret answered in a most ordinary tone as the phone rang and someone knocked. "I said, Turn it off—it makes noises."

"Oh I coulda done that, honey. You shoulda told me."

The man sat up, "Where am I?"

"Well, I guess I know what you mean. But you're all right; you had your shot."

It was that kind of morning, and in the middle of everything Margaret came wiping her hands. "There's something I want to tell you. They can all simply wait a minute. It happened yesterday. Sit down." I sat down. "About that Nordhausen place."

"No." I stood up.

"But to listen." She changed to German. "Sit yourself down." She used the familiar, but we always do—only the old, old Germans do it properly. "I have some money and I lend it out, and this past week two notes—they came and paid off. One yesterday. And I need a safe place to put it out again. On the interest."

"You lend money?"

"Certainly. Lots of people do. Koricanek? At the lumberyard? They say he has more out on interest than the bank has. But he forecloses. If it's a bad year, doesn't give them time. That's how he got all those farms he owns."

"But you lend money?"

"Many people lend money. When they get old, they live on interest."

"Margaret, to buy that place would take five *thousand* dollars, and that's just to start with. Then there's repairs—roof, basement—equipment. Good Lord, and working capital. It's out of the question."

"I know. But all of a sudden people have money. Overnight. Where did it all come from? The war? Do we get paid for killing other people?"

"Sometimes. . . . yes . . . I guess so. God."

"I don't have enough in all. They paid me thirty-six hundred. That leaves fourteen hundred—"

"It's not enough."

"You have some in the bank. Maybe you'd want to keep that for furnishing and fixing it up. So, I was in Borcher's Saloon day before yesterday—"

"Saloon?"

"I didn't *drink.* They offered, but I didn't. I was selling tickets to the supper at the church—yours is in the drawer. I took the dollar out of change."

"But in Borcher's?"

"Nothing wrong with that. With a few beers in them they buy tickets easier. And they should take their wives out to something once. Besides, Father Puziovsky drops in there every now and then for a beer. A little *schluk* never hurt anybody."

"This is all too much for me."

"No, it isn't. Wait. And while I'm there—sold twenty-two tickets—after that I said to them, 'If Dr. Schulze had enough to buy the Nordhausen place and start a hospital, would any of you be in favor of it and lend money to buy it?' I knew old Fritz Newhaus has money he doesn't know what to do with. And right there, out of ten men, seven said they'd each lend you one hundred. And old Fritz said, 'If he needs more tell him to come see me.' "

"Who's 'old Fritz Newhaus'?"

"They all know you. If you agree, I can get the five thousand together easy. My aunt, the one with the slow cataracts? I know she has some—same thing, a man paid his loan off, too. I don't know where people suddenly have so much money!"

"I can't believe this."

"Me neither. Wasn't expecting them to pay off these notes, at least not until fall. So I need to get it out. Doesn't make anything sitting in the bank."

"Five thousand?"

"Yes. Four percent. Same as banks. But this bank'd never lend to you."

"I'll make it five percent."

"No, no. Four is enough. That's what they said too at the saloon. Four. You'd be a safe place, and that's always the main thing."

"Five percent or nothing. You sure you want to lend me this?"

"Where is a loan more safe?"

"Suppose a hospital doesn't earn its way—can't keep up the interest, much less pay off the?—"

"Your practice will. It does nicely already."

"I can't believe this. Gretchen, just why are you doing this? You're my nurse, bookkeeper, you do the office laundry, fix my jackets, now you're my banker? What is it really?"

"As I said, it's plain good business."

"I'm a walking . . . investment?"

"It's business. But the other—as you asked it and if you don't mind my saying it"—she still used German—"that I am some older; I feel like a sister doing for a younger brother. And it helps me, too."

"Thank you, Gretchen, that's lovely. Just the same, I can't believe this."

***

Early morning and raining.

I hate those messages through the operator: "The line is bad in all this rain; all I could catch was 'Come quick.' "

Soft black mud roads. I fought to keep the car on top, sliding, slipping, spinning, twisting the steering wheel this way, then fast around that way. I managed to get up to the house, ran through the rain, and she's in bed right as you come in and—My God! All that blood between her legs, congealed, and a five-month dead fetus in it looking as if it had tried to swim and drowned gasping.

And the woman is dead. She's the color of dead and her mouth is half open—dead. Her eyes are half-open and dry, and there is no heartbeat—you listen and listen—and no blood pressure. And he, a big man, is standing there like a totally blank gorilla, like a zombie in shock, asking over and over, "Is she dead?" And yes, of course she's dead, but I didn't say it. Because there's still blood—live, red blood still seeping out of her vagina and piling up onto the great slab of dark-red jelly.

I visualized pathopathy lounging there, blowing smoke into the ceiling. *One's mine already. Want to try for two? She's dead, too, but doesn't know it yet. She'll be mine.*

How do you get into people?

By their invitation. They open the doors. You know that. How else could I?

I squeezed down grabbing deep into her flaccid abdomen. Squeezed it down hard into a firm knot, and the small placenta slid-jumped out. The red blood stopped as I held tight the fundus of the uterus, and I said, "Open my bag and bring it closer—I don't want to turn loose."

He stood by the door as if ready to leave and asked, "Is she dead?"

And her eyes opened a little—I was holding on hard, cupping that uterus in my hand, squeezing tight as I could. If she had been conscious she'd have been screaming with pain. She looked at me and closed her eyes down halfway again and—God! this woman is dead. She only *thinks* she's alive. And the rain on the roof . . .

There is no way to move her. Ambulance, car, carry, nothing—she'd be dead before we got to the mailbox.

What'll I do?

"Is she dead?"

"Only when you talk to her," which seemed somehow to make sense to him for a while. I shouldn't say something like that. Surely her mind is still listening; it might discourage her into going away completely. "Come on now, hand me my bag," and he did. I'm sure he didn't know it or wouldn't remember. With one hand I got the syringe and sponge and oxytocic ampule ready and turned loose only long enough to fill the syringe and inject, hoping there was still enough circulation going on to pick it up. And the uterus stayed hard, contracted down. Okay, now no more blood, no more running out. Now how do I start putting something back in? Into her veins?

I told him to go to my car and on the floor, back seat, he'd find glucose bottles—select the ones with ten percent—

"Is she dead?"

"No, of course not! She's very tired right now, yes, but she's going to be perfectly all right." I was talking to her mind, not to him. He'd forget it anyway. I listened over the heart area again. No sound. Nothing. Legally she's dead.

I ran out to the car—it was still raining hard—and got two flasks. I set one up, hooking the bottle on a nail, but how was I going to find a vein when the whole arterial system was collapsed?

Using no anesthetic, I cut down through the skin—it did not bleed—and found the vein there, white and flat. I started the glucose and kept a cc of her blood. "Come here. I must see if your blood crossmatches with hers." I doubt he ever knew I stuck him. "Now hold that on there—this sponge. No, no, on your arm. Oh well . . ."

By the big window in the kitchen I smeared the two together on a glass slide and even without a microscope, could see the tiny clumps of cells forming immediately. Not compatible. He won't do.

I tried the phone. Dead tone.

I checked over the sleeping children. Not a one big enough.

So, nobody left but me.

I drew a sample from my left arm; the zombie husband stood and watched. And I could see no agglutination on the glass slides. Neither her serum with my cells, nor my serum with her cells. Not the tiniest clot that I could see. "Wish I at least had a magnifying glass. Would you have one?"

"No."

I have to take this chance—she's dead anyway—

"Is she dead?"

"No! Of course not! She's going to be perfectly all right!" I said it toward the bed. And loud.

But I decided to give the slides more time first, to be as sure as I could be. I felt for her pulse again. Nothing there. And listened to the rain.

The husband left the room. He was in such shock that if he weren't so big-boned and strong I expected he'd collapse, melt into a puddle of protoplasm. And he came back with the heaviest, most powerful magnifying glass I ever saw, with a thick smooth-carved handle. "Is eyeglass."

"Wherever did you get it?"

"From old country."

Maybe he is coming out of it. God, if only she would.

With the glass I saw no clotting. On any of it. Okay. So with the fifty-cc syringe—I had no citrate, so I used a little glucose solution—I drew fifty cc's out of my left arm and, with the needle left in and dripping blood, I injected the blood into the glucose bottle. And washed the syringe—my last—with glucose and took another. And another. Almost a hundred and fifty cc's. Not enough for somebody who's lost so much. But maybe enough to hold on to for now. And listening, I heard a faint, very faint but regular heartbeat. Could barely hear it with the rain. Maybe the heart had just been sitting there saying, if I had something to pump, I'd pump. And now it had a little blood diluted with a lot of glucose, enough to at least act like it was doing something, so it bumped a halfhearted but regular little dub, dub, dub, as I listened through the sounds of rain.

In town Margaret and I typed and crossmatched her relatives, then gave her more blood at home that afternoon.

She lived.

I have always felt that there was one life I really knew for certain that I had saved. Many you treat and yes, maybe you saved some of them, but also maybe they would have survived and recovered without you, too.

But in her case, I felt I had really done what I'm here to do. She had given me a moment of my life that I could keep forever.

But afterwards I wondered why. *If* she chose this, *why* did she wish this pregnancy dead and be willing to risk such a price. She could not, of course, dare say to herself she didn't want this child. And by throwing it out, she must pay the price of guilt.

But why? And willingly?

Is it worth such a price to remain blind? To remain dishonest to yourself?

After she recovered fully, I never saw them again, and finally Margaret drew an *x* through the bill—"Only wastes more postage."

That part didn't matter. Because they had given my life a moment of rare enrichment and strength that I could hold onto until darkness comes. And it would always give me light. But what did I give her in exchange? *She* did the healing, not I, so what did I really give her? "All you can give somebody is a choice—a chance to choose. I think I've learned that now; I believe I know it now. A chance to choose."

"People don't appreciate what you do for them. You'll learn that." Margaret clattered on at the lavatory; washing syringes.

"The most you can give anybody—not just in medicine, but in everything—is the chance to choose: to heal, to grow, to learn, to enjoy—"

"If they do decide to sell—she's the one wants to—maybe you'll still get paid." Margaret had apparently heard news that they'd spoke of selling the farm.

"—a choice. It's the most you can give anybody. I think I know it now. And I thank them."

I have often thought back on it and wondered if either of them, he or she, ever really knew I was there that morning in all that rain.

***

Paint speckled on my chest, swim shorts, and tennis shoes. I stopped singing and held the brush in midair long enough to watch out the window. Vaclav Pechacek's freight truck came swinging into the drive again. Hope it's the operating room lights this time, especially the big center one for over the table.

I dipped the wide brush into the paint, touched the rim and noticed none had dripped onto the newspapers spread on the floor, so far. Hearing heavy steps coming into this vacant room, I continued to stroke the paint on the gray-mottled, spotted wall. "Vaclav," I said without looking, "I want you to drive careful. Shouldn't knock down those gate posts with your big truck. It's too wide. Go slow."

"Vaclav don't drive fenceposts down. Vaclav good driver—fust class. Drive on road, not fence line. Is ugly color." With hands on hips he looked at all three walls I had already finished.

"I did a whole lot already, no? Four more finished."

"Is ugly."

"It's a nice shade of green. 'Decorator's colors.' "

"Better is red."

"Red?"

"Nize red. Like horse barn. I puke me one time something out like this color green."

"Oh nuts! Well, how much do I owe you this time?"

"Thoity-two eighty."

"That would be more than the lights. How many boxes is it?"

"Is plenty boxes. Big, heavy. Is good Vaclav strong mans. I put it you in the back. What is kitchen."

"Was kitchen. That's the delivery room. Maybe they sent the table too. I'll write the check." I laid the brush across the rim of the bucket, balancing it there, and left, wiping my hands on a kerosene rag. I passed a bathroom where Pete struggled alone, hugging, putting in a new commode. The old yellowed, broken one stood in the hall. "Need a hand, Pete? Should call me."

"Oh now." We both looked out to see a car—his car—stop at the side. His wife—looks Indian, like Pete's brother Slim—got out, said something to the children in the back seat, brought the two smallest boys with her. "Comes again. Always money."

"Okay. My pants are in the dining room—I've got to get used to saying operating room. Take five dollars, okay?"

The new phone, on the floor where the nurses' station will be—if I can find nurses—rang and I picked it up. "Okay, Gretchen."

"This one is a Hanslik boy—twelve. Stepped on a rusty nail. I got it cleaned out, ST, then iodine, bandaged. What next—sulfa?"

"Sulfathiozole, for his age. And tetanus. Be sure to test him first."

"Already did. No reaction. So gave fifteen hundred units. And also: Don't forget to bring the checkbook back. A few bills came in the afternoon mail."

"And tell them even with no reaction, he can still break out with welts up to a week later. So it won't scare them if he does."

I opened the door to downstairs and with my big boots almost fell down the steep narrow steps. "How's it going here?" I asked three guys in undershirts, digging.

"The sandrock digs out good." They pitched it out a back transom. "It should make solid the concrete floor."

"When?"

"Tree, four day we can pour it."

"Sure. It works in here if it outside rains or sunshines."

"Good. Good."

When I returned carrying the check, pinching it by one corner, Vaclav stood high on the stepladder painting. He had completed all the space from the window to the corner. "Don't you drip paint on this floor. It's been sanded and varnished."

It's all taking so much time. When will I *ever* get to the upstairs?

Later, through the office door I heard someone telling Margaret, "Go see my mudder. They saying she don't eat; phone to us last night. She don't know nothing for two years. The klappers in her head don't key right, years already. We put her Hodanek's. We don't want to do it. But my wife cannot watch her all day and all night. Can't feed shickens and pick eggs and rub washboard—all outside—with old womans starting fire inside. In nights, we wake up, and she putting iron lids on stove to make supper, and is two o'clock morning yet. We think she burns us yet the house down. Maybe she inside. Maybe us too. So we put her."

"The doctor will go this morning, Mr. Steffek."

Darn it! And I wanted to get finished here so I could get things done at the hospital. Always seems time is on a treadmill.

And you continue, one person after the next, one moment at a time. Connective-tissue times, heart-muscle times, ordinary muscle tissue, or brain-and-spinal-cord-forever times—it doesn't matter. Each is a part of eternity. Each is a part of you.

But the agony of grinding it slowly when you want to go fast!

Margaret came in, checked through my bag.

"Wish I didn't have to make such calls. Want to finish with all that painting. Have so much to do yet, everything needs—"

"While you're there, examine Mrs. Buske, too, and Mrs. Holloway—you know, the ones with private rooms. It's almost time for their checkups. Here's a syringe and tube for the blood sugar. Be sure you take it on the right one—Mrs. Buske."

"Okay, okay!"

"Something wrong? I'm only trying to remind you."

"I know!"

"Because Mrs. Hodanek didn't know what you were doing last time, so she didn't say you had the wrong one. And you had to go back."

I left without my hat and ran through the rain to the car.

❋❋❋

Heard from the new waiting room: "Das right. This here's Cousin Pearly. She come with me. We all come with Jass. She needin' to see the eye doctor in Flatonia. Her seein' glasses ain't so good no more.

"You don't know Aary Silas, do you? He and Dawcy brothers—Cousin Pearly be their sister. They lookin' for Aary to die."

"I ain't sittin' up with him. To dress and go sit up in town ain't in my ways."

"The pains gets on me too heavy."

"They stayin' yonder ways, close at Smithville."

". . . operated him in Austin. Specialists. Now they lookin' for him to die. Oughtn't done it. Oughta waited until the signs moved out of his stomach, down into his secrets. Cousin Pearly can tell you."

"But I jest can't get myself to fit together right. Thinkin' about Aary to much, got this jumpy heart. I wants to take a tremble from it. If somebody walk up on me and I ain't lookin' . . . ! Jest no-account."

Heard from within the drugstore: "Hajovsky, how come you got it peeps-hole in vall? Vy not you come out and stand in front and look in face with the eyes straight?"

Heard from within myself: I need more time! When will I have enough. I'm not getting enough done.

***

If the hospital had been ready—open and operating—I might not have seen it happen. Gangrene! Who would have waited a few days with a case of gangrene?

Charles Watson, black man, about forty-five. Works at the depot, helps haul freight. A gangrened right foot. Suddenly there it is. No complaint, nothing. Overnight, gangrene. The exact demarcation, the characteristic odor, the "doughy" feeling to touch, and the crepitant sounds when your finger pokes or presses into it.

"Charlie, it'll have to come off. I'm sorry." I hate any kind of amputation.

"No, suh."

"What?"

"No, suh. I don't want it off."

"I know, I know. I don't either. Believe me. But it can grow, spread. It's dangerous, so it must come off." I didn't say, It's already dead, we have to cut it off, death can spread. Dead things seem to grow too, like everything else.

"No, suh. I ain't gonna let it go off. The body ought to take care of itself."

"Yes, yes, it should. But this is gangrene. See? You don't feel this. See?" Again I did not say, It's already dead.

"I'll phone the hospital, and if there's an opening in the county room we'll go tonight yet."

"I'll go to the hospital, but not no cutting it off."

"Have to."

I phoned and there was no space. In talking to the head nurse there at LaGrange, when she described what cases were there, it was clear no vacancy would show up for two or three days at least. I drove back to Charles' house and told him we'd have to wait for a day, maybe two. In the meantime, he should keep the foot up on pillows, take vitamin C tablets for resistance, *not* step on it, and I'd check it at least once every day. Also he should rub it gently with mineral oil.

And if in the morning the black edge had crept higher up his leg? And if there was a high fever?

But nothing changed. It was just like the day before. I phoned again, but nothing had changed at LaGrange hospital—nobody had died. Nothing to do but wait.

I got more of the big rooms—wards—painted green. Nice. If this hospital were open we'd have that gangrened foot off right now, not have to wait for it to get worse.

Tuesday, the third day, the black dead part had not advanced, had not grown. It did seem puzzling.

Wednesday, Charlie said a strange thing. "The body—it's a miracle given from God. It ought to take care of itself." That wouldn't have meant much to me except that the foot had improved! Gangrene improved? Impossible. Absolutely impossible. And this old black man lying there and saying the body should take care of itself?"

"How do you mean, Charlie? This takes care of itself?"

"If it makes something wrong, then it makes something else that would correct it, tha's all."

"Well . . . I don't know about that."

"Sure, I knew it be well. I be atakin' the tablets you gimme and rubbing it gentle-like with the oil."

"Those can't stop gangrene—certainly not cure it. This is . . . improved!"

"And I drink all my urine every day warm, just soon as I—"

"How's that?"

"It's what cures things what's wrong. The body do it. It make something else to correct it."

I sat there in his dark shack, listening to this crazy talk, but remembering that if a pregnant woman has diabetes, the tiny foetus manufactures enough insulin for both itself and for her too. Manufactures enough insulin to control the mother's diabetes—and enough for itself too. But did I hear him right? Drink his own urine?

Thursday his foot was totally healed. Friday he walked on it. It had normal temperature in it, felt normal; when you pinched the toenail blank white and released it, it sprang back pink. Perfect circulation. Did the urine do it? Or the vitamin C tablets? Unthinkable.

I never phoned the hospital again about the county room for him.

❋❋❋

Even short of time, you do stop and pick up Mrs. Rosenbauer. It only takes a minute more.

On a grassy hilltop, forty, fifty acres with big oaks around, is the old dead house, the grand old Rosenbauer place. So old that on maps it's called Rosenbauer Hill.

They're all gone now—dead, insane asylums, moved away, and one hanged himself in the barn. Old Joe was ninety-one when he finally died. Ten years earlier he had married an eighteen-year-old country girl. To get free nursing, they said. She's the last one now. Old. Lives there alone, with a thousand cats.

Mostly everybody leaves her completely alone.

I'd often seen her out there. In rubber boots and wearing a man's black hat—probably one of those left over from old Joe—driving the two tired-looking mules pulling a sled with the milk can on it. If it was real early before the milk truck came, she'd have a wet tow sack over the can because the sun would already be coming up, and a shotgun across her knees. She'd be sitting on the milk can, driving the mules. She'd set the can, rolling it on its bottom edge, off the sled next to the mail box, pull up a few weeds and put them over the tow sack, face the mules into the fence and let them graze in the tall Johnson grass. And she'd lie down there beside the road and wait for the truck. Lie there looking at the sky, chewing on a stem of grass. She had to wait for the truck to drop her other can—she only had the two. But as I got to know her better, I found out the real reason her waiting for the can: "so nobody'd have the chance to put me something in it." A real paranoid, I diagnosed.

"Yes, yes. Gotta watch things like that." I'm not about to argue with any first-class paranoid.

And she retorted with "Ha?"

I remember the first time I saw her like that, on the highway, lying down; I remember it as being the first time I ever got a close-up look at her. I came blaring along in a big hurry to get back to the office, pressing up Rosenbauer Hill and there's a woman's body lying beside the road. And I'm squealing the brakes wondering if she's unconscious and from what, already diagnosing—I knew it must be old Lady Rosenbauer whom I'd heard about—and will I be able to load her into the back seat and get her to a hospital? And I'm running toward her and she sits up—

"Oh, oh, excuse me. I thought . . . maybe you were ill."

She didn't smile, didn't say anything. Looked at me like I must be nuts or something. I didn't know at the time that she's deaf.

I kept backing away. "I'm sorry . . . I thought . . . " I got back in the car swearing from now on to mind my own business. If people want to take a nap along the highway at seven in the morning, a good hard bed is fine for certain kinds of back ailments and maybe that's what the old woman had. Anybody as old as that has a right to such a backache.

Then I remembered that face—it was the first time I had seen it close-up, looking at me out of her bonnet. That nineteen-year-old face. Looking at me. Had that really been the old woman? Must be.

After that I often saw her sitting on the milk can, shotgun across her lap, driving the two old mules toward the wire gap at the road, or lying there. I'd wave as I passed and she'd look like, Wonder what fool that is? Or sometimes I'd see her walking to town or back.

When she walked—eight miles, one way—she always carried a big crocker sack on her back that looked full. It couldn't have been, unless it was full of crushed newspapers or maybe corn shucks.

I got so I stopped and picked her up—poor old soul walking, carrying that sack—and I could never see any shotgun. I pulled up beside her—you could see her way off and you'd know who it was,—and we'd go through the same routine every time. First she'd stand there, looking at me like, Wonder what the fool wants? I wouldn't say anything—she couldn't hear it anyway. She'd be dressed in her go-to-town clothes: men's shoes—high-laced things; a black coat of very fine material—also a man's, maybe it was Joe's and he should have been buried in it, or maybe they did have him in it until time to close the casket; and a man's Sunday hat, black, which must have been too big because she kept one hand on top of it all the way all the time. I'd lean over and open the door and she'd stand there looking (this always took a while). Then she'd pitch her sack in the back seat and climb in backwards with her rump way up, showing the bottom edges of all the skirts she had on, a little of the black stockings, and the high-top shoes. She always backed in. Then she'd turn around and, right in my face, give me this big grin. Really something. You see, she'd put her false teeth in—part of the go-to-town dress-up, I suppose—but they didn't fit anymore and the top ones wouldn't stay up at all. They wouldn't even give it a try. So everything she said had to come through clenched teeth. When she'd give me her "appreciation" smile, teeth and all, it was more like she was going "Grrr!"

All the way to town, she beside me with one hand on top of the hat, we'd not say anything. What'd be the use? If I said something, she couldn't understand me, and if she said anything through those teeth, I couldn't make it out. And there was no use of us going "Ha?" at each other all the way—we tried that the first time—so we just drove along.

In town, I knew where she wanted to go; Boaty Kuchynka's Grocery. Boaty told me she always came there first. She sort of camped there, sitting with her tow sack, knees spread out—everybody could see the black stockings—fanning herself with the hat. She'd camp there for hours and finally get up and leave, maybe not buy anything. She bought very few groceries, anyway, sometimes only a can of coffee, after all that walk. He asked me, "What does she live on?" I didn't know. Milk, I supposed.

And then he told me maybe the strangest thing of all. He said, "She always has money—always a tight roll of bills from selling milk—but she'll steal bread."

"Bread? Steal it?"

"Yeh, steal. She'll open a loaf of bread, take out a few slices, slip them into a pocket, and close the wrapper again and put the loaf back. We find it next morning when the bread man comes to take the old ones back. Steals a few slices of bread. Not every time she comes in, but many times. She has money. We never can figure out why she doesn't buy the whole loaf. If she'd ask we'd give it to her."

"Steals a few slices—Somehow that seems very significant to me. A symptom . . ."

"A what?"

"Say, the bread of life . . . "

"Hunh? What do you mean?"

So I'd stop in front of the grocery and open the door for her—she never found out how to do it herself—and she'd back out, never taking her hand off the hat, giving me a thank-you Grrr! and showing all the skirts over her rump to everybody on the sidewalk. She'd reach in the back for her sack and then slam the door shut like hell. Every time. I always thought I would be hit by flying glass. Each time. She must have thought that's the right way to close a car door, these new models. Then through the window she'd give me a final Grrr! and I'd drive on, promising myself never ever to pick her up again—but knowing . . . Once, in letting her out, I stopped too quick and she hit the windshield. In backing out, during the Grrr!-part she added, "Some folks drives like crazy," and slammed the door.

People in town did ask me, "Why do you pick her up, doc? Hardly nobody else does."

"Oh, I don't know, I believe it's that I kinda respect the old girl." I couldn't tell them I thought anybody who has to prove it that much that she needs no one is saying something desperately: and that she's utterly afraid of being open, that she'd rather die than have to know how raw hungry she is; that the risk of knowing is that dangerous to her. I think the slices of bread said it. As if her love had been turned in on her long ago, or she'd been forced to murder her own love, to strangle her own inward child and mold it hard into tiny tombstones of love calcified into fears.

I thought this, but what I said was, "Guess I appreciate somebody like her, more limited, handicapped, than many of us, yet taking care of herself—getting along, pulling her own weight. Guess it's something like that."

But I did pick up the old girl, and we went through our routines every time—the "Grrr!" and the "Fine morning" and the "Ha?" through clenched teeth.

Sometimes, she did try to tell me things.

"Hadda get me some katridges."

I asked, "Why?" You learned to make your sentences short with her, since you were going to have to repeat each one so often.

Finally we got to, "On account that Ferg'son boy—one of 'em."

Ca'tridges? For a Ferguson boy? "Why?"

And we went through some miles of our "Ha?" "Why?" "Ha?" "Why?" "Ha?" like two idiots until it got to her turn for about the twelfth time and she said, "Why? I told you: the Ferg'son boy."

I made a mental note to phone Ferguson's soon as I got back. I'd have hated to see one of those fine-looking blond-headed kids brought in with his guts all shot up just because he sneaked around after cottontails near her house.

"Why him?" I tried, and we went through that for a mile or more.

"Because he turned my milk can over."

I thought of asking couldn't it have been some of the thousand cats or a roving raccoon or one of the mules or something else, but we didn't have that many miles left. I called Ferguson's anyway and Sally Ferguson said, "Thank you doc, but we know her, living so close by all these years."

"But it would be best to remind the boys to stay away for a while."

"I'll do that."

"Say, I wonder if it'd help calm her feelings if you'd take her a loaf of bread now and then—when you bake."

"Did that. Years ago. Once, didn't see her out for a few days—thought she might be sick. Took some soup and part of a cake—chocolate cake. After that she came here every day. Sat around *all* day. She'd come right after her milking and sit here in my way all day. Couldn't get rid of the woman."

Once, a worker for the new Social Security Administration—he came to town the first Thursday morning in every month—wanted to go see her, to tell her to cash her checks. Maybe she didn't understand what social security was for, or something. He asked Ralph Voght, the deputy sheriff, to go with him, so everybody knew he had heard about her shotgun. On the way out there, Ralph tried to brief him about her ways, "I'd suggest you don't try to argue none with her about nothing. Just agree with anything she says."

"No, I don't argue with anybody. Just want to explain to her. Or maybe she's not getting her checks. But they don't come back."

"And you gotta holler at her." So the man did, and he finally got across that his visit was about the checks she had been getting through the mail

"Oh them."

"Yes," the young man sighed, "it's about them."

"Yeah. He keeps sendin' 'em all the time. Must be some crazy feller. Sends me his money to keep for him. I figgered soon-later he'd come for it. Is it you? There they are. All in that drawer. You can take 'em. Sure wisht you'd take care of 'em yourself 'stead of always send it to me. Somebody could come in here when I'm gone and steal 'em or burn the house down."

"No, no. They're yours. To cash. But not those past sixty days old. You'll have to be reissued new vouchers and sign . . ." He was lost. Ralph said the poor fellow really tried. Said there must have been several hundred dollars worth of checks in that dresser drawer. And he said that young man didn't say a word all the way back to town.

Well, that's the way it was. People would see an old woman with a sack on her back and holding one hand on top of her hat. They could pick her up or not—didn't seem to make any noticeable difference one way or another with her. Not that you could tell. Mostly, everybody left her alone.

Every time I saw her, I remembered about those slices of bread.

***

I stood before the huge iron-studded Gothic doors of the Incarnate Word Convent, on the courthouse square in Victoria, Texas. The gates were like you'd dream the entrance to heaven must be. I waited on the terrace in the hot sun, and studied the courthouse, deciding. Should I ring the bell again? Maybe it's not working—I didn't hear anything inside. I'll wait. Such an immense place, a palace, one whole side of the square. And I watched the big clock. Ten minutes past three. It was like waiting for Judgment Day.

Maybe they'll say no . . . and send me to hell.

Not yet. One of the heavy doors began to move, almost mysteriously, and opened enough for me to see its enormous thickness. An eye looked at me across a chain and said nothing. Either she stood bending over—the eye was at keyhole level—or she was a dwarf. "Howdy," I said to the eye. "I'm a doctor; I practice in Schulenburg. I'm starting a hospital there, and I want you Sisters to come take over and run it. The nursing and everything." It kept looking but the massive door slowly began closing, squeezing everything off, and some iron clanked closed.

I didn't know if I had talked to somebody or not. Surely it wasn't the Holy Spirit: I had definitely seen an eye. But should I ring again? Start over? I waited.

The door opened again—same chain, darker eye, slightly taller than the first—or wasn't leaning over so far. I said again who I am and why I'm here and, "So I came to find out: Will you take it over, run it?" This eye kept looking, the door didn't close. "Will you?"

The voice was very young: "I couldn't say, right off. I believe I'd have to ask Reverend Mother first."

"Yes. I should think so, too."

This time, before I could get far in rereading the signs all around the square and the clock in the tower, the door unlocked and opened wide and a nun in long angelic white habit and starched head frame stood asking, "Did you have an appointment with Reverend Mother?"

"No, I didn't think I could discuss any of it over the phone—not in our small town." And I told her too, the whole thing; who I am, where I'm from, purpose of visit, and request. I was getting it better organized each time.

She stayed gone so long I read and reread every business sign around the square five and a half times, faster each time. *It'll make me dizzy; I quit.* Thought of all the many things that still needed doing, waiting at the hospital. Wondered if Margaret could have figured out where I went. Told her I was going to Houston, to see about light fixtures and call-light panel. Reset my watch; three forty-nine. I could have gone across to the Blue Bonnet Cafe and had coffee and sandwiches. But suddenly the door unclacked and swung open wide and easy, as if it had become weightless. "She said she would give you an audience immediately. Come this way, please."

I followed the tall figure, which seemed almost to be floating, through Gothic arches and halls, across handsome tile floors, along porches bordering landscaped courtyards. Everything, I noticed, shone exquisitely clean. On and on we walked, past a courtyard where nuns in long black gowns walked slowly, quietly, back and forth. I followed on through the darkened quiet and coolness and up broad polished stairs that creaked.

The Reverend Mother sat in a chair so tall, so carved, it seemed like a throne. Her chubby round face did not smile, but studied me with frank curiosity.

"Thank you, Reverend Mother. It is kind of you to see me without any previous warning; I should have written."

"This is Sister Aquinas," she answered, indicating a very old nun who was eighty-five if a day and in her white habit looked just like all the others except for her totally wrinkled face, which seemed that of a freshly unwrapped mummy.

All the wrinkles instantly angled into a most pleasing expression and she said, "I am delighted to know you."

"It's certainly mutual," and I liked the old one immediately. "Reverend Mother," I addressed the chubby one on the throne, "I came for a most selfish reason. I am starting a hospital and I want you Sisters to run it. To take it over completely, set the rates, collect the bills, hire the personnel—everything.

"But first I must tell you, I am not Catholic myself—probably just plain heathen, if anything. No, I was raised Lutheran. Don't know how much of it 'took', but I am definitely not religious in any church-going sense. However, the community where I practice is predominantly Catholic. And that is one reason why I believe Sisters could serve it best.

"Another reason is: As a student and as an intern I did work in several hospitals, and I saw that those run by Sisters were always the cleanest, gave the most to the patient, were the most dedicated. The nuns never came on duty tired from a date the night before, nor were they watching the clock, nor squabbling among themselves. And these are the reasons why I am asking."

"Thank you. We've heard that from many. But it is impossible. We don't have enough for our own hospitals. I do wish to ask you: Who sent you to us?"

"No one."

"I mean, who told you to come to us?"

"No one. I knew Incarnate Word operates Santa Rosa in San Antonio, but probably that's a different branch of this order. And I knew your order operates—owns—the Burns Hospital in Cuero. That's all."

Sister Aquinas leaned forward to Reverend Mother's elbow. "We do some nursing, the Burns Hospital and in Yoakum, Huth Memorial. But we are primarily a teaching order. We have schools."

"Oh. I didn't know that."

"But who told you we might even be interested? We have our hands full and not enough active Sisters."

"But no one told me. I came on my own. My own idea—dream, I guess. I didn't know you . . . taught schools."

"Since you requested, we will have to report it and discuss the matter with the archbishop. And he will have to instruct us. Did you contact his office?"

"No. I didn't know how this is handled. I simply thought you decided—"

"But we do so little nursing. We're all teachers. And we keep the church, of course."

"Keep the church?"

"Yes, the cathedral. See that it is clean, altar cloths changed, wine for the Mass—the routines of keeping the church. But we must now ask the archbishop for further guidance. He will decide and we shall let you know."

I followed the same Sister—*so little nursing*—across courtyards—*we are a teaching order*—down steps—*impossible*—across courtyards—*we do not have enough Sisters for our own hospitals* . . . And outside in the hot sun—*impossible*—the great door closed and I heard the iron latch clack closed.

❋❋❋

Her dress looked dirty and had a torn place right in front, her hair was uncombed and greasy wild, and she stood in the waiting room, looking in. Stood with her feet far apart. Stood as if straddling an invisible barrel. The man behind, dirty as she and unshaved, looked ill-at-ease like he wished they hadn't come. "Come, Mrs. Weems, come in," Margaret was saying as if she'd said it before. She handed me a new card: Mrs. Truly Weems, Box 278A, Route. . . . At the same time, in a whispered German, "They use up your time and don't pay. Why do you not refuse?"

"I know I want the time, but I guess . . . this is what time was made for.

"Come in, Mrs. Weems," I said; "Come in, Mr. Weems."

Mrs. Truly Weems. It turned out to be about a prolapsed womb, appreciation, and a pear tree. And, frankly, I wouldn't have believed it either. But it is people.

"Can't pay for it," the woman answered loudly and kept standing.

"Come in," Margaret coaxed.

She stood. "Ain't got no money."

"Come in, Mrs. Weems," I beckoned. "It's all right."

She walked slowly, keeping her feet far apart, like walking down a railroad track on both rails. "Don't cater to no misunderstandin'; we ain't got nothin'."

"That's all right. What do you have?"

"Said ain't got nothin'!" She spoke still louder.

"I mean, what's the trouble?" I didn't ask, What makes you walk like that.

"Hit's my womb."

"Womb?" How could a womb—uterus—cause a person to walk so—

"I said hit's my womb," she repeated louder. "Been thisaway for yars."

Now I really didn't understand how a womb could possibly get in the way of one's walking. The very idea is ridiculous. Not until she lay on the table and I began to examine her and found the whole thing hanging outside. Prolapsed. The entire thing. It laid out there like an old overcoat sleeve.

So of course, yes, a womb can too get in the way of your walking, if it's all hanging outside, baglike, slapping around down there between your knees. It was the oddest-looking thing, with ulcers, filth—I'm sure it attracted flies—and its round cervix at the bottom end like a surprised little circular mouth saying Oh no! In German I muttered to Margaret, "Even in the textbooks it's nothing this bad." Loudly I asked, "How many children did you have?"

"Fifteen—three living. And two misses."

"Oh!"

"Hit's my womb, ain't it?"

"Sure is." Hanging down there like a bag. Womb and your fallopian tubes and bladder and ovarian ligaments and the broad ligaments and maybe the ovaries, all in the bag, all hanging way down. Sure is. Good thing she doesn't ride a bicycle.

Margaret tossed one of the hard-rubber pessaries on the table. Her gesture said: This is the largest size, and it wouldn't begin to fit *that* uterus back up into place. I shook my head and she replaced the pessary into the set.

"Hit's fallen, hain't it?"

Like London Bridge. "Yes."

"Hit's a fallen womb, ain't it?" she asked the ceiling.

Hit ain't just leaning. I stood closer over her face and nodded big, "You're right, it sure is."

"You gonna have to cut it out?"

Out? Lady, this is one we can cut *off.* "It would certainly be best. No use like it is, and it is a possible source of danger." She seemed anemic and wormy and undernourished, not a good surgical risk. "I'll have to build your resistance up some first—your blood. And get the infection out."

"How's zat?"

"You'll have to take some medicine first for a while. But fifteen births! Seventeen pregnancies! I have to do some tests and examine you in a week."

"How's zat?"

When she returned the next week, her condition was much better. That little business of soap and water ("Use this special blue antiseptic soap. It's medicated; it's like a medicine. Use it every day.") had worked wonders, got all the outside infection cleared. And sulfa and one injection of vitamins had all helped clear the inside tissues too. Now it was a rosier color, pink as a baby. But I still couldn't get over the sight of a uterus swinging and swaying around down there like a cow's udder. Her hemoglobin count also improved, a little higher.

"I don't want no more shots. They hurt."

"You're doing much better already. Now continue with everything and let's check again in a week."

"I don't need no more shots, do I?"

The next time, Margaret already had her on the table, her knees up in stirrups, and covered with the sheet. Margaret held out the sterile glove to me. I flipped the sheet back to examine and—It's not there! Gone!

"What? Where is it? Where is your womb?"

"How's zat?"

I inserted my fingers and hit a hard object. "What's that?"

"Hah?"

"What's that . . . thing in you?"

"Hit's a pear," she explained to the ceiling. "They gettin' about right size now. Hit's a old tree—no idee who mighta planted it—old."

"You inserted a pear?"

"How's zat?"

I didn't try again.

"Holds it all up in place right tidy. Used 'em for yars."

And well, yes, a pear would make an excellent pessary: right shape, size, smooth surface, disposable. That is, if anybody would have thought of it.

We had to wait for a space in the county room at LaGrange. The operation went well and so did the post-op period, the recovery. Mrs. Weems was discharged from the hospital and came to the office for weekly post-op checkups, and on the third one I told her she wouldn't have to come back anymore unless she developed some other condition or complaint. I reminded her again not to lift anything heavy for another month. She thanked me "very kindly."

A week later she was in the office, back on the regular date.

"But it's healed," I said. "You didn't have to come. Did something else turn up?"

"Naw, hit's nothin' like that. Jest wanna show my 'preciates. Pears comin' in now, gettin' ripe." With both feet she slid a tattered basketful of pears along the floor, walking somewhat like she used to. "Brung you some eatin' pears." She pointed to the basket. Directly under her it resembled a large nest of setting eggs. "I don't hafta use 'em no more, so's got plenty. Brung you some."

❋❋❋

Susan came in. She showed now.

"How is it . . . with the waiting, Susan?"

"Awright, I guess, Hafta be. Waitin' for a baby, 'es awright. But I don't wanna think about bein' old."

"Are you still of a mind . . . hmm? . . . to let Ora have it?"

"I think so. We decided. She gonna be here when it's born and she can select the name."

"She'll take it to California, I guess?"

"But she be comin' home for visits and bringin' the baby. When this war be over, if ever. Have to. Made her promise."

I had to smile. "Hope we'll have the hospital all going by that time. Let's see: September fifteenth to October first is as near as we got the date. Plenty time yet."

"She comin' on the twelfth, September."

"She? You sure?"

"Ora. Gonna stay with me till you say the baby all right for the train trip. It's two days and one night. She say it ain't no chance of gettin' bumped off in some strange place, like it is by flying, but she'd rather fly home. A friend, goin' to see her sick mother in Hot Springs—she got bumped off the plane by a colonel carryin' a bag of golf sticks. And another—and he in uniform—got put off to make room for a general's dog! But the trains is so crowded. Leastways the back parts, and Ora ain't fair-complected enough to pass for white. I ain't neither."

As I put in two drops of the reagent and heated the test tube over the small blue flame, she sat quiet. "You look pensive, Susan. Something troubling you? You look like you're studying something over. Any questions I might be able to answer?"

"Just that . . . I think Ora'll make a good mother, be a good mother . . . to the baby.

"I can still keep workin', cain't I? I told my white lady I'd have to quit when you said."

And she said again, "I know Ora'd always do good for the baby."

My thoughts said, If this one comes breech, I'm ready, even facedown . . . thanks to a dead baby lying in a heap on a surgical tray. Thank you, dead baby, thank you. So strange that even dead, you can still give to other people . . . sometimes can still give other people their lives.

❋❋❋

Sunday morning. The sheriff from LaGrange phoned. "Can you come see an old woman at the County Farm." The regular doctor who took care of most county cases, Dr. Guenther, was gone somewhere, so he had phoned me.

If I could get back soon enough, I could still work at the hospital later, in the afternoon. "Sure. What's a county farm and where is it?"

"You've never been before." I noticed he doesn't ask you, he tells you.

"Nope. What seems to be the trouble and how do I get there?"

"The county pays only two dollars a call, but they're always behind, so you may not get anything."

"That's okay." Not that it sounded like I had much choice. "Where?"

"I have to take some workers from there to a farm, so I might as well meet you and then you follow."

He drove a pickup truck; I followed, in the dust and along through beautiful country roads I had never seen before, with huge trees tunneling us in their shade. We drove farther and farther into thick growth and great tall Johnson grass and bloodweeds and the biggest pecan trees I ever did see, like redwoods, and the coolness said we were coming near the river. "He maketh me to lie down in green pastures"—you could *feel* it here.

He drove over a cattle guard and past the farm buildings clustered under magnificent oaks, and he stopped at the door of a long shed with rusty tin roof. I followed his big hat and broad hips with the pistol moving up and down as he walked, followed into the dark of the shed, and I couldn't see much but could feel there was no floor, only the dirt. "Where is she," he said to somebody who must have pointed, because I didn't hear anybody say. Could she be in this barn? Why had they moved her out here?

I could see now and I couldn't believe it: Down each side sat a row of old, old people, each sitting exactly beside a long narrow table that slanted downward toward the center aisle. Each old person sat at the same place, near the aisle, each with one hand in his or her lap, and the other at the same place, near the aisle, each with one hand in his or her lap, and the other arm along on the table. Somewhat like Whistler's mother, but long rows of them. And all perfectly still as a picture. As if time had frozen hard still, had almost stopped.

"Why do the tables slant so strange?"

"What tables?" the man asked.

"Those. There."

"That's beds."

"Beds?" I laughed. "Couldn't be. Wouldn't the mattress slide forward—downward—during the night?" We kept walking along the dirt-gravel floor.

"We . . . the county don't furnish no mattresses."

I really didn't understand him. As we passed them, I nodded, smiled; some glanced up and at meeting my eyes instantly looked down or away. "Beds you say? Never saw a table like a bed before. Except autopsy tables are made like that to drain away the— Beds?"

He didn't answer. Nor the sheriff either. I followed. Our boots cr-crunch, cr-crunch, cr-crunched.

They sat dressed in gray or black or dingy blue—not a real white piece of cloth anywhere. Nor any colors left, all faded away. A strong odor of urine. I touched an old woman on the shoulder. "Morning, grandmother," but before my words were out I felt her body jerk into a rigid hardness. *I'm sorry, I didn't mean to frighten you.* That urine odor!

"Oh now I know! The poor farm. So this is it? I'd heard of— But I thought under Roosevelt, all this disappeared, changed—with old age pensions. What is . . . why is *this?*"

"These came from Europe, never took out citizenship. So they don't get it."

"That's odd. I'm sure they lived here most of their life." Wouldn't this line ever end? And the urine odor became so strong now—ammoniac—that it disappeared. God! What is this place? "Surely they must have thought they were Americans."

"They thought it, but they got no papers to prove it. None of 'em talks English." Each old person with one hand in the lap, sat exactly as the last, like rows of something on shelves in a store. How can we do this. "They're foreigners. Of other countries. Some we're fighting. Foreign aliens. They're lucky we don't send them to jail."

"Good God!"

"Foreign enemies. And we feeding them."

A man's lip; swollen, busted, bruised blue. I stopped to look at it. "What happened to him?" and I saw the man's eyes enlarge at me in anger, or fear, and his hand on the wood bed began to tremble and rattle into a dancing.

"Not him," the county man's voice said and continued going. I followed.

These people simply must have an extremely high threshold for suffering. "Where are . . . their families?"

"Ain't got none. That's their trouble. Or disappeared. Wish we knew: I'd send bills for their keep. Or they'd have to take 'em. No siree, if any have families, they're smart enough to stay away." We stopped before a woman; he pointed. "Her."

The old woman also had a swollen lip, lacerated, and two teeth broken off there—the stumps hung loose. "She fell," the man's voice said behind me. The sheriff stood saying nothing.

Why isn't she senile? Why aren't they all senile?

Slowly I raised the thick lip again with both my thumbs. "What do you want me to do about this?" My voice had too much anger; I added, "I'm not a dentist."

"Nothing. Examine her to see if she's got the TB. If she has, she goes to the barn."

I tried to talk with her, German first. No response, tried Czech. She said a few words, something, but with her teeth and lip and dialect, I didn't understand much but *vykaslati* (cough) and *krvavy* (of blood). Why isn't she senile?—she could turn all this off. I listened to the bony chest with flaps of skin for breasts, the large nipples hanging at the bottom like drains. I was going to tell her to cough while I listened, but she coughed and swallowed. While I listened I glanced down at the old dress, rumpled and worn as if she'd been sleeping in it; saw her hard hands; the two sharp knees under the long gray skirt, which down at the hem had caked bowel movement. I looked elsewhere and listened through the stethoscope and saw the shelf of bent tin bowls and big spoons.

Why aren't they senile?

Senile, dear doctor, is not the only alternate level of living, not the only choice.

But what—why are they waiting? For what?

Doesn't everyone? Wait?

I listened. The delicate fine rales—crepitant rales—in both apexes, like thin silk threads tearing, and in the right lower. It won't be long now, little mother. I listened on the back of her chest, between the ribs—how skinny do they get?—and saw the purple bruises with blue-yellow edges. I looked at the sheriff who looked at the bruises, then looked at me, his eyes saying, "I don't see a thing." The fine rales again, on each inspiration.

Why haven't you chosen senility? Why stay and face this . . . this reality? Such a high threshold for suffering. Little mother, your waiting is almost finished. You waited for what? Where is the life you should have had? Always waiting for something to be better?

I listened. Each intake of air ended in showers of the fine crackling sounds. I listened more, here, there, back over the apex of each lung around the gaunt collarbone where the tiny rales crackled the most. Little mother, I do not blame you. I touched the thick hornlike hand in her lap, shocked to feel how soft and tender mine turned back to me. She took the hands away, both, and cupped them together as if to say no, that's the one thing you can't have. You can punch and thump and listen and have me stripped half-naked and shamed with this poor body, and I allow it and shame myself that I do. But not these hands. No, they are wholly mine.

I stood up, folding my stethoscope away, and said mechanically, "She has it," as if I were talking to no one, and looked straight ahead, out the window—barn window, no screen—at a cemetery with no headstones. Only wood stobs, each with a white card on it. And three new freshly dug graves, open. Somewhere I heard the sounds of chains, or something that sounded like chains.

As we started the walk back up to the bright door, I asked, "While I'm here, anyone else I should see?"

The sheriff said—the first time he'd spoken since we got here— "I told doc, the county pays two dollars per person, but that it's always slow in coming, if ever."

"I'm not charging anything—I couldn't. Is there anybody else? She may have infected others already."

"I guess not."

"I'd be glad to."

"No. The county don't like a lot of medicine bills—from the drugstores."

"I'd be glad to."

They didn't answer. But there was a sound of chains, a rhythmic jangle. Through another window I saw a man on horseback, sitting, doing nothing, a rifle across his saddle horn. When we came to the door, I saw a line of men with shovels on their shoulders and chains on their ankles. Each picked up his length of chain which then became silent as they climbed up onto the sheriff's truck.

❋❋❋

Patient after patient, like bee swarms, but of people. I wanted to tell Margaret, ached to tell her, I had driven to Victoria that one day to the convent and asked the nuns. But that I haven't heard.

Patients coming with small disease disguises; sore throat, upper respiratory, infected ear . . . Is it only from the weather changing back and forth? Or is the weather the excuse for saying other "small" things? And those who bring large diseases, one of whom is a middle-aged man with nephritis? What? Why? Nephritis—there's nothing larger; it's finally fatal. Why nephritis? Is life becoming too complicated for him, the dream of rewards and fulfillments fading away? Why such a severe saying as nephritis?

On Fridays and Saturdays some bring Margaret flowers for the church altar on Sunday, armfuls. She's always asking them, "Are your gladioluses blooming? I'll need enough for one more vase." "Sweetpeas, you say? Thank you just the same, but I think it should be something taller, don't you? So it can be seen from the back rows, too. Or larkspurs, would you have larkspurs?" She keeps the flowers in big buckets in the X-ray room where it's dark. I tell her the flowers don't have color in the dark—they're made for light. She says it "saves" them.

"Like 'waiting'? " I asked. She didn't know, of course.

But I dare not tell anybody. It'd get out somehow. She'd be too pleased. She'd have to whisper it to somebody, maybe even to her card club, and it'd get all over town ("Now don't breathe it to a soul, but *nuns* might . . . ").

Patients of all ages and all languages of disease. An older woman who has to walk to town. Had five children; now has varicose ulcers and the danger of phlebitis. Patients come along in this unclassified, jumbled, unselected way, for this is general practice and is the way of life, all life. One doesn't know what's next. Could be a skin rash or an incurable tumor of the spinal cord. Mexican child with diarrhea—they probably have no refrigeration and the child ate something spoiled. I won't ask about an icebox. May only embarrass them. Black child with sickle-cell anemia. Why?

And if the nuns should refuse to take over the hospital?

I want so for it to get off to a good start.

Boy—emergency—with a live bug in his ear. "Open a can of ether, Margaret. We must kill the bug first with a few drops, then wash it out."

"Crawling, clawing in my head. It's driving me crazy."

"Yes, son."

And that phone will drive me insane for sure. "Hello!"

"Hello?"

"Yes, hello."

"Hello?"

"Yes, yes. Hello!"

"Doktor?"

"Yes."

"You behind Hajovsky?"

"Yes. What is it? What can I do for you?"

"You hexamine my brudder if we bring him by you?"

"Sure. What's ailing—what's the matter with him? How is he sick?"

"He's sometimes and sometimes not."

"How is that? Come again?"

"What?"

"How is he sick?"

"He's sometimes here and the odder half not so much."

Is he describing epilepsy? Or narcolepsy? Syncope? Whoever he is, and whatever, he certainly must be turning it *in.* "You mean, his mind? Comes and goes?"

"Maybe yes, maybe no. I don't know so good."

Don't tell me it's catching. "Okay then. You bring him in anytime."

"What?"

"Bring him in. Is he cooperative—will he let you bring him in?"

"I haven't asked him yet."

"I mean, do you think you can bring him in without trouble?"

"What?"

"You implied that sometimes he's not— *can* you bring him in to be examined?"

"When?"

"Any day. I'm in the office every day."

"Sundays too?"

"No, not on Sunday. I want to quit that. I want one day off."

"Sunday is gut time. You not so busy."

"Any day except Sunday."

"Sunday gut time. Go to early Mass and then nodding to do all day."

"Not on Sunday."

"Is no working in field on Sundays. Gut time."

"Not on Sunday. You know that."

"Is gut time. Is already dressed up for going to town."

"Not on Sunday."

"What?"

"Any other day. Good-by."

"Gut. Then we bring him Sunday. Sunday morning? Vot time?"

I sighed into the phone. "Oh all right! About nine or nine-thirty. Right after Mass."

"We should come Sunday?"

"Yes, yes!"

"Vitch Sunday?"

⁂

The same thing all over again! Someday she's going to come in here blind.

"Now look, Mrs. Schneider. I don't know what to do for you. To prevent it. Something is giving you this. It doesn't make sense. Your're doing something that starts it off. Else it wouldn't come on so suddenly. Try to remember. What do you think causes this? Do you know? Have you thought about it?"

She looked at me, looked down at her feet. Margaret stood waiting as if she'd like to know too. Mrs. Schneider looked at her, nervously wiggled her big shoe with the buttoned straps across the bony instep. She crossed her thin ankles with the big knotty feet and recrossed them. Finally she looked squarely at Margaret.

"Oh yes, Margaret. Please go take care of the waiting room." We waited until the door closed. "Now what is it that causes this infection? Do you know?"

She kept her greased lip stiff over her upper teeth. "I guess I'll have to quit it." She pulled slightly on the wide new brown ruffle added to the hem of the faded yellow dress.

"Quit what?"

"It's all my husband's fault."

"What is his fault?"

"My so-called husband."

I waited.

"But at bedtime I sometimes put a few drops of milk in my eyes."

"Milk? I don't understand. Is it a home remedy of some kind? Whatever for?"

"Well it—it makes the eyes sparkle a little the next day. Or maybe you didn't notice." She smiled, nervously, big.

"Huh?" I stared at the missing tooth, the skeleton hands and thin legs, the bony face powdered into a white skull. How in heaven's name? . . .

She began to fidget more. Glanced at the door. Wrapped a handkerchief around two fingers; unwound it. "It's hard, doctor, it's very hard to be . . . " She never finished. Just pulled at the handkerchief.

I called Margaret loudly through the closed door. She stepped in so quickly she must have been just outside. "Fix the usual for Mrs. Schneider."

Then I caught myself and tried to be a little kinder. But even though I made efforts to be accommodating to her and to say pleasant, unimportant things and be gentle with the salve application, she said nothing more the whole time.

After she left, I kept trying to understand my aversion. "Why would anyone risk going blind again and again for so little!

"Now I shouldn't judge, that's not my job; I should try to understand her.

"Then why am I judging?"

Margaret said nothing—let me keep on talking.

"What did her actions say? What has this pathopathy told me, taught me? Surely pathopathy says its purpose simply by performing it. Why is it so hard for me to hear it, to see it?" I guess I was talking to myself.

"So she feels alone, a failure. One should have pity for her—sorrow for all in that need. She wants acceptance, friendship, safety in those around her. So in her own limited way, she asks for it. And maybe: the greater the need, the more desperate the try."

Now, how could I help her to get a little more confidence in herself so she wouldn't need to blame and push other people around.

I couldn't think of a thing.

Stayed blind to it.

⁂

Wearing only my swim shorts, I came backing down the ladder, holding the bucket in one hand the brush in the other, and looking down, I saw Mrs. Fajkus, Vincent Fajkus' wife, sitting in the ladder.

She'll want something, it'll take time, and I won't finish painting.

As she got up, standing, she pulled the skirt out of her buttocks. "I'm vaiting for you. The Mexican boy I tell him and he say he don't know vere is you. I tell him I need me nudder shot for hot flashing. I think he don't vants to call you from roof down, so I am vaiting."

"Why didn't you come on up and help?"

"I'm phoning for you, and operator is saying she can see you on the roof—is no use phoning. I tell her I need me nudder shot for hot flashing. She say her oldest sister got it too."

Wiping paint from my hands and elbow, and trying to get some off my stomach. "Well is there anything else?"

"Is shots. Hot flashing is coming back so I need me more shots."

"I don't have it here. Margaret's gone by now. Can you come in the morning? At the office? I want to putty around some windows yet before it gets too dark."

"But tomorrow we begin cutting tops, and Vincent can't bring me and is already hot flashing, and so in head, *se touche,* too. Ye-siz Maria."

"Okay. We'll go to the office. Pete," I called, "Pete!"

He looked out the upstairs window.

"I'm going and probably won't be back. Anything you need before I go?"

His head went back in.

Then it came out again. "I told John come help—he's here. Says he can use five dollars."

"I'll leave it in the dining—under the telephone."

I dressed in the future operating room. It's eight days now and still haven't heard anything from the Sisters. Should I tell Margaret anyway? Tell her I asked and they're probably not coming?

When I got back to the office, Mrs. Fajkus sat in the car, in front of the drugstore, fanning herself.

When I'd finished with her, a pharmaceuticals house detail man came in. He piled a stack of samples on my desk with literature about the new drugs—always bright colors—and closed his bag and said, "I notice you don't smoke those new filtered kind."

"No, I prefer these."

"I asked one doctor why he didn't smoke filtered ones. He said, 'That would be like sucking a nipple through a nightgown.' "

Detail men are always full of jokes like that—goes with the territory. It takes time to listen to them, but I hate to be impolite.

Still haven't received a letter from Reverend Mother.

Won't I ever hear from that convent? Have they decided not to come? Dropped the whole thing? Seems like they'd at least tell me so.

Where the hell am I going to get enough nurses?

❋❋❋

A man alone, so Margaret stepped out. Edwin Winkleman. Middle aged. Took care of his parents after all the brothers and sisters left and married. Now alone on the farm, which is gradually deteriorating; the roofs, the pens, fences. The others gone, married off, living in the city. Edwin home alone.

"Have something up my rectum." He did not look up at me. His clothes were washed but not ironed. "Can't get it out. A hoe handle."

"A what? Oh. Well. Let's see. Bend over."

A hoe handle. About eight or ten inches of one, near as I could palpate in the abdomen without pushing too hard. By rectal exam my finger could feel the flat, sawed-off end. "It'll be tricky to get a hold on it. What instrument will? . . ."

I didn't ask how it happened—no use to embarrass him more. He didn't come here to be hurt more.

But how'm I going to get it out? A corkscrew of some kind might get into the wood . . . But no, it'd only make the wood turn. There is a forceps called "snake-tooth" that has two small sharp teeth at the top, two at the bottom, and it opens wide like a snake's mouth. Now if I could get that pronged into the wood without snagging the intestinal lining . . . My finger held it off—he was being very cooperative—to protect it well. It worked! I pulled the wood handle out easily and the rectum mouthed itself closed like a puckered kiss and seemed to swallow.

"Now there, Edwin, all done. Didn't hurt any now did it?" Had been in him for days, the thing stank.

I wrapped it in a newspaper without touching it and handed it to him.

***

Margaret kept talking while putting the samples away. "A new family. They only just arrived, moved to town." She knows everything. "Reillys. That's Irish. Saw them at Mass. Big family—must be six or seven children. Several are big, grown. So many. Took up a whole bench."

"What on earth is an Irishman gonna do here? You have to be German or Bohemian—I mean Czech—to even talk to somebody. Do you know his job?"

"Jim Harrington is Irish. Worked here for years—works for Eastern Seed."

"Yeah, forgot him. But what's the new one do? Did you find out?"

"Certainly. You don't think if I'm going to pump a gossip I'm only going to get a little bit?"

"Yes, and whoever she is, she'll pump you about patients in return."

"Do you want to know what I learned?"

"To tell the truth, I do. But I hate to ask."

"He's an auditor for the county. Like a bookkeeper about where the money goes to. And for several other counties around here, too, and chose to live here so he'd have about the same driving distance to any of the courthouses. He's something or other in politics. They've got that big old Sengleman house."

In the afternoon I saw him walking—knew him immediately—near Mike Goldstein's Store and Shaeftner's Hardware, toward Olle's Barber shop. Fat man. Very fat. I honked and waved and he didn't know me but instantly waved back, smiling—waved big. So different than when you honk and wave to Germans or Czechs. They just stand and look, like they're trying to remember if they've ever seen you before, trying to place you. And you know they know you. Even those in the fields sometimes do that, and they know your car a whole hill away. Maybe he and I did know each other from that moment on.

And I went to see him that same evening. I knew I shouldn't take the time—but yes I should. He sat reading on the porch. Fat man. Very fat. Round. His head seemed much too small now for his body. (You could always tell Olle's haircuts—he wanted to be sure to give you your money's worth.) "Howdy, Mr. Reilly. Welcome here. I'm a doctor and want to ask your advice, if you don't mind."

"First, I want to say thank you, doctor, thank you. And then to say

I'm good at giving advice, on anything from childbearing to Supreme Court decisions. Advice, you know, is the cheapest, or maybe costliest, thing around. But let's try. What is it?"

If we hadn't liked each other this afternoon on the street, we did now. For certain.

"I can't discuss this with anybody in the town—it'd probably be too close to them. But this anxiety I'm carrying is getting too close to being, becoming, hate. Getting too heavy to hold." And I told him about starting a hospital and that I asked the nuns—it being an almost totally Catholic place—and how I haven't heard from them since. And that I really wanted them, that maybe I could possibly run it without them—although nurses are impossible to find out here. So, should I go see them again? And they had asked if I contacted the archbishop's office; so should I go there? San Antonio. And that I'm getting shaky about the whole idea of starting a hospital anyway. Yet on the other hand I really wanted to . . . well, because I felt it's simply one of the most important things a person can do in this life. "It's costing more than I realized; we can't get some things. Right now we're so snagged because we can't locate enough wire for the call lights to each bed."

"You have to understand, doctor, they can't jump right into something. When they ask the archbishop's advice, he'll say, 'Have you acquainted yourself with the situation?' They can't go there with half-answers. Sit tight. They're investigating you. And assessing the entire situation. I'm sure it's a good indication, very good, or you would have heard by now—in the negative. You go right ahead with your hospital. Do you like beer or whiskey?"

If we each had sounded his own inner tuning fork, the vibrations, if not perfectly identical as one note, at least would have hummed closely in harmony. "Whiskey, please. Although you make me feel like I've already had some." And in silence I wondered . . . if someday I might not tell, dare to tell, him about the blue baby. No, no, probably never. No one.

❊❊❊

Sister Aquinas, the old shrinkled one with the delightful brown eyes, leaned forward again, saying, "All of this is rather unbelievable, for it happened only a week prior to your first visit, that our archbishop, Archbishop Lucy, told us we should start a hospital in Schulenburg. Did you contact his office?"

"No, ma'am, I haven't." Or does one say, Your Grace? Before I could think, I repeated, "No, ma'am."

Reverend Mother's small round face had a way of pouting. "We had to have his permission first, and put forward your request." She was not in the tall throne chair this time.

Sister Aquinas added, "But with his stated wish, there's no difficulty there."

"I see. You had already given it some thought before I came?"

"Yes, some." The lips puckered in the round face as if in deep thought. "However at the very most we have only two nurses available."

"And one of those is not an RN. We are mainly teachers."

"And keep the church."

"Oh that will be perfectly all right. Just so long as one of them is. She can do the actual charting. Anybody who is kind makes a good nurse. We can hire other nurses, lay nurses—if we can find them."

The old one spoke quickly, "But the Sisters would be in charge over them?"

"Definitely. In fact they would hire and fire them."

"Are they available?"

"Not easily. I have found one RN there—wife of a member of an oil crew. How long he will be stationed there, I don't know."

Sister Aquinas said, "Additional help would certainly be needed."

"Certainly."

"You will have to give us some time before we can be fully organized."

"Certainly."

"And the Sisters will be in complete charge?"

"Everything. Set prices, collect bills. I want to have nothing whatsoever to do with it. Saves my time. However, there is one thing, one request, I would like to ask. Only the one. And that is that they would never turn anybody down. Regardless of whether they could pay for it or not. I think that's what a real hospital is. Admit anyone who asks."

Both Sisters looked at me and said nothing. Then at each other and Sister Aquinas nodded her hood.

"And if we accept, doctor, there are a few things which must be arranged for the Sisters: They must have a room for their chapel."

"Chapel. Certainly. The chapel couldn't be part of the nun's sleeping quarters? A room adjoins—"

"No, because the chapel is open to the public."

"All right. There's one—it could be on the second floor, couldn't it?"

"Yes. They also have to have a private dining room. There are certain prayers at meals."

"A private dining room? Separate from the lay nurses? It means two dining rooms—giving up an extra room, and I need all the rooms possible."

"Yes, doctor."

"I'll arrange that." Seems all I've said since I got here is "certainly." I wonder if people who give in to others all the time get diabetes? They hold their anger in, smile, are always nice—and pass sugar in their urine. Are they trying to turn their very body waste into sweet syrup?

"Also you must understand: The salaries of the Sisters are to be paid directly to the convent, in one check. Not to the Sisters individually."

"No? I see. Okay. Now what about social security and withholding?"

"None. We are a tax-exempt institution."

"Certainly."

Sister Aquinas nodded and Reverend Mother pushed herself up out of the chair. "It seems we are very much in accord."

"Certainly," I said more or less automatically. I hope I don't get diabetes.

Standing before me, short. "Would you please stay for dinner?"

"Cer—I'd be most happy." (It didn't occur to me I'd have to eat alone—be served a delicious dinner of roast chicken in a vast paneled dining hall like in a castle. Alone. Butlered by a middle-aged nun always standing behind me. "Wouldn't you please like to sit down? There's plenty chairs." At least forty. "Oh no, no.")

"In the meantime I must attend to some matters out at our villa. Perhaps you'd care to see it."

"Villa?"

Sister Aquinas explained. "It's rather only a farm. But some of the Sisters do live there, temporarily. Resting. A bit of a retreat."

"Yes. I'm very interested in farms. I'm a country boy, born on a ranch. Would you please let me take you in my small car?"

Reverend Mother looked toward her wrinkled associate. "Would you go . . . too?"

"Yes, yes I will." She began to rise, slowly.

"Do you really feel—?"

"I don't have to get out of the car."

The two Sisters sat in the back seat. In the rearview mirror I saw their hoods waving, so I rolled up the window. "Who founded your convent? Was it pioneer settlers?"

"No," Sister Aquinas leaned forward, "The Mother Order is in France—Lyons. Nine nuns came here to start it."

"Sounds like a dream to me. Like starting a hospital."

"They landed in Vera Cruz."

"But that's a thousand miles away. More. They traveled by horses?"

"They walked."

"That's impossible!"

"All the way. They may have been given short rides on passing wagons or carts. Only three arrived here. The others died—of malaria, one from snake bite. Two were murdered by bandits."

We drove, quiet for a moment. "And I thought of starting a hospital as being difficult! Is it still connected with the Mother House in France?"

"No. The communications were so slow, often when they requested permission for this or that, by the time they received a reply it was of no practical value. Also, after the original three passed on, there was a language barrier, as no one here spoke French. It was then placed under the San Antonio diocese."

"What a fabulous history!"

"We have been interested in the history of your area. We find—and it is significant to us—that the people, Central Europeans, became transplanted there in groups, in colonies. In that manner they retained their European culture, religion. One such transplant consisted entirely of neighbors from one village—a full shipboard—and they brought their priest, an older man who had baptized most of them at birth."

"I didn't know that either. About us. But nine nuns walking! From Vera Cruz!" I parked under a tree and opened all the doors. Reverend Mother started for the farmhouse, a two-storied building with a screen porch all along the front, both upstairs and down. With four or five nuns on the porch, sitting or walking slowly.

"We unfortunately had several cases of tuberculosis among our nurses. They are here now, recuperating. Possibly contracted from their own patients. It is why we are at this time so limited in our nursing. Please do not repeat it."

"Certainly not."

But tuberculosis? Why choose tuberculosis? Is it against the "imprisonment" of convent life? The others seem to accept it. Against orders coming heavily down from dogma? Is obedience a difficult vow? Are their coughings complaints against something?

"We have milk, vegetables, fruits—"

"But that brand, VI—six? Six what?"

"It is Incarnate Word. In Latin. *Verbum Incarnatum.*"

I laughed and a nun on the porch turned to look. "Sister, I have seen a lot of cattle brands, so many—the Circle K, the Lazy W. My dad's was the Triangle S, which Indians called the Hat Snake when his father used it. But this is the first time I ever heard of a cow branded in Latin!"

"Yes, all things are possible. Here we are: I am English, the convent's founders were French; you want nuns for a Czech-German community; there are the Spanish, the black ones, tuberculosis victims, a young doctor who calls himself heathen—we seem so diverse. However, it is merely on the surface. Underneath we are all alike—all wishing, hoping. And all forgiven and all protected and purified in the divine light of His grace."

I turned, half ready to answer with "Certainly." I looked into her face framed in its white box hood. The late afternoon sun shone obliquely on half of her habit, making it radiantly white. Her eyes were wrinkled smiling. Before I knew it, I was smiling back, but saying, "I'm glad if it has worked well for you, Sister. As for myself, I can't believe in someone else doing my life for me, giving me . . . *me.* That is, paying my debts. Using my sorrows. No. Simply doesn't work . . . for me. Maybe I've had to be on my own too soon or too much—or something. Just doesn't hold . . . for me. Amounts to nothing. I feel we receive 'divine grace' only when we *do* 'divine grace.'"

"Then you are one whose work must prove it. Small wonder we have heard such extraordinary stories about your extravagant charities—"

"Charities? I'm sorry. You've been misinformed."

"I distinctly recall: A woman driving through your town began having a baby in a filling station restroom. When the owner phoned you, you came immediately."

"Oh that! That was Miloslave—we call him M. J. Yes."

"Similiar to the Christchild, born while traveling. Today's service station is the modern barn, no less.

"And we know of an incident where a man with his family, looking for work, had a sick baby—under a tree on the highway. Hot weather. He walked to your office and told you he had no money, not even for gasoline. It is the very story of the Good Samaritan, the modern, living one."

"Oh now, it was only an injection and some sample pills. But I didn't find work for him."

"And you bought him gasoline—at the same station where the baby was born. Do you still joke with the owner about his 'maternity ward'?"

"It's M. J. Pulkrabek. How do you know such things? About me? I hope you don't know my miserable facets as well. I certainly have them too."

"Doesn't each of us?"

"Suppose so."

"Our work at the convent is dying."

"What do you mean?"

"Yes, in its present form it is dying: No girls are joining convents today. Perhaps you noticed how few young ones. Surface realities change—but only on the surface." Now there were four or five more nuns on the upstairs porch, maybe one was Reverend Mother, checking individually on the others. "No, today girls go to college, to business schools, nursing school, and find well-paying positions readily. Or young men easily have work and can afford to support a wife. After the old ones all pass on, the convent, as we know it, will be dead. It has been much like a mother to us all. But now it is passing on."

I said nothing.

"We envision that those still cloistered can, by going out, as into your hospital, there by their example, their work, inspire others to live a more dedicated, fuller, richer life—those whom they come in contact with: patients, employees, visitors, all persons. So instead of *dying,* one might say *changing.*"

"I understand. And I like that. Isn't that really a form of resurrection—constant change?"

Reverend Mother went down the walk under the oaks. The wide sides of her hood flapping slightly in the breeze, the long chain of beads at her belt clicking together as she came.

"I do hope I haven't bothered you with my excessive talking."

In the car, I reached over the seat and touched her hand—the one with the gold wedding ring on it. "Thank you, Sister."

❊❊❊

"Come over anytime," Jim Reilly had said. But I have so much to do at the hospital yet.

Why is he so fat?

I need slip covers for the hall furniture, a kind that could be washed; I need bedside lamps, all alike; and shelves in the little lab. Need a sink in there too.

Finally did get a guy to do the rewiring and put in the call-light system, him crawling around under the house and in the attics at night. Sometimes I held the flashlight for him. I didn't understand all he was doing—hoped he wouldn't electrocute himself.

But Reilly phoned, asking me to stop by after work for a drink. I explained my "after work" is often nine or ten, but I did go and we listened to the news and talked too late and long into the night.

Late was also the only time things calmed down at the Reilly house, with eleven people there! A daughter, divorced, lived there, too, with her small daughters; she was Jim's secretary. A teen daughter, Pat, had had rheumatic fever when they lived in Chicago; I listened to her heart—loud mitral systolic, told her not to take PE, I'd write the teacher a note. One son in college studying law. The youngest boy wouldn't study—all sports. The two oldest sons, Jimmy and Francis, were draft-age.

Each time I went it was always a busy place, and I stumbled over toys and baseball gloves and tangled with stockings hanging all over the bathroom. Scattered everywhere lay a clean clutter. All over, the huge dining table especially—had school satchels, a catcher's mask, opened letters, a *Life* magazine, a few of the new paperback pocket-sized books, volume twelve of the *Encyclopedia Britannica* open at "Gettysburg, Battle of." And a young voice, "Don't lose my place!" Could hardly find an open spot to set your drink down. Mrs. Reilly, always a pleasant person, seemed always in smooth, easy control of the constantly fluxing multisituations. She walked through it all with a confidence that always said, It will all turn out all right.

This family was a warm place. And I instantly had been taken right on in as if I had always belonged.

I told him so. "Yes, seems we either have the best time together a family could have, or we have the damnedest fight you ever saw."

Fortunately they left me out of their fights. Or maybe I wasn't allowed to be that close, not one-hundred percent.

Why is he fat?

But I shouldn't be here—have so much to do yet. Curtains—where do I get curtains? The carpenters have finally dug out the basement under the house and poured the concrete—that'll be kitchen and nurses' dining room and nuns' dining and two large storage rooms with shelves. And who can I get to build the dumbwaiter?

We talked. About his early life, shanty Irish and lace-curtain Irish; about his devout mother, who lit candles during any storm; about his father, "himself" who would get magnificently drunk and sing Irish ballads all the way home waking everybody, and people loved him anyway. How his younger sister became a cripple gradually after a sad love affair, and how she wouldn't try to walk, and during a period they forced her to and she did walk, and when they stopped making her, she stopped too. About his defeat in politics—he had worked with Roosevelt way back, long before anyone considered the man presidential, and that, too, was long before he had polio. Wished he had saved correspondence from Roosevelt.

Jim Reilly. He and I never finished talking. It was always a glow to be near him. It was here I heard many of the Fireside Chats.

That Friday, Jimmy, the oldest boy, received his "greetings."

***

"Good morning." I was still wiping my hands. Something about her seemed familiar. "Oh yes, Mrs. Schneider's sister. How is she these days?"

"About the same, doctor; she doesn't put milk in her eyes anymore." She laughed jerkily. "She complains a lot."

"Yes, I imagine. What can I do for you? You certainly don't look sick."

"No, I'm not." Laughed again, nervously. "I came to ask you for a job. At the hospital. I haven't worked out for so many years. Just washing and ironing at home. I could do the laundry. There's a good wash house out there behind. I could even take some things home. And if it comes too much at one time to keep up, Mrs. Schneider can help, too. She can do the particular things real good, even better than—"

"Excellent! She needs to be kept busy. But you'll have to ask the Sisters. They'll be coming soon now. And we still don't have everything finished."

She started to speak but I continued, "Would you help Mrs. Zapalac and James' mother do the final cleaning and waxing? Upstairs? I want everything, especially in the Sister's quarters, to be shining. And we don't have all the basement finished, kitchen, storage, two dining rooms—the carpenters are working every day, building the walls and shelves. Upstairs is finished and I'd like to have it all *glanzend* clean." I forgot she doesn't speak German. "They're used to it."

"Mrs. Zapalac? Doesn't she do the cleaning at Frank's Place, one of them?"

"Yes. However, she's consented to help us out too, after work, until the Sisters get here. They'll do all the hiring."

"Oh. Oh, they will do the hiring. But I'm not Catholic." She streaked a finger along the desk top and looked at her fingertip.

"That doesn't matter. Don't be afraid. I know they'll like you."

"You think so? My sister's husband—he was Catholic, and for a while she went. For instructions. But I'm not. Catholic."

"That simply doesn't matter. You'll see. Look, I'm not either. And they're going to work with me."

She looked directly at me, still holding her finger up in the air.

"And a little later—after everybody gets settled and accustomed—then if Arnold would come around often, I'm sure the Sisters would teach him how to do some laboratory work. You know, blood counts and urine analysis—the more routine things at first. I believe Arnold would be good at something like that."

She stood and stared, her mouth half open. "You mean? . . . " She stared at the finger cross-eyed, and began to laugh and to wipe tears away with the back of her wrist as if she had soap suds on her hands.

"Why? What—is something wrong?" I held out the towel almost as if offering it to her.

"Oh no. Oh no. It's hard to believe; Arnold needs so to get out. But we have no money to send him to school, and we don't know anybody—I am going to get my sister right now and don't you worry: That place is going to shine from top to bottom and every corner. Nobody will find a speck of—" She still laughed, a jerky, sobbing laugh, as she left.

But I have to get some kind of heat dryer for laundry, sheets. During rainy weather sheets will have to be dried indoors, and fast enough.

Margaret ushered a man in, "You remember Narcis Pospisil's back."

"Good morning, Narcis—Nick." He has a dislocated—

The sister's head came back crowding in front of Nick. "I forgot—" she leaned around the door—"to thank you."

"You certainly already have. And I thank you." I hung up the towel. Nick has a dislocated vertebra—disc—pressing on the nerves to his right leg. "How's our back doing? Holding up?"

Joe Schovajaca wearing his hat, came in next and asked, "You make it horspittle, no? So should I bring gallon milk every morning when I am bringing Wiolet in for school?"

I frowned. "But Joe, doesn't the school bus go right by your gate every morning? The new school buses?"

"Yass, but I am so close to town—only little ways. And bus is beginning by my house first, picking oop first Wiolet—like five-forty-five and she ride almost two hours. No, I take her eight o'clock school—like now. Bring milk to horspittle."

I asked how much this wonderful special delivery service would cost, and Joe appeared puzzled. "But nothing. So long as cows be fresh, is milk. When cows go dry . . . is no milk."

I insisted he be paid for the milk and the service. He answered, "If you paying something, I won't bring milk. Give it to peks. When Sisters come, I start it bringing milk with Wiolet."

❊❊❊

All the mail lay stacked to one side. "Anything this morning from the hotel-supply house? Want to get the dishes and trays wholesale if I can." One letter had been laid squarely in the large green blotter. Margaret, scrubbing, leaned over the basin in the examining room washing instruments from yesterday. (We soak them overnight.) But her sounds came hard and clattering. The letter lay addressed to me; the return:

Procurement and Assignment Board
Medical Society
Suite 85
1201 Summit Ave.
Fort Worth, Texas

"Open it" she ordered. "I've got to know."

I didn't move.

She came, wiping her hands. "Don't sit there like a tombstone. Open it."

"I've always received deferment—before." I muttered. "Without even asking."

"That was always the *local* draft board. If you don't open it, I will."

" 'Dear Dr. Schulze,

" 'It has been brought to our attention that you are of military age and available for duty. Since there is more than one doctor in your community—' "

Margaret snatched it out of my hand. "Just as I thought. Kotzebue. *Doctor* Kotzebue." She read aloud, " '. . . Friday morning at ten. If you cannot arrange to be present, please contact my office immediately.' I knew it. I knew it. The whole thing! Not only the hospital!" Her hands jerked up over her eyes; she ran into the examining room and closed the door.

But there was no time to worry or wonder. The waiting rooms were already occupied with patients waiting.

"Good morning, Auntie Callie. And how are you?"

"Only half tolerable—between a nug and a tug. Hafta push myself along. Don't look so well youself. You comin' this time? Watch Night?"

"Why, Auntie Callie, that's more than half a year off."

"But you comin'?"

"Oh, sure, sure."

"Bet you ain't."

"I . . . I . . .

"Here, let me help you off with your coat, there." She stepped up on the table.

"Brought my pills along. Only a few left. Honey—I mean, Miz

Margaret—you bring me a drinkin' glass of water, please? Jass come by for me so early, didn't have no time to take my morning one afore we done drove off."

As she unpinned the blouse and unbuttoned it all the way down, "Nursed all my chillun on the breast. Nine." And in spreading it apart she showed the knotty edge, and red, where the flat shriveled left nipple should have been. "So tell me what I done got here. If I'm in a danger, you tell me. It always oozing a little blood. All the time. Gotta keep somethin' over it. So tell me what lonesome thing I got myself here now. Tell me true. Is it bad? My very best friends are all gathered in. There ain't no one close to me still walking. It gets mighty lonesome. So what I got here? Tell me true. I always puts my trust in you."

When we finally finished for the day, Margaret latched the side door, and I drove her home. The picture show was already dark.

Coming back I took a different street and, getting to Reilly's house, I saw lights on in the living room and Jim sitting there reading. As I got out, the car door slammed, and without looking, Jim got up and went into the kitchen. And when I entered he was coming back with two glasses and ice and a bottle of Scotch.

I had to tell him, no use holding it back. "Hate to come weeping about having to go—when you have a son going."

Jim didn't say a word, passed me the Scotch and bowl of ice cubes and let me tell it all: how I hated to go, how I'm a son of a bitch for not going: it serves me right that now I'll have to: I hate to; how I'd like to "stay in my own self-centered little dream and escape being sucked up into the clanking iron machine of. . . ."

He never said a word, just listened, got more ice.

On and on.

How I should kick myself; how "I wish there was some way—I'm a coward—don't want to be where they kill each other . . . Would rather be here where they . . . Seems *they* —these—have a high tolerance for suffering . . .

"I ought to hate old Kotzebue, but it's strange. I don't think I do. I feel even a touch of sorrow for him. Sympathy—a very slight touch anyway."

And finally, "Well, thank you, Jim. I feel better now. Slightly anesthetized too. I'm ready now. Guess I never . . .

"I'll tell the Sisters. After Friday. Tell them first. Margaret already knows. I'll have the carpenters stop. Just board the hospital up. Until later. Still do it later. That's all this is, a delay. I can't afford to think of it any other way."

Jim did not interject.

"Another thing, Jim: I believe a person should either learn or earn. If not learn, then at least earn. From every experience. And this whole thing is good for me—teaches me I was being too damn serious about myself. Like I was too important. Too much of the world became 'me'. Starting one dinky little country hospital—one two-bit shoestring country hospital—pretending it was something great. Huh!

"Well . . . I hope I don't start crying: It *was* something great."

And the next morning the very first person made me feel worse again. Old Mrs. Sembera—strong garlic odor—sat on the examining table and cried, dabbing at her eyes.

"Something happened, Maminko?" I noticed the pterygium growing in the inner corner of each eye.

"I know so it is mine blood bressure. It goes round in the head. I know so is making it myself, by worry. Is coming from mine brodder Bohus his son Josefek," and she wailed softly and sobbed.

"What happened? An accident?"

"He going. Going army. Have to go. Is getting the paper and have to go." She continued weeping. "*Popecni streda* [Ash Wednesday] he is getting it. He got to go."

"Maminko, maybe there is a good side to it. He will see more of the world, learn things. Maybe go to school yet afterwards. Maybe it—"

"In first time, I am little girl and mine two brothers is going, first time. War is same place as now. My papa needing them for farming but has to go. Two brothers—only brothers—Yon and Josefek. And both is dead.

"Yon they shoot him right avay dead, in Nemecko [Germany]. When he come home in box, Papa want to see is Yon is no mistake. Is Yon and we bury him. And brother Josefek is in horspittle in France. They cut him first the legs off. In horspittle. But only few days is die anyway. When they sending him home in box too, like Yon, Papa want to see it is Josefek. And inside is Josefek but is no legs. No legs put in box. Somebody is forgetting to put in." She wiped her eyes and nose.

"And Papa he is writing and writing letters at night with the lamp, to Presidents Vilson and congressmans and General Pushing, asking where is legs. And getting nize letter alvays back but not saying where legs is."

She blew her nose, honking loud.

"Pappa alvays think legs is coming later, in separate box. Somebody finding them und put in box and is sending it. But legs never come."

I waited with the blood-pressure cuff.

"And now mine nephew Josefek is going. Is walking on his legs. But is going. Army."

I wrapped the cuff around her arm and started pumping it up. With her free hand she wiped her eyes and blew her reddened nose again.

"Going army. Walking on his legs."

❋❋❋

Margaret insisted I take the Saint Christopher medal; I pitched it in my suitcase.

The city traffic and buildings, the immensity and noise, were strangely frightening. I had forgotten. And you had to pay to park. The new things, parking meters, resembled old-time hitching posts, but made of metal. The office building loomed large with blank glass walls. Inside were huge pot plants like small trees, and carpets. At a desk a woman with a high hairdo told me the Procurement Office was down an inner hall by the next secretary. There I waited.

I studied the paneled walls, mahogany, and the odd pot plants and a large gold-framed picture of a battleship, the *Maine.* And I waited. My watch now showed past the time of my appointment. I smoked, one cigarette after another. The chairs, of richly grained leather—real leather—stood around empty as if watching me. The wide gold-leaf frame of the battleship *Maine,* seemed wealthy and remote to me. The secretary ignored me.

The door opened and two men stood shaking hands. One wore a tailor-made uniform—it fit him perfectly. He carried his cap, so he might be the one leaving. Yes. He left. The other, in a pin-striped suit, did not look at me nor come over to shake hands. He returned to his office and the secretary went in. When she came out, she said "You can go in now."

He sat behind a large, shiny desk with thick glass all across the top of it. The American flag, with a gold eagle at the top, hung down its large staff. As we shook hands I saw a folder open on his desk.

"I'm well acquainted with the situation there in your town—we made inquiries. Two doctors. You're the newcomer." He took a cigar out of a mahogany box with silver hinges. "And we find you were planning to open a hospital. I'm certainly glad I caught all this before you got it going. You couldn't very well do all that with this uncertainty hanging over you. Oh yes, have a cigar."

"Thanks, I only use cigarettes."

"And, I'm certain, too many of those."

"Well . . . yes."

"Therefore"—he blew smoke toward the mahogany-beamed ceiling—"it all depends on what you decide to do. Of course, if it was me, I know what I'd be doing—I certainly wouldn't be sitting here. I'd be down to the nearest enlistment center right now."

"I've always received deferment from the draft board," and I reached for my wallet. He waved the idea away.

"I presume you have thought it over. So what have you decided? The board prefers for the individual to decide voluntarily."

"I . . . I hadn't thought about it. I didn't know it was up to me."

"It isn't. This board decides. I'm the chairman."

"I have a friend, Ted Chambers; we were same class, same fraternity. He's in the Pacific and writes he's doing nothing but reading old journals, playing poker, and taking showers three times a day."

"Yes, yes, but the next day he may be doing ten surgeries, one after another around the clock. Others are."

"I'm sure you're right. He's thinking about staying in after the war."

"Yes. Certainly. You see? A fine career. A retirement pension coming in at forty-five. In your case"—he glanced at the folder—"forty-seven."

"But I'm sure Ted won't stay in. That's only to—"

"But we don't have time to discuss your friends, do we."

"I only mean, I think I'm doing more—working every day—where I am."

"Your area raises foodstuffs. Raises food and ships it east. Hogs, beef, grain. Primarily corn and sorghum. Right?"

"Yes."

"But they don't ship out any big amount. No real tonnage."

"It's no big farms—no corporations—"

"Then mainly they're only feeding themselves." He closed the folder.

"It's a poor area. There is no big production. It's all small farms; they do the best they can. But they're never a drain on the—"

"I see. So what do you decide?"

"I . . . hmmm . . . "

"You know the board has the power to draft you."

"Yeah—yes. I know."

"You seem to be hesitant. Speak up."

"I want to stay where I am. The thought of going scares me. Maybe it scares everyone . . . who has to go. I know that insane hostility can only be stopped by more hostility. It has to be done. I guess there's no other way. Our area is not a rich one, but it's . . . my place. And I'm doing a good job—mostly. Sorry. I can't volunteer to leave it. Sorry. You will have to draft me, after all. I'm sorry."

"You are the only fully active man in four small towns there, aren't you. Weimar, Schulenburg, Flatonia, Moulton."

"But there's Dr. Kotzebue—"

"Yes, yes, we know Kotzebue. Doesn't take everybody, does he—not fully active. And to replace you would take someone who speaks either German or Czech or both."

"What?"

"You see we have to be thorough—had to check you out. And if for any reason things get all that bad, we know where to find you."

"What?"

He was standing, holding out his hand. "Sorry we have to rush. And good luck with your hospital."

Four Small Saints . . .
and Me

I stood on a box in the basement painting shelves. Fast. Slapping it on. They're coming today, and I still have one whole side to do. Thank heavens, the dishes finally got here: I kicked at a barrel with the top off and a few plates peeking up out of the straw. I had opened and checked it. And all the cardboard boxes.

Mr. Jurecka came down the steps, stooping in. "My wife and I we finished the chapel. All ready. Nice prayer benches you got them." He's a retired bank employee, and they've been working here full time for days. Came on their own—I didn't ask them.

"Prie-dieux. Got them at Sears in Houston. Didn't know they had religious things like that."

"We painted the old altar. Looks nice. Want to see it?"

"Thanks, I will later. Let me finish these shelves. They're supposed to get here before dark. Is everything ready? Take a look in the dining room—do you see anything missing?" While he disappeared I called to him, "Pete finished the ceiling yesterday. He didn't splatter on the table and chairs, did he? I gave him a drop cloth."

He came back. "We have a picture at home of the Last Supper. I'll bring it tomorrow. Be nice in there."

"Fine. I have a picture in my room of a nude woman hugging a rock cross in an ocean of wild waves. I don't suppose that would be quite appropriate."

"No"—he's always so serious.

"It belongs to the hotel anyhow."

"Father Puziovsky will bless the altar stone."

"Like the Stone of Scone, or the Blarney stone?"

"Mustn't joke about a thing like that. It's holy."

"I see. Where do we get the stone?"

"He'll bring it. There's a hole in the altar. It fits. Every altar has one."

"Didn't know that. Very interesting."

"Shouldn't we put a lock on the chapel? I can get a good one at the hardware."

"Why?"

"I notice you have that John working around here."

"The good-looking one? How can a man be that good looking and still always get himself in jail?"

"He's a thief."

"Probably worse than that." I was making headway with the shelves, but so many to go yet. I swear I'm tired of painting. After all day yesterday. And all speckled up. Probably never get it all out of my hair.

"We'll go now. If you can think of anything, call us."

"Thank you most sincerely. And be sure to tell your wife I do indeed thank her. Haven't seen it all finished yet, but I thank you for taking over the chapel and doing it yourselves." I had seen the curtain all across behind the old altar—crushed velvet, bright red, with huge dime-sized pearls sewed on at random spaces, like stars maybe, but looking more like earrings dangling. The ceiling was painted a dark blue, probably intended as a blue-skies effect, but this was almost purple.

"It's for the Sisters."

"I know. Yes."

It seems I painted and painted and painted. Shelves are a nuisance to do, lots of trouble and all you see is edge. I heard the boys working in the yard, chopping weeds, talking Spanish that I couldn't understand. Paint, paint. Ivory. I'm tired of ivory. Suddenly they were quiet outside. Pete's head leaned down looking into the basement window, upside down. "They here."

Good heavens, what'll I do? Well, stop and go meet them, what else?

Taking the kerosene rag with me, I went out to the curb. An old used car, but shined up, with cardboard boxes tied on top and on the back, and four nuns in black gowns with starched white around their faces floating out and half blowing away. I approached them. "Howdy Sisters."

A small, dark-eyed one said, "We thought Dr. Schulze would at least be here to meet us.'' Each had a big cross embroidered in red on the front.

I realized now I had no clothes on, only swim trunks, and was speckled all over. ''I'm it—him—I mean, me. Trying to get the kitchen finished before you came. I think we've got everything else done. You'll have to inspect it. Shall we take your things in? The fellows can help.''

Pete, John, Natividad, and the ugly one who looks like a sleepy Indian and never says a word—he's working with his shirt on because he still has a wide white bandage on his back and left arm. And he wouldn't want that to be seen, in case a Salas drives by and looks. All stood as if waiting. They had been working in the yard, but all had dropped their hoes and came and took off their hats, and I thought they were going to kneel and kiss the Sisters' hands or hems or something, like in a picture of natives welcoming Columbus.

I said, ''This is Pete Immaculate Conception Estrada and his brothers, John Holy Word and Natividad Blessed Sacrament and—I don't know Slim's whole handle. They have unusual names.'' I had no idea why I introduced them except they were there. ''They'll help carry your—''

A little fat one stepped forward and her pouty little mouth said, ''We'll manage that ourselves, later.'' I looked close at her little round face. I knew she wasn't Reverend Mother, but I'd swear she was a carbon copy.

''Well—well okay, I think I'd better be getting those shelves finished.''

The dark-eyed one said, ''White, I see.''

I looked down at my stomach and navel. ''No, that's the operating room and delivery and scrub room. This green is—well, something else. It's this ivory.'' To be polite I didn't show it on my left nipple, but on the back of my hand. ''Ivory. Do you think you'll like it?''

''Nice color.''

''You make yourselves at home now. Your quarters are over on that end, if you want to rest after your trip. Or explore around and see where everything is; and the chapel is upstairs. Make yourselves at home. I hope you'll like it.'' I started for the basement. At the door I turned and all four were following right behind me. ''I'm painting down in here,'' I explained. ''You ought to go in the front.''

''We're going to help you,'' the little fat-faced one said.

"Now?"

Holding a hand on their heads, they stood there billowing in the breeze, everything flapping and flying, full sail, a big red cross on each. Coulda been the Spanish Armada.

"Well, okay. But shouldn't you first change into something more—oh, oh yes," and they followed me down and rolled up long black sleeves, and while I painted away they opened boxes and unpacked dishes and pots and trays and glasses and began washing all the pieces and drying them. And we talked. And I finished the shelves.

❊❊❊

"Good morning, Sister. Hope you all slept well?"

"There are no crucifixes."

"What crucifixes?"

"There should be one in every room. I made out the order last night."

"Sure. Anything you want."

She opened a catalog; there I saw church pews and altar cloths with coiled wire fringes and memorial windows in colors and, "There! Best to have a nice one."

"It's very nice, I'm sure," and glanced farther down. Twenty-eight dollars!

What? Good God! And here I had always been under the impression Sisters took vows of poverty.

"One for every room. There are thirty-nine rooms in all—I counted." She slapped the catalog closed, while I, in a state of shock tried to multiply twenty-eight times thirty-nine, thinking I've somehow got to get more money in the hospital account if she's writing checks like that. That's more than the operating room . . .

If it's going to be like this all the time, I may not be able to support their brand of poverty.

But there were no further religiously necessary items, and within a few days everything seemed in order. I shared that optimistic conclusion with the Sister who reminded me of the Reverend Mother.

"I guess that's everything, Sister. Now we're ready. All set for Sunday? Gus Strauss gave us a nice write-up in the paper. You see it?"

"It's a little difficult to read."

"All those x's, yes. Do we have everything? Can you think of anything else?"

"I think we're ready. At least the Lord hasn't brought to mind anything lacking."

At the office I told Margaret I'd be right back. "Have to do one more thing first. Going over to Dr. Kotzebue."

"Him? For heaven's sake why!"

"Have to. I'm not going to go around carrying any hate." Nietzsche stood waiting at the screen door; I patted and reinforced my determination by telling him I wasn't going to pay the price of keeping any of that stuff—neither the anger-out nor the sorrow-in.

As I entered Dr. Kotzebue's office, the receptionist, without looking up from her writing, automatically asked, "Did you want to see the—?" Her mouth stayed half open.

"Don't worry." I smiled. "I'm all right this time. Just going to invite him to use the hospital. But I would like to slip in. And out."

It was only a whisper. "Go down to the third door. I think they're having coffee."

I whispered back, "You know? I think you're a right nice old girl."

"Is that a compliment? Or is it?"

They were having coffee. "Good morning, Dr. Kotzebue. No, don't anybody get up. Sit down, please. Just wanted to personally invite you to use the hospital whenever you wish. We'll open day after tomorrow. And for any type case—up to you. Except we can't manage isolation. I'm ready and willing—most willing—to help you with any surgery. You supervise it; I'll do it and as you say. Or any OBs. Bring your own nurse, or I'll come if you say so. I have given orders that when you come, you're to have anything you want, that everyone is to give you their fullest cooperation, and that they must open every door you head toward so you won't have to ask. The doctor's scrub room is in the back—used to be a pantry—and you can park just beside it.

"I wanted to personally deliver this invitation. Please come. It's yours. Thanks." And I left. As far as I could remember, he never said a thing. But he didn't have much chance to either.

"Thanks," I said to the receptionist, waved, and winked.

And she smiled back—the cutest, quickest smile.

Margaret said, "He'll never come."

I had to tell Jim all about it. "*Now* the hospital is open. I feel that now it *is* open. No, I don't think he'll ever use it. But that doesn't matter. That's him. Feels like we've really opened the door. Officially not until Monday, but I feel it's done already.

"But this is a strange thing, Jim—I feel it doesn't belong to me anymore, that I don't have to own it. I know it's mine, but . . . "

"That it belongs to everybody? Melted—melded—into the community?"

"I don't know exactly. But I don't feel any ownership there."

"That's strange. Because you put so much of yourself into it."

"I'm thinking that if it goes well, pays itself off, I'd like to donate it to the Sisters—give it to them. I guess it's really theirs anyway. We'll see."

And I had to tell Jim about the aunt:

Margaret has an old old aunt who lives near the hospital, across the street. Has cataracts, bad, both eyes. Can't see anything during the day—only at dusk and at night. (The pupil enlarges in the dark, letting a little sight come in and out through the edges of the lens, around the center where the cataract grows. The specialist I sent her to is having her wait until they "ripen" fully before removing them.) She told Margaret I had put up a headboard—from a bedstead—out on the hospital lawn.

"No, auntie, that's a sign. A signboard. For the hospital."

"Oh, a sign! Hospital sign. Yes, I understand. But my! How clever of him to put it on a headboard."

On Sunday afternoon we held open house. Everybody came. Cars parked for blocks around. I had asked a dozen women in town to be hostesses to introduce people to the Sisters. Margaret made me a list of women to ask—some had never been in my office. And I sent identical corsages for each of them. Everyone came to see the Sisters. The expensive crucifixes hung all over the place. It was all a big success. Officially, we had opened the doors.

And Sunday night, late, our very first case was Molly.

***

Molly. An unfortunate affair. Always had been. She'd hang around the saloons, get drunk, beg money for beer until they'd make her leave.

Slept with anybody for anything. Came into the office once looking like her hair hadn't been combed in weeks, and people got up and stood rather than sit next to her, because she kept scratching—here, there.

She got into fights—always had bruises. She was put into the small city jail regularly. They couldn't let her smoke because it was wooden, and each time she'd threaten to burn it down—and she tried to twice. She had had a daughter, three or four years old, who they say never had a clean dress. The court took the child away, saying Molly practiced sexual acts with her, which I doubt ever happened. More of a legal "necessity" to get the child definitely away and transferred through orphanages into a home somewhere far off.

Although I couldn't find any signs of it in her reflexes or retinas or anywhere, I feel certain she had some degree of organic brain injury. Maybe from birth, maybe from a childhood illness such as measles or whooping cough. Minimal brain damage at least, it seemed to me.

She had often been found sleeping drunk in the weeds along the tracks. People said it would be best if she slept on the tracks, then the freight train would finish all her problems. She staggered down the street, one stocking collapsed around an ankle, stumbling, leering at any man, asking twelve-year-old boys for a nickel and old men for a quarter. Sometimes a person, passing, would turn red in the face and pretend not to hear her.

And she was our very first hospital case.

When people saw her in a ditch, drunk and trying to crawl along, or sleeping there—or what looked like her or a dead body—they'd phone the law, Ralph. They sometimes found her still unconscious drunk with her skirts up, where some passing tramp or someone had found her there, and had left her so. With the skirt up over her head, a person couldn't tell right off whether she was still breathing or not.

This time somebody had phoned and Ralph came, crawled under the bridge, looked at her and felt of her, and said, "Goddamn, she's dead." The coroner and some friends had gone to Rockport, so they called Marvin Brosch's Ambulance Service (and Funeral Parlor) to come pick the body up. Marvin drove the big, long ambulance with its red lights on into the drive and called, "Doc, got a customer. The county'll pay for burying her."

"It's Molly," he grinned. "She's dead. Found under the bridge by the pump station. Just brought her by so you wouldn't have to come down to pronounce her dead."

His young assistant—a kid—added, "I'm going to get help. Embalm. Marvin promised."

The embalming place is a small room under Marvin's house—a half basement, small; you can barely squeeze in past the table.

"It's most thoughtful of you, Marvin, to bring her by." (And entirely illegal. She should be pronounced dead first, before the body can be moved. But in Molly's case, who will there be to question or object?) I climbed up into the back.

The assistant snapped on the ceiling light. "See how dead she is?"

Marvin said, "You shouldn't sound so eager."

"Can't help it. My first!" I think he's Marvin's nephew and visits here often from the city.

The Sisters came out, all four, looking in through the ambulance door and windows.

She lay completely flaccid, not even a corneal reflex—you could touch her right in the eye. Grass burs in her hair and dress. I listened over the heart—you're supposed to in pronouncing them dead, to make sure. Pity, she was still a young person. I didn't hear a heartbeat, but . . . did a few bubbles go by? I pressed on the chest, listened. Nothing. I placed a fist under the ribs and hit it flat with the palm of my other hand two, three times; the young nephew stopped drinking his Coke and turned around to watch. I listened and her heart was beating regular with normal sounds. She groaned and, without opening her eyes wiped the slobber off her nose with the back of her hand. The nephew yelled at me, "You brought her back to life!"

Marvin stared, "You started her off again!"

"Get ready. Roll out the oxygen, Sister. Bring her in, Marvin."

The two glared at each other; Marvin said "Goddamn! And for nothing!" The young man slammed his bottle into the rack and they wheeled her on in.

What the Sisters did with Molly! First they bathed, deloused, shampooed her; scrubbed her nails; went through the box of donated used clothes and ironed a nightgown for her and later a white blouse and gray pleated skirt. With black stockings and high-heel shoes, Molly became a very decent-looking woman. The Sisters had her help wash dishes and sweep and took her up to chapel. Why it looked almost like a miracle.

They tried to get her to help bathe and comb Pinky Viser, who had come in with a severe case of diabetes and was on insulin, but Molly only stood back and watched. When one of the Sisters asked her to she did take a bedpan to Mrs. Zemlichka, who had our first baby Monday afternoon. (Sister Barbara did not encourage Molly to come into the small nursery—we had taken a Wasserman on her, but the report wasn't back yet.) But, unless they kept her busy, she sat and leafed through the magazines, looking at the pictures and chewing gum.

About the fourth day Molly decided to leave. She didn't say anything like Thank you, but she did say Good-by. Sister Jean Marie and I stood at the door waiting for the family to bring "the old gentleman, our father, Mr. Crockett" from Muldoon, which is almost all black. And Sister Jean Marie said to Molly, "You be sure and come over and visit us here. Anytime."

Molly, chewing gum, answered "Sure, sure," and we watched her walking down the drive. A car turned in and Molly stayed right in front of it until it stopped. She stepped to the driver's window, up to a broad-shouldered black man, and asked, "You wouldn't give me enough for a beer, would you?"

"We bringin' our father to the hospital, ma'am."

"Would you?"

"Excuse me, we'd like to pass."

And she walked on, swinging the pleats, chewing gum.

Sister and I stood waiting. "There she goes. Our first admission. Not lovely, especially, but beautiful nevertheless. Beautiful as any other simply because she's real. She's as real as anyone else on earth. Aw, I don't know what I'm trying to say."

Sister's pouty little mouth, with a quality like doubting seemingly built into it, spread into a large smile.

❋❋❋

As I hurried into the dimly lit front hall, Sister Joan of Arc's long white figure came silently out of the low night lights and floated smoothly along beside me. "I felt you should see her immediately because they said she had a convulsion at home. Pressure is two hundred thirty over one twenty."

"Oh no!"

"If you remember her, she's in the last half of the eighth month, as near as I can get it from her. She's still dazed and not too coherent." Sister's quiet movement floated abreast of my long-legged strides going straight to the operating room, where they had laid her on the table.

Three men stood in the hall, wearing clean white shirts, dark trousers, and good hats and smelling of garlic. They watched big as the nurse and I hurried past.

The white bright room stood crowded with fat oily-faced women in clean faded dresses and uncombed hair, fanning themselves and the patient. A garlic smell here, too. A woman beside the table leaned over, crying and wringing her hands and dropping her head down on the patient's breasts while twisting a pale blue rosary through her fingers. "Oh no mine Maria," she wailed. "Mine Maria." Seeing me, "Oh doktor, doktor, she vill not die—no—mine Maria?"

The others fanned her. Her uncombed hair blew back in jerks. One of the women picked at trying to straighten the mother's collar but couldn't—the dress was on inside out.

The patient, a young woman, I didn't recognize. Oh yes, remember her now. But her round swollen, moon face already told much of the diagnosis. Eclampsia.

"Get a specimen and do the albumin."

"Sister Jean Marie is doing it now."

"Good. But—you mean she's up, too? Can't always do this—be up day and night. Maria?" I spoke loudly leaning down to her. "How do you feel now?"

"In the head, is such hurting. Oh. And it looks me all such fuzzy things—nothing straight, like should be."

"You mean the lines—the edges of everything—look hazy?"

"Such kind fuzzy growing along everything."

"Yes." I patted her arm.

"I think I fall down. I go to spit and the stove lid fall me on the foot. I know nothing. Maybe I break me a bones?"

The women all began to fan her right foot. I reached into a pocket for car keys. Both swollen feet were still bare and unwashed. With the key I scratched the sole of the left one. "It fell on her right foot," said one of the fat women, wiping the sweat from her forehead up into her hair. I watched the toes responding, spreading apart automatically, beyond her volition, and the big toe drawing back. Then all toes came forward grasping downward, as if through some ancient prehensile instinct a hand had come alive after centuries, trying to reach, to hold onto . . . Positive Babinsky. Yes, she has had a convulsion. At least one.

"It's this foot," the woman repeated. "I seen it."

"Yes, I know. We'll see about that later."

Sister Jean Marie appeared, holding up a test tube with something like clabber in it. "Four plus."

"Mine Maria!"

I took the tube carefully by the clamp, knowing it would still be hot, and stepped into the hall to the three men. One of them, the young man with the full thick neck and large shoulders spreading tight into his shirt, had been crying. "You are her husband, are you not?"

"Yes he is," answered an older man. The husband nodded and his face cried more.

"Maria has this poison of pregnancy. We must take the baby right away." Sister Jean Marie stood silently beside me. "We have to do a section now," I said to the crying man.

All the men nodded. All still had their hats on.

"Have to take the baby out, through the side."

They nodded Yes again, all in unison, automatically.

"Do you understand?" I asked the husband, wondering if they did under so severe a strain.

"Mine Maria," came from the operating room. "She no die!"

"He understands," said the man who had spoken before, and suddenly my left hand felt grabbed and squeezed by two strong hairy hands with short dirty fingernails, and the young man with red eyes kissed it. I almost jerked back in surprise.

I hate this worship of the doctor. It isn't real. I don't have that magic power he's trying to hand to me. Maria's choice in the matter is bigger than mine, absolutely. I said to him, most patiently I think, "I must tell you clearly: I do not do the healing. I only help provide that chance—that choice." To Sister Jean Marie I added, "Call Father Bohac—they're from his parish—for Last Sacraments, just to be on the safe side. And get her blood type and theirs and crossmatch while I change. On second thought—as toxic as she is—it's best if you call Father Puziovsky. He's nearer." She knew that I meant Maria could go into more seizures at any moment.

"Thank you, father—I mean, doctor." Her little mouth looked pouty even now.

Shortly thereafter, wearing a crinkly sterile gown, a cap, and mask, I stood, my gloved fingers covered by a sterile towel, hands clasped almost as if in prayer. I waited and watched Sister Barbara's long, pale fingers stay touching the lumping pulse near the ear. The odor of ether fumes. Her soft voice flowed, "I think you can begin, Sister Jean Marie. She's under, but light."

Through the mask I said, "Good. Let's try to keep her light. She's too toxic to take deep. Blood pressure?"

"Two hundred forty-two over one twenty-three or four," Sister Barbara answered with the stethoscope dangling from her ears.

Good God! From over my mask I watched Sister Jean Marie start painting the large mound of pregnant abdomen. She painted carefully, beginning in the center, at the navel, and working in concentric circles toward the outside of the surgical field. This she did with ether, then repeated it with alcohol, and finally with the orange-red antiseptic. Two shiny medallions near Maria's throat blinked against the light with each breath. I checked the other preparations: the suction machine, the resuscitator, the table to receive the baby. And there was Sister's special preparation, too: a small glass of water. In case the child did not breathe, she would baptize it while its heart still beat alive. Maria, don't die on me.

I reviewed the various steps of the operation and mentally checked if the proper instruments were ready for every eventuality. First the long incision, one long, straight, quick cut beginning at the base of the ribs, rising up over the smooth mound and down almost to the pubic crest. That would be through the skin and fascia, and there would be minor bleeding. Plenty of small hemostats lay ready for that. The scalpel so sharp that you did not feel it touching against anything, as if the flesh melted apart before the blade touched it. Like you only pointed the scalpel and the flesh obeyed the thought. *Maria, don't die.* Then the uterus would lie exposed, this huge bluish-red glob of egg.

Maria, do you choose this illness? To say what? Is it a disguise, only a reflection on the surface of something deeper, or above, or farther off?

Why choose this?

You were about to be a mother. Maybe you tried to be your mother. Try only to be you. Don't fear it so much that you decide to leave it all. I ask it for selfish reasons, yes: I do not want to carry a dead mother in my mind. But I ask it too, in the name of . . . yourself.

To me all diseases are disguises. All the world wears disguises. Even our dreams are disguises. It is said this is so we do not wake up, for without the disguise we would see ourselves real.

Do we drip drops of disguise in our eyes to veil our vision into seeing what we wish to see? So we do not wake up to what is real?

And is it for the same reason that we wear all other disguises: power or goodness; fame, and love and anger? Like disease? Don't we see only what we want or dare to see?

What is there so terrible, Maria, that you must wear this horrible disguise, to hide from yourself? To keep from seeing what—knowing what?

In any case, you have translated your fear into this organic language and now we must deal with that.

I will slide my hand over the hot surface of the huge slick egg, feeling for the baby's position, rechecking. Before making the cut into this blood organ I will look again: Are the two large clamps ready for the cord? And the scissors? While I hold the slippery baby up—with both hands—Sister Joan of Arc will snap the two clamps on the cord and cut them. Then I'll hand the baby onto the table and Sister Jean Marie will take over. Are the respiratory stimulants ready? The infant resuscitator? And the open gauze and the suction bulb? Yes. And in case I have to leave the operation to work with the baby (toxic), the extra pair of sterile gloves lie ready so I can return later to the operating table, where Sister Joan will be compressing the uterus together, as Sister Barbara gives the injection to contract the uterus firm. Where is the hard tube for the cervix? Ah, there. Ready.

"Mine Maria, no die," came from the hallway.

I hope the baby lives.

And the cut into the uterus. First there will be great gushes of blood. I will have to ignore that and plow ahead through the thick vascular uterine wall, then carefully enter the cavity. A lake of amniotic water will begin spilling out over the bleeding wall and drenching the sides of the table, and my abdomen, my gown, will be red from the chest down. The suction machine will be nozzled into the uterus against the back of my hand by Sister Joan, but the fluid will still be spilling over anyway. I'll plunge my hand into the hot, bloody water, feel quickly for the little legs, and pull the infant out. There will be blood up to my elbows.

Will the infant live? So far its heartbeat can be counted—one hundred fifty-six—but that's fast, toxic.

Or has it already been programmed to fail by the toxic chemistry?

"Doctor, she's ready."

Blood will soak through the sterile drapings, down the sides. The floor will run thick with it, and Sister Jean Marie has already spread newspapers and mattress covers there to sponge some of it up.

It seems each life must be born in blood. Must each rebirth also come at the same cost? Through blood? Not organic red blood, but the bursting and baptizing of spiritual blood? What is the organic reflection of spiritual blood? Tears or laughter?

"Doctor, she's ready."

Maria, don't die. Do not demand so much from yourself that there is nothing left.

Or, if you must die—if you see no other choice—then go ahead. I'll give you the chance. *You* choose. Either way.

"Doctor, she is ready," repeated Sister Barbara, holding the can of ether with a safety pin through its lid so the cold liquid dripped from it onto the cloth mask. I saw Sister Jean Marie give a short sideways shake of her large white hood. With my hands still folded, she probably thought I was praying. Well . . .

Stepping to the side of the patient, I reached to the tray and took up the scalpel, knowing already its exquisite sharpness.

❋❋❋

Even with the hospital, the established office routines continued.

I clipped the X ray onto the view box. "That's me?" Susan asked.

"This is your pelvis here, hipbones each side."

"Where's the baby?"

"Here. This circle is the head, and here you see the backbone."

"It's standing on its head!"

"Sure. Supposed to. Means it'll come head first. That's perfect."

"They all look like that?"

"Supposed to. See there's enough room for the head to enter the pelvis. No bone tumors or old fractures, nothing in the way."

"What's all those spots and things?"

"Here? Intestines and pockets of gas, things like that, uterine wall and such. Arms and legs don't show up too clear yet, bones are still too small, fine, but you can see legs here and arms here. Perfect."

"I'm thankful for it. I mean the baby, that it be . . . all right. That it don't be born and then suffer no kinda way." She studied her fingers. "Guess I done plenty things ought not to, but I don't want none of it to go on the baby. If I done it, it oughta come on me. You sure the baby all right? Ain't gonna be marked?"

"Everything checks out perfect. Urine, blood, chest X ray, this, everything."

"Had it on my mind so."

"If you don't mind my saying it, you've changed. I think you act more serious than you used to be. You were so young."

"Some tells me that, and I don't know what they mean. 'Cept I make more plans: After the baby born and I'm well, I'm going to beauty school. Learn to style heads, skin care, all such as that. And work somewhere."

"See? Sounds great."

"Ora wants pay for it, tuition and all. But I savin' my money, I think I make it on my own all right."

"I think having a baby is giving you a new life."

She laughed and waved the empty specimen bottle for next time.

And George Taylor with all his deformities. I'm helping him undress enough so we can get to his hydrocele. Unbutton and unbutton, layer after layer. First through three layers of pants, now two layers of long underwear. "George, you stay dressed for a blizzard."

Margaret said in German, "You can practically tell what month it is by how many layers he has on. Next month one more layer comes off."

"Gosh it's big again." In a hydrocele (*hydro,* water; *cele,* cyst) the inner lining keeps producing too much fluid, too fast, making the cyst larger and larger.

He said something. I thought he meant that it hurts and pulled.

"I'm sure it does, George. Next time don't wait so long. Come get it drained before it's so heavy."

Instead of sticking each time to fill the syringe, I put in one needle and left it in, taking the syringe off to empty it and then locked it back on the same needle. This way I only had to hurt him once.

Margaret held the pan and counted as I squirted out each syringe full of the clear yellow fluid. "One hundred twenty cc."

The first time I drained it, he thanked me for not sticking him but the one time. Said before he'd get stuck so many times at each draining he almost fainted. In German, I said to Margaret, "That's hostility. Pure hostility. Taking it out on a helpless . . . using him."

"One hundred forty."

"You mustn't let it go so long, George." And back into German. "Would like to operate it, for good, but he's such a bad risk."

"It turt o'right," and more I couldn't even guess at.

"One hundred sixty."

"There. All collapsed. That's got it for this time. When did we check your blood sugar last? You staying on your diet?"

I understood more by his nod than his words.

"What's in this package you have here?" She was already peeping into the home-wrapped parcel.

" 't a take."

"Why, it's a cake. You shouldn't be eating sweets. Who baked it this time? People shouldn't do this. Who?"

She understood him. "Mrs. Hodanek? The one from the rest home? She did? That's it," she explained to me, "Alfonzo has been drinking worse again. She had to call the law—afraid he might hurt the old patients. Screaming and breaking things. And she brings George a cake. People shouldn't do that! George, you give this to Miss Emily the moment you get home; don't you eat any of it—only a taste. I'm going to phone her right now." And she stomped off, leaving me with all his buttoning-up.

And women come for vaginals. Want to be examined "inside," and it is a good idea. I'm slipping a Vaselined speculum (also called a "duckbilled") into vagina after vagina to look at the cervix. Looking at cervices so much that Margaret has a time getting the speculums washed and resterilized in time. When the women get depressed they want to know if "cancer is inside—if eating-cancers is starting me inside. You can tell me. I want to know if it is. Don't hold it me nothing back, you can tell me."

Slipping the duckbilled speculum in, opening it, and seeing the entire cervix, and, if there is a cervicitis, painting it with Merthiolate. We now routinely say it may get on their panties later, because once one phoned back: "Now? I am getting it monthly in technicolor?" Margaret always adds, "It will wash out, don't worry."

Cervix exams, vaginals—so many that I told Margaret, "I'm going to get rich after all, simply because women haven't got it outside like men, where they can examine it themselves."

I don't see how a middle-aged woman blushes as easily as Margaret.

***

Early morning now, after Mrs. Mersiovsky's hysterectomy. The sun is coming up already hot. I'm wiping my face with the bottom of my scrubshirt, forgetting that I'm showing Sister Joan of Arc my naked stomach and navel. "Vaclav? The leg? Doing any better at all this morning?" I reached for his chart.

"None, doctor. Temperature is higher than last night."

"We've waited all we can. I told him. Schedule it for tomorrow—no, day after tomorrow. I explained to his wife, but I don't think she realizes it will be off. I hope she knows it. He does."

"Yes, Father—I mean doctor."

"If we're completely finished now with the surgery, I'll change his dressing. Anything else I should do first?"

"We admitted a sad case now."

"Oh?"

"Little Negro boy. From Flatonia. Hundred three and eight-tenths fever. Breathing in fast grunts. Seems very sick to me."

"Sounds like pneumonia. Let's go see him."

"The saddest part is he's like an orphan; the people he's living with have six of their own. I don't think anyone is really interested in him."

"Maybe that's why he chose to tell it this way."

She walked beside me quietly. I knew she didn't know what I meant.

I thumped and listened to his chest. Lobar pneumonia. In the base of each lung. Solid. "Coughing up blood?"

"Yes. Now his temp is a hundred four and two-tenths. Rectal."

"When did he get sick?"

A voice behind me, "Two-three day back." There was only the one person with him.

"Shoulda brought him sooner. Gotta get some sulfapyridine in him—let's use double doses—and aspirin, and sponging. Can he keep medicines down?"

"He vomit all day yestiddy they said. I was workin' out."

Little son, why so severe? Are you saying you breathed in of this world, took in that which should give life and found it toxic? Those you needed—when you breathed them in, did they become the poison of rejection?

Is this what you say?

Please, son, let this medicine work.

I shut out the other thoughts that would have said, But this case is too severe, too much solid congestion, too far . . .

As Sister and I walked back, I remarked quietly, "Better find out whether he's baptized—he's too sick."

"She thinks he never was."

"Better do it."

"Thank you, Father—I mean, doctor."

"I'm sorry"—my voice sounded apologetic—"I'm so sorry for him."

At the double front doors, several people came helping a woman limp in. She was holding her side.

"Did you send her in, doctor?"

"No. Don't think I even know them."

Sister Barbara already came up the hall with the wheelchair. One of Dr. Kotzebue's patients. A complete surprise to Sister and to me too, only to find the patient had come on her own, not through his office. She asked Sister to call him to come see her here.

I stayed in the scrub room, stayed out of sight lest he think I was prying, but stayed near so if he wanted me I'd be right here, ready. Sister interviewed the patient, got a urine, phoned, and he came right away. And Sister met him at the door, remembering to have it open, and led him to the patient.

Before the patient could tell him anything about the pain in her side, which began in the back and came around and down into the groin, and that Sister Barbara, suspecting kidney stone, already had taken a urine sample and Arnold has it ready under the microscope and it shows many red blood cells and positive albumin—before the patient can say a word—he says, "You are not sick enough to be in any hospital. Go home, and I'll send you the medicines." And he turned and left.

Sister Barbara told me herself how he'd come and gone. And I think she tried to say something to forgive his action. That would be her nature, to be forgiving. "The man's hands are terribly scorched."

"His hands? Or his heart?"

I shouldn't have said that.

After all, I don't know his reasons, nor what he's saying.

I suppose she forgave me, too.

Before I left, all dressed to go, I went back to see the boy again. The woman with him was sitting up in the chair, her head to one side, snoring softly. Sister Joan of Arc sponged his arms slowly; he didn't seem to know it.

Without a sound I questioned, Temp?

She held up four fingers.

When I arrived at the office, Margaret had the morning mail in a stack. Usually it's just a lot of junk—advertising, samples—but there—at last!—with an enclosure saying now there is enough to release some for civilian use, lay unwrapped a clear waterlike twenty cc vial of penicillin! And a tract giving information and instructions.

I drove straight back to the hospital, showed it to Sister Joan of Arc, and said, "Let's give him—the little pneumonia boy—one cc intravenously every eight hours." Together we walked and I found the vein in his arm, gave him the first dose. He lay relaxed. Didn't flinch. Didn't seem to know much of what was happening. *It's too late.*

Back at the nurses' station. "I'm afraid for him, Sister. He's too sick. That fast breathing, grunting. Guess he found the world too hostile, too hurting. Somehow has chosen to leave. He is dying."

Singsong chanting came softly from upstairs, like an aroma drifting down.

"Let's make it one cc every six hours. That's four times a day, okay? And keep trying to get the sulfapyridine down him too." He's going to die anyway. "Unless he checks out . . . If he does, just let me know. I don't have to see him to pronounce—I hate to have to look at him dead. Skinny kid."

As the other three Sisters came down from chapel, walking quietly and slowly behind them is Pete.

Next morning at the hospital. "You didn't call about him. The boy? He's still alive?"

"Even some better. Much less temperature too."

But I didn't really hear that, couldn't really know that, until we came in his door and—I can't believe this!—the kid jumped up, standing, holding his arms crossed. "Ah don't want no more them ole shots."

"Son! This is beautiful!"

"Ah don't care. Ah don't want no more."

A sound behind me chuckled.

"This is a miracle. It can't be! In twenty-four hours?"

"An Ah don't want no more ole 'mometer stuck in me neither."

"Hesh now. They tryin' to hep you."

"Ah don't care."

Sister Joan of Arc asked him, "Will you hold a thermometer under your tongue? And not bite it? For me?"

"Ah don't know."

"Okay, okay, son. This is too beautiful to believe!"

"Ah don't care. Keep them ole needles and things 'way."

"Hesh. Talk nice to the doctor and nurse."

And his lungs—he let me listen only because I promised him a dime—sounded almost perfectly clear. Only a few moist rales, where before it had been solid exudate. You couldn't believe!

We kept him another day on sulfapyridine, powdered and mixed with jelly, and he took it okay and began eating everything off his tray, every meal. Sister Barbara—our "kitchen" Barbara—brought him extras, "betweeners."

I talked to his auntie alone and she said his mother stayed in California and had written that she was doing real well and would send for him soon. But they didn't know for sure, because she also sent some money, "so maybe she ain't."

"Ain't what?"

"Gonna send for him."

I said no more. Maybe I should have.

***

Still in my scrubsuit and with powdery white hands I wrote orders, as they rolled the patient out to her room. There was an atmosphere of ether about us all. With her mop and bucket Mrs. Zapalac, as always in her black-stockinged feet, started into the operating room. Sister Jean Marie stood beside me, waiting to have the orders.

I looked up toward the front doors to see someone standing outside looking up at the hospital, one hand holding on a hat, a sack on the shoulder, and teeth like saying "Grrr!"

"Sister, I don't know what ghastly sins you have committed to deserve this, but there's Mrs. Rosenbauer."

"Who is she?" and she started for the door.

I stayed behind and let Sister try.

"Are you Mrs. Rosenbauer?"

"Ha?" she growled.

"Are you sick?"

"Ha?"

"Come in."

"Ha?"

"Won't you please come farther? Come in."

"Ha?"

Sister stood quiet. I'll bet she's praying—for patience.

"It's a horspittle, ain't it?"

"Yes."

"Ha?"

Sister's hood nodded big, and her hands made a "come in" gesture, but Mrs. Rosenbauer stood.

"I got the peu-monia."

"Come."

"Got the peu-monia at home." Said it like it comes in cans and you store it on shelves. "Makes me cough and pee same time."

"Please come."

"Ha?"

Sister went down the steps, took the woman gently by one elbow, hugged an arm around her, and simply brought her up the steps and in. Took her to Number Six, which is semiprivate, but had nobody else. She turned back the top sheet, patted the bed and made signs of ironing it, like "lie down," I suppose. Mrs Rosenbauer looked around the room, pitched her sack into a corner, sat down beside it, and that's where she remained her whole hospital stay.

We examined her there—she did have it, lobar pneumonia—gave her penicillin injections there. Then we wrestled her up and onto the bed and took her big shoes off. But moments later, after going out for a pan of water and a gown, she's back in the corner. "Leave her be," I said.

Sister made a pallet for her there. The old lady pitched her sack on it, and that's all the use it ever got. She took her first medicines, completely cooperative. I ordered extra large doses of cough syrup. "You folks go outside? To the toilet?"

Good heavens! "In there!" I pointed. She did use the bathroom but never closed the door and never flushed. When they gave her clean clothes she stuffed them in her sack.

They'd place her tray on the floor in front of her. She'd carefully take her teeth out, eat everything, then put the teeth back in.

"But she looks so young," Sister Joan of Arc said.

I put my hand on top of my head and through clenched teeth asked, "Ha?" Even Sister Jean Marie tightened her pouty lips together.

"If your theory—that when people suffer disappointments, hurts, they show it by getting sick—is a truth, what made *her* sick?" Sister Joan of Arc is the only outspoken one.

Sister Jean Marie admonished her slightly by saying, "Number Three B is calling," and pointed to the light.

In leaving, Sister Joan, with one hand on her hood, said, "Ha?"

"Sister." But the lips were partly smiling.

Nevertheless, I wondered. And decided the best way with Mrs. Rosenbauer was to do it direct. So I tried:

"Why did you get sick?"

"Peu-monia."

"I know. Why?"

"Ha?"

I pointed to her chest.

"Peu-monia."

I nodded. "But why? Why did you get it?"

"Because my mule died."

"Huh?"

"My mule got sick on me and died. Could be I caught it from him. Stayed beside him too many nights in that windy barn. Tried every liniment. Nothing helped." She kept grinning "grrr!" "Too old. Had that mule twenty-two years. Laid there five days before he died." The face kept that grinning young mask, but two tears came evenly down. "Couldn't get him up."

Suddenly I remembered the slices of bread.

I patted her hand and told her the lungs were clearing fine, in fact were almost perfectly clear—that she'd be all right.

"Ha?"

A couple mornings after, she swung the sack up on her back and by way of explaining, I suppose, muttered as she passed the nurses' desk, "Crazy horspittle. Been here almost four days with the peu-monia and they never did put me a plaster. And no liniment. Plum crazy." We watched as she opened the doors and began backing out, pushing the screen doors open with her rump. Sister Barbara, the tall one, came along from the other side.

"Oh? Are you leaving us?"

Mrs. Rosenbauer either did not hear or ignored her and walked on out the driveway.

"Well." I said with relief, "glad we didn't have to put anybody in with her. So now, that's that."

❋❋❋

Elton Niemeir is home and in the hospital. Got hit by a car, late last night. Maybe he did have a few Shiners or Schlitzes too many—I wouldn't want to say—but with it so hot and everybody glad to see him . . . And right out in front of Rietz's Friendly Tavern, as he went around the back of his car, blam! And he's in the street trying to get up and can't manage his leg.

And later I'm trying to clean it and get the tendons and muscles straight and the gravel cleaned out, and we find that a whole V-shaped piece of bone is missing. Gone. The tip of the V was at the front of the shin, with the broad part toward the back. So the question is, actually how wide was the tip? Did it come to a point? Or was the tip wide as an inch?

So we measure both legs—you do it from a tubercle on the crest of the ilium (pelvis, hipbone) to the inner ankle, laying both legs straight—and yes, an inch and an eighth shorter, missing. Sisters and I checked it three times.

So, at the operation, we simply leave the space open and screw steel bars, braces, across this space (which will naturally fill in with bone later). Two such bars and twelve screws, all Vitallium (which doesn't have to be removed later), and the next morning I talk with a bone specialist at Brooks General explaining how I had fixed it and say I wish we had had at least loose pieces, chips of bone to put in the space to "seed" it, so it would fill faster with bone. He replies they don't go too heavy on bone banks, only in essential places. Says they'd have done nothing different, and to give Elton a few days' rest or so, and then they'll send the ambulance.

With his leg up in bed, he's telling me, "I think . . . I might have accidentally got in the way on purpose—not knowing it—because the truth is I don't want to go back. This might get me a desk job. I wouldn't like it, but no more combat duty."

I immediately say it is most admirable, courageous, when one can see deeper into himself than only the surface layer, can see down into the murk and muck too—to have the guts to be that honest. And brave.

He says nothing about that. Guess nobody wants to look into themselves. So I ask how it was in Germany. Since he speaks the language, could he communicate with the people? Or do we speak it here too differently now?

He repeats, "I don't want to go back." He tells me about being in a forest, the battle. And he sees a German soldier—recognizes the typical helmet—behind a tree. The soldier's back is to him, and Elton puts the sights on him, right between the shoulders. Begins tightening up on the trigger when he holds it there and calls, in German, "Hold still! Exactly! I have you in the back. Drop the rifle, hold the hands up, and turn around slow. You are my prisoner." And the man does.

As Elton is marching his prisoner in, the prisoner says, "May I ask you a question, since you speak our language?"

"Okay."

"Where do you learn to speak it? In school?"

"No, at home. My people came from Germany. My name is German: Niemeir."

"So is my name Niemeir. It is a common name—lots of Niemeirs. If you allow me to say so."

"Yes. In the States too. Keep your hands up. In the telephone books."

"Yes sir. May I ask what part of Germany your antecedents are from?"

"From near Munich, the southern part."

"I'm from a village near Muenchen too. Niederdorf."

"Is that so? I have an uncle yet. Lives at Kleinderhoff, a small place, wherever that is."

"Not Albert Friedrich Niemeir?"

"Yes, that's his name. You know him? And don't try anything foolish."

"Know him. He is my father."

"He's my uncle. Papa's brother."

"Your papa must be August. In Texas."

"Yes." And Elton, with his rifle in the German's back, says, "You are my cousin."

And with his hands up in the air, the other says, "Yes, you are my cousin."

"And we don't know what to say. With my gun on him I am marching him in, prisoner, and I say it again, 'You are my cousin.'

"And he is my prisoner and his hands in the air and he says it too, 'You are my cousin.'

"We don't know . . . what to say . . . more."

❋❋❋

"It ain't only that I gonna be good for her or him—this baby gonna be good for me too. I'm tired of this goin' here, goin' there, runnin' around life. I'm trying to settle. I need this here baby, and she gonna need me. I knows it," Ora said.

Sister redampened the cloth over Susan's eyes and replaced the rubber mask and its corrugated hose.

"And my husband—he so anxious to see. Wants me to call him the day it comes. He gonna be a daddy! Hope it's a girl. He'd like that best." In the delivery room and standing against the wall, Ora looked smaller than usual, dressed in the sterile white gown and cap and mask. "Sure thank you again, lettin' me watch. Hope it ain't too much against the rules."

"Not at all. Fact, I believe in the family being present at births. Makes them all more part of it—as it should be. No, I'm especially glad you could make it."

"Y'all talkin' 'bout me?" Susan asked, drunkish.

"Course not, honey."

"You know how the gas works now, Susan, so be sure and take deep breaths of it when they first start."

"Oh I will I will I will . . . " she slurred.

Watching her perineum bulge with the pain, "You're doing fine, Susan. Not—" What the? What's *that?* "Not much longer now." A tiny foot, not an inch long, and flat. I began working, massaging busily. Ora leaned forward and frowned. Sister Barbara's eyes were questioning over her mask.

I don't know.

Everything's been normal—all her exams. Now this.

Sister asked calmly, "Susan, how do you feel?"

"Feel just fine, nurse, ain't nothin' hurting." She's half asleep.

"How old are you now? I'll be getting all the information we need for the birth certificate." And while she kept Susan talking, she watched across the big abdomen toward my hands where she could see this very small foot, much too small for a full-term baby.

"Where were you born? Careful, Ora, that you don't touch anything there: Step back a little."

Now there were two such feet.

"In Lafayette County."

"What was your mother's maiden name?"

"Clayberg."

There were now two flat legs. I was gently trying to deliver the rest of it.

"And . . . er, where was she born?" Sister kept staring at the thing coming into my hand.

"Mean what county?"

"Yes . . . yes."

Two flat arms appeared.

"Don't rightly recollect. Do you, Ora?"

"No, I can't imagine," Ora answered, never taking her eyes from it. Its flat chest and head were now also delivered. She stared at this flat, rubbery doll-sized thing. The thing no longer than my hand. I covered it with a towel and Ora looked questioningly at me.

Looking straight at Ora but talking to Susan, I said, "Everything is all right, Susan. You'll be finished in a few minutes now." And I nodded to Sister, who then gave her continuous gas, and I locked the forceps on the baby's head and pulled evenly and slowly, relaxed for a full minute by the large clock, then pulled and delivered a husky squalling baby.

"It's a girl," Sister Barbara said.

"I wanta . . . wanta see her."

"Later. After. After she's cleaned and the doctor has finished sewing. Breathe this deep now."

As soon as Susan was taken out of the delivery room, Ora pointed to the towel. "Can I see that?"

"Sure. Let's."

"What is it? The war didn't have nothin' to do with that, did it?"

"No. It's really not too important, but it teaches something."

"What say?"

"Let's start at the beginning. Susan's baby began as twins. About the third month this one died—I don't know why." The baby lay on my hand like a flat paper doll. "But nature didn't let this one rot. If it had, it would have meant the death of the other baby and would have poisoned the mother's blood too, with its decaying toxicity, poison. Maybe enough to kill her. At least the womb would have had to empty. So nature mummified this one—I don't know how—and let it stay in the womb until the other one was ready to be born. Of course, when the healthy one grew, it took up the space, and flattened this one out against the inside of the uterine wall."

"Does this happen often? Never heard—"

"No. Very rare. Ordinarily it would have been twins."

"Does it hurt anything about the other—about my baby?"

"No, not at all. Except when she has *her* children, there would be a possibility of twins."

"Is she all right?"

"Susan?"

"The baby, my baby."

"Sure. But I haven't checked her heart yet."

"It won't lead to nothing later?"

"Oh, no. Not at all."

"You said it teaches something?"

"Oh that. Well, to me it does. It teaches that we can—must—discard our life if it is inadequate, incomplete. Then we stand the chance of having another full, healthy life."

"I don't know what you sayin', but it sounds good." She laughed big.

Sister Barbara entered carrying the bundle. "Oh there's my baby." She watched Sister smile down on the fat, oily face, clenched fists, and squeezed little eyelids, closed tight. Sister's face smiling down at the infant made a picture like some painting of the Madonna.

Ora sighed from deep in her large bosom. "Nurse, you have such a lovely complexion."

"Oh, do you really think so? Thank you."

"Here, let me hold my baby. I want to know how it feel to—"

"Now hold her right." Sister handed the child out slowly. "And don't drop her."

"Why of course I won't drop her. Oh ain't this something? Oh, us, Jesus, I just knew you'd give me a baby someday. Oh, Lord—say what's she goin' to do, cry? Did I talk too loud? Did mama scare you, honey?"

"You are not holding her right," said Sister trying to take the baby.

"I'll do it. I'll do it. Just listen to that voice. Ain't it beautiful? She be a singer some day. Wonder if I ought name her Marian Anderson Tar? Or Ethel Waters. I know. Me and my husband already decided. She goin' be Ora B. Tar, Junior. That's it. That's what it'll be. Yes, I like that best. Little Ora," and she chuckled and swayed herself and the baby.

※※※

Wet and windy. The kind of late-afternoon cold and early dark you'd never want to go out into, unless you have to.

They phoned that he was dead. Would I come out and say so. The undertaker had told them it must be done first.

In the almost-dark, the black plowed fields were like the squares and triangles of a patch quilt laid out smoothly over the rolling hills of prairie land. And when the wind came swooping, you could feel its gentle force strong against the car; you could hear its clear, cold voice.

At the farm I entered the large empty room; no curtains; no rugs; bare, clean unpainted boards of the floor and of the walls; the ceiling; the doors. Like only the important things mattered here.

The stove had a rose-red spot glowing. They were all sitting near it when I came, and a rocking chair, too, in its usual place also near, but covered with a quilt, humpy. The little old man was under the quilt. Old dead man sitting in a rocker by the stove, like any evening. His long white hair hung almost like a woman's. Once, long ago now, he had asked me, "Is this the time?"

I cupped the stethoscope bell against the hard ribs and listened for the heart. Even through it and the silent chest I heard the wind outside. Suddenly the sound of geese, flying low over the roof and gables. Their sounds honked happily along and down the flue into this room too, filling it. The woman smiled, smiled big.

"Geese," she said, speaking English. "He always like it to hear geeses." She smiled so genuinely that it seemed he wasn't dead, but still sat here, alive in the rocker. "Always by his birthday they already coming." She pointed at the little dead father, still smiling. "Today birthday. November second. Eighty-four today. He wants it that he should make eighty-four. And always by his birthday is still some geeses coming home. All day already."

She still smiled big.

As I swung the quilt back up over his head, it started the chair rocking, as if he were doing it.